Praise fc

"When you think of our most successful athletes, main stream media typically highlights years of personal sacrifice and demanding physical training. *The Gold Medal Mind* takes you on a comprehensive and step-by-step journey through the psychological challenges and necessary, teachable strategies for achieving high-level success in sport and in life. A great read from a veteran sport psychologist."

— N. James Bauman, PhD, former Senior Sport Psychologist, US Olympic Committee

"*The Gold Medal Mind* provides as clear-eyed a look as I've ever come across at what it takes to train your mind like an elite athlete. Doug Jowdy is smart, skilled, and passionate about teaching athletes how to hone their mental game. He suffers no fools and tells it like it is, and his personality permeates this book. If you are looking for a quick fix to get that gold medal mind, this is not the book for you. But if you are prepared to do the work, this one-stop shop book will help get you there."

— Kirsten Peterson, PhD, former Senior Sport Psychologist, US Olympic Committee

"Dr. Jowdy has struck gold in guiding us toward maximizing control of our mental state for peak performance. Intertwining interesting first-hand stories with specific techniques and tools, he provides the roadmap for everyone to get into the 'zone.' Whether you are an athlete, a performer, a business leader, or even a surgeon such as myself, this is the book for you! Read it and live it and you will be a gold medal winner in whatever you do."

— Eric McCarty, MD, University of Colorado Professor and Chief of Sports Medicine and Shoulder Surgery

"As an acupuncturist working in the field of sports medicine, I know the importance of understanding the psyche of the athlete. Being a successful competitor involves the entire spectrum of body, mind, and spirit. In my 40 years of clinical practice with elite athletes, Doug Jowdy stands out as a masterful sport psychologist who embraces the importance of this wholeness. *The Gold Medal Mind* is appropriate for all who train and compete, regardless of age, event, or level of mastery."

— Whitfield Reaves, OMD, LAc, author of *The Acupuncture Handbook of Sports Injuries and Pain*

"When near-term goals shift due to injury, illness, or other factors outside their control, athletes are forced to navigate uncertainty as they prepare for whatever comes next. Filled with practical suggestions and an array of foundational mental skills, *The Gold Medal Mind* is a must-read for anyone interested in the ever-changing landscape of sport and successfully managing the common pitfalls athletes face throughout their careers."

— Dr. Sara Mitchell, US Olympic and Paralympic Committees

"*The Gold Medal Mind* is a treasure trove of resources within the chest of a creative and helpful idea. Athletes practice physical skills until they develop muscle memory. Practicing psychological skills until they become mental muscle memories makes a great deal of sense. I encourage you to take advantage of this wonderful book and the associated resources."

— Dr. Everett L. Worthington, Professor Emeritus,
Virginia Commonwealth University

"*The Gold Medal Mind* is essential reading for all athletes and sport science professionals working in the field of performance enhancement, particularly at the high school, intercollegiate, and elite levels of competitive sport. Starting from an evidence-based foundation, Dr. Jowdy provides sequential steps for the practical application of his successful 'gold medal mind' approach. Having been a colleague of Doug's for many years at the US Olympic Training Center (Colorado Springs), I was fortunate to observe how he put his concept into practice with multiple Olympic medal winners."

— Randall L. Wilber, PhD, FACSM, Senior Sport Physiologist,
US Olympic Committee

"*The Gold Medal Mind* is the conversation every coach or athlete wants to have with a sport psychologist. It's casual and understandable, more like a meeting in a coffee shop than a stuffy lecture hall. With funny references and personal stories, Doug lays out truth after truth about sport performance, and more than that, life performance. Open this book and read the last paragraph of the first chapter. If you are seeking information on breakthrough performance ideas in sports and life, I bet you can't stop reading!"

— Pat Manson, retired US pole vaulter and three-time Pan Am Gold Medal Winner

"Inspirational! A compelling, thought-provoking read! This book skillfully guides you to the realization that we all need to do more to completely understand the mental training approach required to unlock our true potential, especially when dealing with the roller-coaster ride that is professional sport."

— Steve Guppy, Assistant Coach, Nashville SC, retired professional soccer player, and former assistant coach of the Colorado Rapids (MLS Champions, 2010)

THE GOLD MEDAL MIND

THE GOLD MEDAL MIND

BECOMING A PSYCHOLOGICALLY SKILLED ATHLETE

Podium Press
Boulder, Colorado

Podium Press
Boulder, Colorado 80306
www.goldmedalmind.com

ISBN: 978-1-7356462-0-6 (book)
ISBN: 978-1-7356462-1-3 (e-book)
Library of Congress Control Number: 2020916305

This book is for informational purposes only and is not intended to be used as a substitute for medical advice or counseling. Please seek the advice of a mental health professional if you are experiencing symptoms that make day-to-day living difficult or if you have a problem with alcohol or drugs.

Printed in the United States of America

DEDICATION

To George and Dennis,
who served as my sport psychologists
in their own loving ways.

How often do we forget that the losing team made it to game seven and overtime?

— Spencer Jackman

Engrave this upon your heart: there isn't anyone you couldn't love once you heard their story.

— Mary Lou Kownacki

Records are made to be broken.

— LeBron James

CONTENTS

FOREWORD

As athletes, we're given a certain deck of cards to work with. Some say your variance of improvement across those genetics can go only so far. I disagree. I believe you can affect every aspect of your body and performance with training and time. If you feel you have weaknesses in certain areas, or even if you think you're fine and are "crushing it," I guarantee there are levels to the game that you're not yet aware of. But here's the thing—those levels are mental, not physical.

I was essentially unbeatable during the 2000–2001 season. I felt like Neo in "The Matrix" when he starts dodging bullets in slow motion. It is no coincidence that 2000 was the year I began training with Dr. Doug Jowdy. Working with Doug gave me a unique ability to "suffer" during practice so that competition became easy in comparison. But the most important thing Doug taught me was how to quiet the noise between my ears to create a hyper focus on the present moment and the task at hand. This alone gave me the ability to physically alter the way I responded to training, stress, and recovery.

Doug and I started working together in Calgary in the summer of 2000, when he was the psychologist for the US Olympic speed skating team. At the time, I was very skeptical of many people. I had a major distrust for authority. Doug seemed to be someone I could trust enough to share my weaknesses and vulnerabilities—as well as the immense and outrageous goals I had for myself. I was honest with Doug and told him I wanted to be the greatest short-track speed skater of all time. I said I was willing to do whatever was necessary to achieve the level of commitment and performance required.

I told Doug I thought I needed a greater threshold for pain. I wanted to be a machine, able to give 110 percent of myself 100 percent of the time. If I could develop a capacity to handle pain significantly longer than everyone else—every hour, every day, every week—I could transform not only my own performance, but also the way people think about speed skating and skating in general. Athletes are human, but we want to be machines. We want our legs to function like pistons in an engine that never gets tired as long as there's fuel in the tank. But how do we go about training for that if we are dreading a particular workout that we need to thrive in? I wanted to possess the power of those monks you hear about who live at extremely high altitude and go outside in frigid weather to meditate for hours in nothing but underwear. I thought, what if I can train myself to go toward the fire instead of away—to actually *thrive* through the pain?

Doug said, "Okay, I can help you achieve those types of physical goals. I don't know if you're going to win this season or not. But I do know we can impact your training right here, right now. I'm going to help you create a new set of habit-forming mechanisms that are going to become your new baseline. And actually, it's got nothing to do with you training harder on the ice. It's going to be you sitting in front of a computer screen and actively, intentionally learning to control your heart rate in real time." But he cautioned me I would need to leave room for error: a bad workout, a strained muscle, fatigue, problems with equipment or the ice. In short, I would have to learn to have compassion for myself. I needed to accept that I was not a machine, but a fallible human being.

Doug introduced me to several biofeedback devices, including a handheld device I used daily. The feedback from this particular device was a loud buzzing noise that would slow to a metronome-like ticking when I got control of my heart rate. I could instantly tell when my mind was in a state of calm focus instead of bouncing all over the place. I think that's what started a real change in me. Whatever

Doug asked or prompted me to do—I dove in headfirst. I took to the training as if there were no other options. I still remember preparing my mind for training as I walked to his office. Walking back to the dorms afterward, I thought about biofeedback, visualization, and concentration.

After training with the biofeedback devices, I was able to create a mental state during competitions in which the crowd would go fuzzy and all that mattered was the ice rink. I trained myself to drop into a Zen-like trance state at will. What I relied upon during those competitions was my mental training—the initial setup, implementation, and methodologies that Doug shared with me.

That seriousness and intensity remained with me throughout the rest of my career, until I retired in 2010. Mental training was a game changer for me, because it helped me recognize that we are complicit in the creation of our own reality. If I had accepted what I saw as my limitations early on and believed I had already done as much as I could do, I guarantee you I would not have won medals. I would never have broken out of the cycle of just doing what I was told and going along with the system like the rest of the team.

Looking back on my career now, in 2020, I am convinced the single greatest tool I had in my arsenal was right between my ears. I believe I won most of my races before I even set foot in the arena. When I did lose, it was due to nothing but my own state of mind. Yes, training is essential. Yes, technical mastery, diet, rest and recovery, coaching, and support are all important. But whether you are able to overcome the inevitable hurdles we face in sport may depend entirely on your ability to focus and refocus again and again in spite of distractions like pain, frustration, impatience, and discouragement.

To me, sport was the world's greatest movie, the most challenging and fulfilling experience of all, exhilarating and powerful. It was every human emotion imaginable. It was life. I recognize now I may never find a replacement for that, and the transition has been difficult. But it turns out that for me, mental training is the catalyst that makes all the other dominos fall into place. Even now, when I'm pursuing some form of daily practice that makes me feel mentally dialed in—even if it's just a five-minute mindfulness meditation—or if I go for a run and I'm just concerned with that one activity, the rest of my life seems easier to navigate. Whatever problems I have seem to dissipate and fade in importance.

The beautiful thing about this book is it teaches you that potential exists within you too, and it can be trained, improved, and sharpened. Your mind is probably the most important tool you will ever have as an athlete. When I told people I planned to become the greatest speed skater in history and change the sport forever, they thought I was arrogant and naïve. You know the rest of the story. What will your story be? It's up to you to light the flame within and start the journey, one step at a time.

— Apolo Anton Ohno
Eight-time Olympic medalist

PREFACE

Dreams do come true. As a young athlete, at the age of 14, I already knew I wanted to work with Olympic athletes and help them with the mental aspects of the game. One thing led to another, and many years later, there I was, standing in front of members of the US speed skating team, talking about what I now call the gold medal mind. But even as I stood there, part of my brain did not believe it was happening. For such a long time, my self-limiting beliefs—my demons, if you will—had other plans for me, none of which involved my dreams coming true.

According to my self-limiting beliefs, I did not have the intellectual and emotional horsepower to work with Olympic athletes. Unconsciously, perhaps I did know that I had what it would take. But in the "oceanfront property" of my mind, I was more doubtful than confident. After all, who was I to think I could do postdoctoral training at Stanford Medical School after having earned a meager 2.3 grade point average for my sophomore year in college? By conventional standards, I was not supposed to "win a medal" or "be on the podium." For me, working for the Olympic Committee would be like being on the podium professionally.

But life had other plans for me. Annihilating self-limiting beliefs in order to perform beyond expectations became a central focus of both my personal and professional work. Self-limiting beliefs are thoughts, sometimes dwelling deep in the recesses of our minds, that lead us to self-sabotage. In my work with athletes, I commonly share the following scenario to make crystal clear what I am talking about when I use this term: some Olympic athletes believe they can make an Olympic team, but never win a medal. Some believe they can win a bronze, but not a gold. And then there are those who will believe they can win one gold, but never two. You get the idea.

We do the same thing in the game of life. In the spirit of rigorous honesty, one of my most vicious self-limiting beliefs, harbored for years, was that I would not be able to write a book. I had published scientific papers and book chapters with colleagues. But when it came to the idea of flying a solo mission, my inner demons went for the jugular. See, I thought I was a team sport guy, and writing a book was like playing an individual sport—more threatening because I could not hide behind coauthors. However, with dedicated practice of the techniques I describe in this book, I smashed those limiting beliefs. Although they did rear their ugly heads at times, I kept my psychological immune system a well-oiled machine, so at the very least, I held the negative beliefs at bay while I was writing.

Through the years, I became a bit possessed with helping myself, and later athletes, develop the ability to smash self-limiting beliefs (a.k.a. inner demons). In my work, I teach a range of skills to help both amateur and professional athletes transcend self-imposed obstacles on and off the field. My approach is based on my conviction that wanting to perform beyond our wildest dreams is what drives us to become competitive athletes in the first place.

By the time I was 13 years old, I was reading just about every book ever published on sport psychology. Dickie Nolan, my hockey coach at the time, exposed me and my teammates to concepts such as mental practice (a.k.a. visualization) and relaxation training. I could not get enough. My quest to figure out if these methods were a form of black magic led me to begin using them on a regular basis. I learned they made a significant difference in my performance. Most important, as I got better at enlisting my mind as an ally, being an athlete became more fun. While in graduate school, serving as assistant coach of the Pennsylvania State University men's ice hockey team, I incorporated the skills I had learned as a kid with what I was learning in the classroom. Again, I found the techniques worked, and athletes enjoyed the challenge of developing a gold medal mind. They readily accepted that if they wanted to win a national championship, the timing was ripe for a little humility, and they realized mental training was the answer to winning more. Some athletes still feel that seeing a sport psychologist is a sign of weakness. This is usually a result of the ego fueling self-will and self-reliance, not wanting to depend on anyone. If you are reading this with a bit of skepticism, I welcome that, and I am grateful you are considering another way to become the athlete (and person) you have always wished to be.

How did I get so absorbed in all this sport psychology stuff? I was absolutely lost and depressed after my competitive sport career ended when I was 19. I immersed myself in my studies for many years after my career as an ice hockey player ended. Learning to understand human nature and help others strive for excellence started to provide the rush I once got through sport. All these experiences together led to my embracing this area of study as my new "sport."

After completing my formal education, I went out to test the theory and practice of sport psychology with athletes of all ages and skill levels. More and more I saw how profound was the impact of mental training on performance. The evidence was undeniable: a commitment to training the mind resulted in dreams coming true. Today I use similar techniques in my counseling practice, working with people dealing with addictions, struggling with anxiety or depression, adjusting to the death of a loved one, or even coping with physical illnesses, such as cancer. There is something about these skills that helps people perform better in many arenas, with a range of issues.

Here is an example of how the benefits of my working in multiple areas played out in the world of sport psychology. When I interviewed for my job with the Olympic Committee, the director of human resources asked me, "You have been working in a hospital with drug addicts for years. How does that apply to athletes?" I replied, "It's all about performance. One person is trying to win a gold medal. Another person is trying to achieve 30 days of being clean and sober. The biggest obstacle in either case will be the person's mind. Whether it is winning a gold medal or achieving 30 days of sobriety, engaging the mind in ways that enhance performance makes all the difference." My interviewer looked at me and said, "If you get the job, can you take time to work with my staff too?" That was good to hear, after feeling I was under mild attack a minute before.

My involvement in the recovery movement was one of many driving forces in my writing this book. Immersion in the Twelve-Steps of Alcoholics Anonymous (and Al-Anon) on both personal and professional levels has demonstrated to me again and again the power of the mind as an ally. Living a life of recovery has confirmed for me that there really is such a thing as a gold medal mind, a state of mind that allows a person to perform beyond his or her expectations, on and off the field. For example, by developing a gold medal mind, a high school athlete can annihilate self-limiting beliefs and realize his or her dreams of being a state champion. For a person with an addiction (athlete or non-athlete), reaching a year of sobriety is an achievement that can seem like winning a gold medal.

The focus of my education and experience has not been limited to athletes, which I believe has complimented and taken my work with athletes to a higher level. Today, in my private practice, I work with both athletes and non-athletes. Variety and challenge is what attracted me to psychology in the first place, and helping people with a range of issues keeps my work rewarding and meaningful. Perhaps more important, there are many similarities among athletes striving for performance enhancement and non-athletes learning coping skills to navigate the ebb and flow of life. Which brings me to a crucial point: developing a gold medal mind is as much about living a meaningful life as it is about winning in sport. I wrote this book because I am passionate about helping both athletes and non-athletes embrace the journey of the gold medal mind. People who know me will tell you I often say, "Expect to surprise yourself." I say it because I believe it. My hope is that after you embody what you learn in this book, you will surprise yourself in more ways than you can imagine—and have fun in the process.

ACKNOWLEDGMENTS

A virtual team of people has been instrumental in my professional and personal development and ultimately inspired me to write this book. Tears come to my eyes as I reflect on how they have touched my life. First and foremost, I am indebted to an ice hockey coach of mine, Rich "Dickie" Nolan, one of the three most influential people in my life. Dickie inspired me to go to any length to "leave it all on the ice" day after day. His immense passion for athletics and the game of life served as fuel to keep my "North Star" goal of writing this book in the forefront of my mind. John Catalano, PhD, my undergraduate advisor in psychology, was tough as nails, inspiring me to put every ounce of effort I had into my dreams. Sally Farnsworth, a classmate, encouraged me to persist and accomplish more than I ever imagined I could. The late Dorothy V. Harris, PhD, my advisor at Pennsylvania State University, allowed me to continue the study of mental practice (a.k.a. visualization) from a psychophysiological basis. Renate Forssman-Falck, MD, a psychiatrist and clinical supervisor, taught me in an artful way that the only way to truly understand human nature is through the psychoanalytic tradition. (Believe it or not, Freud was a natural-born sport psychologist.) The late Dennis Bonney, LCSW, who became a father figure, best friend, coach, brother, and friend in recovery, helped save my life. While I was in treatment, he said to me, "The pen is in your hand. You can write your story now." His advice was figurative as well as literal, but on a certain level, I think he knew I would write a book. George Einhaus, a mystic, spiritual advisor, and sport psychologist in his own right, helped me understand what a gold medal mind really is. Although both Dennis and George have moved on to paradise, I have felt their spirits with me throughout the process of writing this book—especially when my inner demons would scream, "What are you doing? Who do you think you are?"

Then there are the athletes and coaches I have been blessed to work with. The speed skater Apolo Anton Ohno took my understanding of excellence to an entirely different level. After coming close to letting go of my career at one point, my experience working with him served as a constant reminder of what it takes to truly soar. Axel Wessel and Rachel Feiltz, two athletes I had the privilege of guiding through vicious injuries, taught me just about everything I know about dealing with injury and what it takes to move through the healing process with grace. Bart Schouten, whom at the time I met him was the head coach of the US long-track all around speed skating team, embraced the use of psychology to enhance performance in a textbook-oriented manner. Having Bart join the speed skaters and me for visualization training sessions was a testament to his dedication to making psychology a part of his coaching repertoire. He confirmed for me that, yet again, you cannot teach what you have not learned. His use of psychology demonstrated that coaches have a wonderful opportunity to act as sport psychologists for their teams, if they are willing to become students of the gold medal mind.

And in closing, some random and not so random people, places, and things that have had a direct influence on my writing this book. Prolotherapy and plasma-rich platelet treatment held my body together when chronic injuries made it difficult to sit for extended periods of time. Dr. Whitfield Reaves, my acupuncturist and author of *The Acupuncture Handbook of Sports Injuries and Pain*, helped by leaving a needle in the top of my head (Du 20, or Governing Vessel 20, a.k.a. "the Valium point") so I could stay in a zone-like state for hours on end and write long after my treatment with him was over. My editor, Evelyn Leigh, has been a guiding force for me throughout this process. There were times I almost retired this book before even sending it to training camp. Her words of encouragement inspired me to rage (a word my brother and I used to stoke ourselves for a fierce attack). And finally, I thank God (or, if you would prefer, the Spirit, the Light, the Source, or the Great Pumpkin) for divinely inspiring the creation of this book.

INTRODUCTION

I was immersed in the world of sport growing up. Our motto was, "It doesn't matter if you win or lose, as long as you win." Yes, we gave lip service to "how you play the game," but the idea of winning trumped everything else. After a particularly bad performance, my father would scream at me, "I don't care what anyone tells you, it is about winning! You are out there to win! Don't let anyone fool you!" That is just a snapshot of how outrageously competitive my dad was. The crazy thing was he thought sport was an absolute waste of time. An immigrant from Lebanon, he was all about being practical—becoming a doctor or lawyer and "putting points on the board" by making lots of money. About a year ago I asked him, "Why were you so hard on us in sports?" He exclaimed, "If you were going to be an athlete, I wanted you to be the best!"

There you have it, a glimpse into the "locker room" at my house growing up, which shaped how I see *and don't see* life and sport today. I was raised with winning as the alpha and omega of the whole pursuit of sport. My professional experience over the last 33 years has confirmed that we all love to win. And what athletes are willing to do to win sometimes seems to defy reason and logic. Just think of the grueling Tour de France bicycle race and the risk some athletes take to beat the competition.

I have yet to meet someone who plays to lose. But I am sure you have watched a competition in which it seemed as if an athlete or team was playing to lose. We all know losing was not the intention, but the player(s) seemed helpless to change the course of the performance. A classic example is the Seattle Seahawks' massacre of the

Denver Broncos in Superbowl XLVIII (final score 43-8). Even though I am not a fan of football, it was painful to watch. But from a sport psychology perspective, the game was a textbook example of how any of us, at any time, can be our own toughest opponent, on or off the field. We have all been there, and know what a nightmare it can be. At the risk of letting my pride get the best of me, I will declare right now that as a result of what you learn from this book, that never has to happen to you again!

How can athletes prevent or handle situations like the one just described? What does it take to win more? My years working with athletes have convinced me that in order to win consistently on the scoreboard, an athlete needs to be just as psychologically skilled as they are physically skilled—perhaps even more. I am determined there is a psychological state, what I have come to call a gold medal mind, that leads to winning—winning medals in the world of the Olympics, world championships in the world of professional sports, national championships in the world of intercollegiate sports, and state championships in the world of high school sports. Yes, the objective is to win, but an athlete with a gold medal mind knows there is more to winning than the scoreboard. Achieving and maintaining a gold medal mind is a victory in its own right, one with benefits that carry over into the game of life. A gold medal mind helps an athlete perform beyond his or her expectations on any given day, on and off the field.

At the heart of the matter is a real paradox. The fact is that letting go of the scoreboard (the outcome) and focusing on the gold medal mind (the process) will result in winning more. This philosophy runs counter to the typical modus operandi of an athlete hoping to win: trying, striving, grinding, contracting, pushing. My message stands in opposition to the conventional, competitive approach. I will elaborate on this truth in many different ways throughout this book. It is a truth that needs to be embedded in your heart and mind, because the gravitational pull to be overly identified with the scoreboard—to be obsessed with winning at all costs—is so innate and so strong.

Leaving sport for a moment, let us take the example of a musician playing in a symphony. I have worked with many extremely talented musicians who take propranolol prior to performances, especially big ones, to prevent performance anxiety from getting out of control. The medication keeps the cardiovascular system from running amuck. That is important to a musician with the jitters, because heart rate and blood pressure getting too high will impact the sound of the instrument. Overactivation of the nervous system causes excessive tension in the facial muscles, including tension in the muscles around the mouth. For those who play horn instruments, this affects the seal around the mouthpiece and can cause the sound to vibrate—a musician's worst nightmare in an audition, for example. It all starts with a specific area of the brain generating thoughts such as, "Am I good enough?" "Will they like me?" "What if I mess up?" and other variations on this theme. And it is all the result of worrying more about the outcome than the process.

I believe the psychological skills that create and maintain a gold medal mind have the potential to change the culture of sport. I think these skills can help athletes maximize their performance, meet their goals, and achieve more wins—and even if they do not win, still feel satisfied. We are approaching a new era in which "the agony of defeat" will become a thing of the past. One of my hopes is that this book can help young athletes develop a gold medal mind before they become overly obsessed with the scoreboard. I work with too many kids whose parents bring them to me because puking before competitions has become a regular event. I see miserable young athletes sobbing after a loss, shutting down, having sleep difficulties and impaired focus in school, feeling perpetually unsatisfied, and taking themselves to the whipping post even after a bad practice. I have seen young athletes with suicidal thoughts after beginning to lose hope they will ever compete at a division I level. This is tragic, and I want to change it on a large scale.

Situations in which soccer, for example, starts out as fun for a kid and turns into a torture chamber are happening more frequently. I know of a kid's rock climbing gym that produces national and world champions. They hold tryouts for the seven- to eight-year-old team. Yep, kids are being told they are not good enough even at that age. I guess an argument can be made either way for whether that is tragic or fantastic. But I will not get into intellectual analysis now. I want to focus on the fact that there is a better way to help kids excel in sport. I want athletes, coaches, and parents to know there is a more productive approach to increasing the odds of winning championships—and more important, to helping kids learn to enjoy sport. Experiencing the waves of winning and losing on the scoreboard is actually part of the athlete and coach's job description. Even LeBron James's job description says somewhere, "Be prepared, because there will be times you will lose. Furthermore, it may sting really badly!"

When I first start working with an athlete, I often ask why he or she plays. I say something like, "This might strike you as an unusual question, but why do you play lacrosse?" We then explore the question on a very deep level. It might take a few sessions to get at an athlete's real intentions and motivation for choosing to devote their precious time and energy to their sport when there are so many other possible ways to spend time, energy, and money. Often the answers I hear include getting a division I scholarship, playing pro, or going to the Olympics. In fact, those are the top three answers I get from the young athletes I work with. In the course of the conversation, I suggest the athlete entertain, for at least six months, the possibility that the reason they are playing is to learn about the outrageous power of his or her mind. I encourage athletes to get enchanted with the idea that focusing on the development of a gold medal mind is the real key to realizing dreams. I recommend they lock in with single-minded attention on what I call "psychological victory."

I tell them this is what will lead to becoming the *Sports Illustrated* athlete of the year. How do I know? Not from books, but from lessons learned at the University of Life, working with athletes for three decades. One of those real life experiences was with Olympic speed-skating medalist Apolo Anton Ohno. He wrote the foreword to this book and talked about our work together in his autobiography *Zero Regrets: Be Greater Than Yesterday,* so I am privileged to be able to share this experience with you. (Under normal circumstances, of course, I protect my clients' right to privacy at all costs.) The long and short of it is that Apolo embraced the philosophy and worked harder than any athlete I have ever seen on his mental game—on developing a gold medal mind. While I did not call it by that name at the time, in essence that is what we worked to actualize together. Apolo "crushed it" when it came to practicing what I share with you in this book. Becoming the most decorated winter Olympic athlete did not happen by accident, chance, or luck. It was a result of intense physical training, but perhaps even more a result of warrior-like psychological training. My hope for you is that you embrace the challenge to develop a gold medal mind with the same commitment, determination, and discipline you devote to your physical training.

I encourage athletes to develop a fascination with the role the mind plays in their pursuit of excellence. The mind is by far the most potent factor in the ability to achieve goals. Unfortunately, we are not taught in school or at home how to develop a gold medal mind. Among many other things, cultivating a gold medal mind involves shedding old beliefs about oneself, the nature of competition, and how to win. A gold medal mind is about freedom from negative self-talk that fuels doubts, fears, worries, insecurities, and concerns. But again, becoming as psychologically skilled as you are physically skilled requires a commitment to training your mind as a weapon.

Consistent and correct mental practice is required to develop a gold medal mind. Becoming a warrior does not happen if you use visualization training just once in a while prior to a competition, or set goals only when you feel like it. You must train mentally at home, during practice, in the weight room, with dietary habits and sleep, while stretching, and in all aspects of your daily life. In order to go to heaven, you need to die first (a topic I will expand on in chapter 14).

One of the most important characteristics of the gold medal mind is the ability to consciously get into and maintain a zone-like state. Everyone reading this book knows what it is like to be "in the zone." It is that state of mind and body in which you are absorbed in the present moment, performing effortlessly with little or no thought. This happens both on and off the field. You can probably recall being there during conversations with friends, for example. When in the zone during a conversation, emotional connection occurs and flows, with no effort required.

I use the term "zone-like state" because being completely in the zone is a rare event, one that seems to happen outside our conscious control. I believe the zone exists on a continuum from low to high. On a 1 to 10 scale, a 1 would represent a state of mind with which you might have been better off staying at home, and a 10 would be the zone in the purest sense of the word. But instead of waiting to spontaneously be in the zone, I believe there are things you can think and do to get into a zone-like state. For example, when I work with athletes, I usually have them monitor their zone level in practice and competition. We spend time figuring out what leads to a higher level of "zoneness," what interferes with it, and how to get back to it. It goes without saying—higher levels of zoneness are correlated with better performances. A primary reason is that when in a zone-like state, an athlete is absorbed in the present moment and free from worry or self-doubt. In this state of consciousness, an athlete's confidence radiates throughout every cell of his or her body. The athlete is able to trust and let go—with no trying, grinding, striving, or contracting. They can simply let it happen based on trust that they have what it takes. I know you have been there, and you want to know how to make it happen more often.

I believe the promise of this gold medal state of mind is why athletes keep coming back time and again, why we train for hours on end. The gold medal mind allows for that sweet spot in time in which everything comes together in perfect harmony. And what brings us to the sweet spot is winning the internal battle that rages in our minds on most days, most of the time. Winning that battle is a skill that can be learned. Once this skill is mastered, a scoreboard loss will not sting nearly as much, because we will know every ounce of mind, heart, body, and spirit went into the contest. When the gold medal mind is at front and center stage, we can feel euphoric regardless of the outcome of the game.

Nearly everyone in the world of sport claims to understand the value of what is commonly called "the mental game." But this aspect of sport is addressed much less than it could be, given the resources available. Through the years, when I have asked athletes and coaches what percent of performance they think can be attributed to an athlete's mental state, I get responses that range from 50 percent to 99 percent. Then I ask, "What percent of the time do you spend training for the mental side?" The highest number I have heard over the years, and this includes pro- and Olympic-level athletes, is 10 percent—and that was from an athlete who simply listened to music before running races. Is that not a big discrepancy, given the fact that most people would say that confidence, for example, is crucial to athletic success? Most athletes do not deliberately train to develop confidence, let alone learn how to maintain confidence. But doing so is essential to making it through a long and grueling season that can be filled with injuries, burnout, and slumps, among other conditions that can destroy confidence.

USING THIS BOOK

In this book, I define the characteristics of the gold medal mind and describe in detail what interferes with this state of mind, how to achieve it, and how to maintain it. I provide examples and analogies to explain the challenges that seek to destroy the gold medal mind. I offer tips, techniques, and training methods for you to practice, allies that will empower you to prevent your own self-sabotage. It is my hope that this information will touch your heart and create change in the way you think, feel, and act for years to come, not just while you are reading it. The techniques have the potential to do that, but not overnight. Change and transformation will be directly correlated to your rehearsing the techniques to the point you embody them and make them yours. Get ready to practice them over and over again. After all, you did not develop your physical skills over the course of a few years. You became phenomenal as a result of at least a decade of practice and thousands of hours of training.

Changing thought patterns and developing your ability to concentrate will be more challenging than improving your second serve in tennis, for example. Learning to soar, and being able to keep soaring in high-pressure situations, requires that you internalize new psychological skills. Think about it. When does an athlete break down and fail to win? Under pressure. I see many athletes who are "practice players," performing better during practice than in an actual game. Why? During practice, they can perform without thinking because they are not preoccupied with the score or with disappointing coaches, parents, or teammates. My hope for you is that you are able to achieve that state of mind when it counts most, not just during practice.

Approach and work for the development of a gold medal mind with recklessness and a heart that is fully alive. I use the word "work" because that is what we are accustomed to doing as athletes. But what I really mean is enjoy the transformation, and have fun making it happen. Become amused by the mystery that is involved in mental training, because the goal will be elusive at times. Your brain has been wired a certain way as a result of years spent thinking a specific way, and it will rebel. Enjoy the work, and watch out for your competitive tendencies, because there is no winning or losing here, just practice. As they say in Alcoholics Anonymous, "Progress, not perfection."

At the heart of what I am talking about is change. Performance enhancement is about change, plain and simple. This is an area of study that a former professor at Penn State, Dr. Michael Mahoney, wrote about extensively throughout his career. The culmination of his work was published in a book entitled *Human Change Processes: The Scientific Foundations of Psychotherapy.* This masterpiece is 455 pages and has approximately 2,648 references. It is one of my favorite books of all time, and I frequently go back to it for answers to the tough questions I face in the process of helping people change. It is equivalent to a "play book" that informs an athlete how to execute defensively and offensively. The good news is you do not have to read Mike's work of art, because in my book I explain in simple terms how change happens. What I say is based upon research and theory, but only occasionally will I write from an academic perspective.

The late, great, and outrageous author M. Scott Peck, one of my favorites, starts his book *The Road Less Traveled* by saying, "Life is hard." His book *Further Along the Road Less Traveled* starts with, "Life is complex." Well, after reading both books, I made a promise to myself that I would start my book out by saying "Life is meant to be fun, really fun." And that is how I would like you to embrace this process of change—as fun. Yes, it is work and requires practice, but try to put a smile on your face when you are practicing concentration training and find you cannot sit still for more than three minutes. This mental training stuff is the next frontier. Allowing yourself to smile when the journey gets hard is part of the process.

My friend Simon Martin, who has competed internationally as a runner, is training to run a sub-5-minute mile at the age of 62. Simon read chapter 8 of this book ("Thinking Less: A Psychological Lobotomy"), which explains the technique and benefits of concentration training for athletes. Simon was intrigued by the idea of using concentration training as a way to better handle pain and fatigue during races. So he decided he would give the concentration exercise a whirl. Just last week he told me he got up after practicing, assuming 20 minutes had passed—and his wife pointed out that it had only been 4 minutes. In his British accent, he said to me, "It is bloody hard to sit there." Yeah, man, I thought to myself. This mental training stuff is the next frontier compared with what we know about conventional physical training. I would not say it is the final frontier (that being spiritual fitness), but it is definitely the next frontier.

Please read with an open mind and heart. Be mindful of your assumptions, any preconceived notions you may have based upon what you have heard or read. This book will be unlike anything you have been exposed to before. Consider it an adventure in self-discovery. The better you know yourself, the better warrior you will be in training, in competition, and off the field.

CHAPTER 1

The Gold Medal Mind

In the beginning...men and women were created, along with all the animals and everything else. (I am not insisting you believe this, but please go along with it for now.) As the story goes, men and women were rebellious by nature. Competitiveness and a desire to run the show were noteworthy characteristics. In fact, men and women seemed to want to assert their will against the very Dude who created them. Yep, all the way back to the beginning of time, men and women liked to fight, to be right, and to win, whether it was an argument about eating or not eating an apple or a competition to see who could pick the most fig leaves in an hour. They wanted to win. So the story goes. I am sure you know the rest, or if not, know where to find it. (Hint: it is in the part called Genesis of the best-selling book of all time.)

Here is a story that drives home this point about winning. A couple of years ago I attended a conference sponsored by the Gold Crown Foundation, based out of Lakewood, Colorado. The organization was founded in 1986 by basketball star Bill Hanzlik and Colorado business leader Ray Baker. In 2001, it provided more than 35,000 opportunities for kids to be involved in various sports. The group does tremendous work, and is truly changing lives for the better with their sport and enrichment programs.

Speaking at the conference were professional basketball players, former professional coaches, college coaches, and ex-college players. The great all-pro quarterback Archie Manning was the keynote speaker. During one presentation, a college basketball coach talked about summer camps for kids. He noted they would let kids around five years of age scrimmage for short periods of time with the scoreboard turned off. No one would keep score—except the kids themselves. Yes, even with no emphasis placed on the score, these five-year-olds kept score and made sure they all knew who was winning and by how much. This is no surprise to me. I see it when shooting hoops for fun in the driveway with kids. They keep track of how many they make. Recently, I helped coach a nine-year-old girls' basketball team—Moon Star was the name of the team. Again, there was no scoreboard, but I knew who to ask for the score: Lucy, Elle, Sophia, and Hope. These little ones were intense, and I loved it!

Is keeping score part of human nature? And is our emphasis on the scoreboard healthy? I don't have all the answers, but I do know that focusing on the scoreboard *too much* can have detrimental effects on how we play the game. I thought long and hard about using the words "gold medal" in the title of this book. Gold medals are associated with being the best of the best—on the highest platform on the podium. According to a close friend of mine, Dick Moscati, the silver medal is the award for the first-place loser. But I have worked with many athletes through the years who have won gold medals that will never appear in the record books. They did not step up to the podium in the end, but they knew, in the deep recesses of their minds and hearts, that their performances were podium material. These athletes played because they were madly in love with the game, and basked in the joy of the journey.

Five-Ring Fever

When I went to work for the US Olympic Committee, I met someone in the international relations department who had coined the term "five-ring fever" to describe the addiction many employees and athletes developed to the Olympic rings. This person had an interest in the medal count like the rest of us, but also realized how insane the focus on the scoreboard could be. He pointed out that obsession with the medal count was not always in the best interests of the athletes. He was an amateur sport psychologist in his own right (and a person in recovery), aware of the paradoxical nature of winning without being able to completely explain it. In brief, the paradoxical nature is this: if one places focus on the process of playing the game (and letting go), the outcome will take care of itself. As they say in Twelve-Step programs, we need to "put forth the effort and let go of the outcome."

Most of us in sport science roles could easily get caught up in the quest for winning, because the Olympic medal count has always been the alpha and omega. As you are no doubt aware, months prior to the Olympic games, predictions are being made about who will win what medal. And for the athletes, there was no escape from the focus on past medal winners, record holders, and Olympic athletes who became household names. Videos of all the greats were showing 24/7 in the athlete and visitor centers—powerful stuff. The reality of playing the game was too often lost in a sea of past medal counts and predictions of future medal counts.

I have witnessed five-ring fever becoming an epidemic across all sports and at all skill levels, and I feel strongly that the gold medal mind is the antidote. Embracing the simple concepts I lay out in this book will result in achieving goals beyond your wildest dreams. Best yet, there is wisdom in this stuff with far-reaching and enormous implications for playing the game of life.

The Language of Winning

Shortly after I began working for the Olympic Committee, we all had to attend a departmental meeting. The emphasis was on the allocation of resources and the development of what were called performance enhancement teams, or PET. A PET was a staff of sport scientists (a biomechanist, nutritionist, exercise physiologist, and sport psychologist) assigned to work with a particular national governing body (NGB)—US figure skating, for example. Those of us working with US speed skating were to meet on a regular basis to review all aspects of the program. Each of us would provide input based upon our evaluations and propose steps to achieve future goals. This worked quite well and allowed for an integration of services. Teamwork at its best!

However, the other aspect of the departmental meeting focused on allocation of resources, which teams and athletes would get what. The director of coaching and sport science explained that teams would be identified based upon their potential to win medals. Services would be divided into gold, silver, and bronze levels. Obviously, gold medal services were the 12-course meal, the mother lode of services. Gold medal services would be available to the NGBs that had the greatest potential to win medals. When I heard this, questions started dancing around in my mind. Isn't there something wrong with this picture? I wondered. Who can predict who will win a medal? Does this system not reinforce an overemphasis on the outcome (a.k.a. five-ring fever)? Does it not sabotage the potential for developing a gold medal mind? What about the detrimental effects of labeling sports and athletes as potential winners or losers? The whole idea seemed to send the message that our every move was about producing champions. What would the athletes on the table tennis team think when they learned they were only entitled to bronze medal services, if that?

The reality, as we know it, is that the medal count and who has the most golds at the end is what counts. Right? I am not trying to completely devalue what intrigues the masses and puts political points on the board. But I am devaluing five-ring fever to the extent that it leads to our having blind spots, and nurtures a tendency within us to become our own toughest opponents. In my experience, only a small percentage of performers win by focusing on the outcome. Take the game of pool, the art of rock climbing, or the precision sport of diving. Performing at one's best is typically a function of focusing on one shot at a time, one handhold at a time, one dive at a time—not the potential outcome of the performance. In the mind of a champion, the process of playing the game takes center stage. The champion's psychological state is strong and resistant to the distractions, both external and internal, that will take them out of a zone-like state.

Watching nothing but the scoreboard distracts administrators, coaches, athletes, and parents of athletes from the true path to winning: the establishment and maintenance of a gold medal mind. These well-intentioned folks may say they understand the importance of an athlete's state of mind to his or her performance, but place little emphasis on speaking the language that helps athletes improve their mental game.

Each sport has its own particular language, whether it is dance, archery, bowling, or baseball. There is a language associated with physical conditioning, words such as aerobic conditioning, lactate threshold, fast-twitch muscle fibers, power output. There is a language we speak when referring to the mental game: negativity bias, self-fulfilling prophecy, choking, self-serving bias. The fact is the language we use when working with athletes can make the difference between helping an athlete develop a gold medal mind approach and becoming a slave to five-ring fever. Using the wrong language can lead straight to what all athletes train to avoid—losing, defeat, failure. The way we define winning, victory, and success can sabotage the very thing all athletes strive for—the podium.

I am not proposing we revise the language we use in a conventional sense. But let us consider redefining a few words. Sportscasters, when covering an athletic event, constantly use words like success, failure, victory, defeat, winning, losing. This is understandable, but the conventional definition of these words can crush the essence of a gold medal mind. These words are all linked to the scoreboard—the outcome. Who wins and loses is based on the number of points scored or who has the fastest time.

With a gold-medal-mind approach, *victory is defined as achieving and maintaining a state of mind that leads to winning on the scoreboard*—being in the moment, for example. And defeat is defined as being sloppy mentally and becoming prisoner to all the doubts, fears, and worries that can lead to paralysis during an event. The difference between the two is a choice. Making the choice to perform from a gold-medal-mind perspective is what I call a psychological victory. And that type of victory is independent of the scoreboard. But the beautiful paradox here is that achieving psychological victories is also the true path to winning on the scoreboard and earning a medal in the conventional sense of the word.

Simple but Not Easy

This is it, in a nutshell: winning the inner game as a result of having a gold medal mind will lead to winning on the scoreboard. Taking most, if not all, of the emphasis off the outcome is a major characteristic of the gold medal mind. When we are operating from a gold medal state of mind, the outcome will take care of itself. Make your performance about the gold medal mind and let go of the results. It will be impossible to "block and delete" the scoreboard, but the idea is not to give it oceanfront property in your mind. In other words, let it play cowbell and not lead guitar in the orchestra of your mind. Hint: the mental gymnastics involved here require achieving not by trying, but by letting go. This can be one of the most challenging concepts to internalize, because as competitive athletes we are wired to go to war and aggressively fight and strive to achieve.

In sport vernacular, the words would be something like, "Relax to swim faster." Lloyd "Bud" Winter, the legendary coach of the San Jose State track and field teams, 1941 through 1974, makes this the focal point of his book, *Relax and Win.* During his tenure at San Jose State, Bud coached 37 world record holders, 27 Olympians and NCAA All-Americans. Because of the impact of Bud Winter on the coaching of sprinters, San Jose State earned the name "Speed City." Bud was the first person to prove the idea that the key to winning in sports was not "110 percent" effort. "Far more can be achieved with four-fifths effort," he said, and he proved it.

From a Buddhist perspective, I am talking about the concept of non-striving, something Bud Winter would have understood instinctively. The Buddha was full of essential paradoxes, but he did not address the paradox of winning. From what I hear, sport did not have the power to wreak havoc on the soul back then the way it does now. In the Buddha's day, what they did instead was chop wood and carry water. For those of you unfamiliar with that concept, chopping wood and carrying water is the gold medal mind in action. We must chop wood and carry water without giving thought to how bright the fire will burn or how sweet the water will taste. Get the idea?

The long and the short of it is that getting a seat on the podium starts with getting mentally prepared for *practice.* Let me say this again—getting a seat on the podium starts with getting mentally prepared for practice every day! It starts with keeping it simple, a day at a time, and focusing every ounce of gumption on having the highest quality practice "just for today," as they say in the Twelve-Step world. Just for today, without much thought about tomorrow, let alone the next Olympics. For the athlete infected with five-ring fever, living just for today can feel a bit like an "emotional Olympics!" But fortunately, by focusing on developing a gold medal mind, any athlete can learn to navigate the fine line between dreaming of the podium and busting ass one day at a time.

Finding the Sweet Spot

The gold medal mind is about the sweet spot. It is a state of mind that is aware of the scoreboard when there are 2:35 minutes left and the score is 1–0, but at the same time, is even more aware of staying in a zone-like state. It is about concentration, and where an athlete (or coach, for that matter) is focusing his or her attention at any given point in time. We already know that too much attention on the outcome will lead to getting hijacked by your own brain, to being your own worst enemy. A gold medal mind is about training your mind to be an ally. Your mind is so much more powerful than you realize. Sport is one of the best mediums for learning this reality.

Knowing how amazingly powerful your mind can be and how best to use it will be assets long after the dance (i.e., your competitive career) is over.

The gold medal mind is also about having dreams, wishes, hopes, desires, fantasies, and direction. Just think of the three-year-old boy dressed in his favorite pro-baseball jersey, dragging a big bat around because he wants to be a real baseball player. That kid is gold-medal-mind material. Look at his bedroom wall covered with pictures of pro-baseball players, the blanket depicting baseball hats and bats and gloves, his St. Louis Cardinals pajamas. What's his favorite bedtime story? It is about a player named Jackie Robinson. And what does he dream about? Not sugar-plum fairies, but home runs, double plays, outrageous catches, and the roar of the fans as they run onto the field. You remember those days. Where have they gone? I hope you still have pictures of your heroes on a wall somewhere. And if you do not, my hope is that reading this book will take your dreams to another level and lead you to put pictures of your heroes back on the wall. These heroes do not have to be athletes. I have a picture of my personal rock stars, Dennis Bonney and George Einhaus, on my wall at all times. If not for them, I would have never thought of writing this book, let alone been able to complete it.

We have all experienced the state of mind that is the gold medal mind. But for many of us, it is elusive. It seems to happen randomly, and then we have an outrageous day. What I propose and explain in this book is that achieving a gold medal mind is within our conscious control. I believe, based upon what the science says and what I have learned working with athletes, that this state of mind can be created and maintained during even the most intense training sessions or competitions. Just as there are factors that lead to winning a state or national championship, like the execution of a specific offense or defense, there are factors that lead to producing and maintaining the gold medal mind. And not just in sport. The gold medal mind applies to how we live life.

CHAPTER 2

Becoming Psychologically Skilled

In the book *Blink,* Malcolm Gladwell discusses a concept called "thin slicing." This concept measures the accuracy of an expert in a particular field in predicting a specific outcome in the blink of an eye, without putting much time or thought into the prediction, as compared with crunching the numbers based upon complicated statistical analyses. For an example of thin slicing, Gladwell reviews the work of John Gottman, a psychologist who has spent his career studying relationships—what destroys them and what keeps them thriving. After analyzing a husband and wife having a normal conversation for an hour, Gottman can predict with 95 percent accuracy whether the couple will still be married in 15 years. If he analyzes them for 15 minutes, his accuracy falls to 90 percent, a drop of only five percentage points. This is thin slicing at its best. Gottman can quickly identify the ingredients that make a relationship last or lead to divorce based upon his study of couples. (For those of you who are curious, contempt is at the top of the list of the variables that destroy relationships.)

Are there experts who can identify a psychologically skilled athlete, who after watching an athlete perform for 15 minutes can tell with 90 percent accuracy if that athlete has what it takes mentally to be a champion? In other words, after watching an athlete for just a short period of time in a tournament, might a coach be able to tell if an athlete has a gold medal mind? I am not sure, but I do not think so. I know in the world of what is called talent identification, experts in football, for example, have identified physical characteristics that are associated with success: speed, strength, agility, and the like. But when it comes to psychological skills, we can guess, but we cannot know for sure. Psychological abilities are harder to measure than physical. Still, some sport psychology professionals are trying to use psychological testing to help with the identification of psychological skills. They have athletes take a range of personality tests and make predictions based upon their scores on various factors, such as neuroticism, for instance. The following example is based upon a true story. In 1989, when I first worked for the Olympic Committee, a national team coach requested us to test the level of neuroticism in his athletes. Although those of us who did the testing avoided making predictions, the coach believed the level of neuroticism measured would separate the good from the great. Is there truly a correlation between neuroticism and performance? From a scientific perspective, I do not know. However, the coach claimed that based upon years of experience, the test predicted performance. He felt that the higher the score on neuroticism, the worse the athlete's performance would be.

It seems possible this could be true, because in general terms, high scores on neuroticism means that a person worries a lot, and we know worry is the antithesis of a gold medal mind. But this by no means proves the predictive power of psychological testing. Tests need to undergo rigorous psychometric scrutiny in order for us to be able to confidently say something like, "If the athlete scores a 52 on this test, they will be championship material." This has not happened yet.

In 1991, I met a psychologist at a national conference who was working with the Portland Trailblazers. He was using psychological testing to help with player selection, and shared with me that he used the Rorschach inkblot test for the purpose. At the time, I was taking a course in psychological assessment and learning how to use this test. I remember wondering, "What does this test have to do with predicting athletic performance?" After all, the test is supposed to determine whether a person is acutely psychotic. The psychologist told me he used the Rorschach because athletes could not figure it out. Compared to other tests, it was close to impossible for them to guess what the right answers were to make themselves look good, because there are no right or wrong answers on the Rorschach. However, saying card number six looks like a dead cat (which it does) does not, in my opinion, mean one is psychologically skilled, or vice versa. But according to this psychologist, the amount of human movement an athlete saw in the inkblots determined how psychologically healthy he was. Based upon that result, the psychologist concluded that the athlete would be a good team player, as opposed to a psychologically unhealthy athlete who might be selfish and self-centered. Who knows if that test had that amount of predictive horsepower? From a psychometric standpoint, it was just another unproven attempt to predict athletic behavior. But if I put my scientific mind aside, the test may have provided data that was more useful than might appear on the surface when it came to player selection.

In a book chapter we wrote years ago, Sean McCann, Judy Van Raalte, and I discussed this issue of using psychological testing in sport. I will not get into the details, but in general, there is a lot of misuse of testing with athletes. Professionals take scores from a particular test and try to thin slice the results into something relevant to the world of sport. There are more and more sport-specific tests, but even these do not have predictive validity (the ability to demonstrate a correlation between test scores and actual sport performance). Designing a test for athletes that predicts psychological skillfulness, and ultimately, physical performance, is a huge challenge.

In *Mental Toughness Training for Sports: Achieving Athletic Excellence* (an applied sport psychology book that came out in 1982), the author offered a psychological self-report test that purportedly measured psychological skills. He called the test the Psychological Performance Inventory. Scores were broken down into ranges that translated into various conclusions. For example, a score between 6 and 19 on the self-confidence scale meant that the attribute of self-confidence "needs your special attention." The test was total nonsense, because it had never been evaluated for what is called reliability in the field of psychometrics. Reliability refers to the consistency of scores; one such measure is called test-retest reliability. Without it, a person could take the test one week and achieve one set of scores, and take it again a week later and have totally different scores. Reliability also involves measuring what is called internal consistency, or whether a specific scale (self-confidence, for example) actually measures that variable. Again, given that the internal consistency of the Psychological Performance Inventory was not established, the test's self-confidence scale might actually measure what the scale called "positive energy" purported to measure. Thus, in the end, no one could say for sure what the scores meant. The potential danger of such tests is that an athlete could conclude he or she is strong or weak in a certain area based on a scale whose results mean nothing. This is why one must be really careful when taking unproven self-help-type tests.

Psychological Skills and the Gold Medal Mind

The good news is that research has identified psychological skills that are strongly correlated with high levels of performance. These studies do not analyze the predictive validity of psychological tests, but they do reveal how specific psychological skills affect performance. For example, loads of research studies examine the impact of various types of self-talk on performance. Other studies look at the effect different types of goals or imagery training have on performance. And many, many more studies lead to a verdict that these skills work and are highly effective. Meta-analyses have supported these results time and time again. (A meta-analysis is a statistical analysis that looks at a bunch of studies at once to determine the effectiveness of an intervention.) There is much more to this topic, but again, the moral of the data is that the gold medal mind is alive and well—in robust ways, to use statistical terminology. My conclusions about the gold medal mind are based upon this research, on what I have learned at national conferences, and on my own experience dating back to 1983.

Just as elite athletes have fine-tuned physical skills, an athlete with a gold medal mind has a range of psychological skills. Take an elite pole vaulter, for example. Some of the necessary physical characteristics include sprint speed, kinesthetic awareness, and mechanical consistency. These are the characteristics a college coach would look for in a high school pole vaulter. Of course, the athlete's physical skills will not be as finely tuned as a pro's, but based on thin slicing, a coach can see the tendencies and know there is potential. But physical skills alone are not enough to make a national champion. To have that potential, a national champion must also be psychologically skilled. For example, a champion pole vaulter would have the ability to concentrate and stay focused when dealing with a headwind. If a pole broke during a jump, he or she would approach the next jump with as much aggressiveness as ever.

Over the last 25 years or so, I have asked athletes, parents of athletes, coaches, and administrators what they believe are the factors that determine psychological skillfulness in an athlete, and I have listed the most profound of these below. The list also includes characteristics gleaned from some of the sources I just discussed—the research, outcomes of national conferences, and my own experience. If there were a John Gottman in the sports arena, after watching you for a short period of time, he would be able to tell with a high degree of accuracy the degree to which you possessed these important psychological skills. They include the ability to:

- Maintain emotional composure.
- Stay in the present.
- Refocus when distracted by internal (thoughts) or external (crowd, weather, equipment problems) factors.
- Support teammates during practice and competition, regardless of how you feel about them.
- Have humility (the ability to keep the ego in check) and understand the ugly side of pride.
- Keep aware of and mentally control tendencies such as entitlement, selfishness, and self-centeredness.
- Know that perfectionism can be both good and bad.
- Rise to the occasion when it really counts.
- Resolve conflict with a teammate, coach, parent, or friend without blaming, justifying anger, rationalizing, being stubborn, or feeling like a victim. (Being psychologically skilled is also associated with being able to forgive.)
- Stay internally motivated, willing to go to any length to succeed, and knowing that half measures lead to substandard performance.
- Cultivate personality traits such as perseverance, commitment, discipline, dedication, determination, resiliency, optimism, courage, hunger, and passion.
- Be a leader, someone who inspires others both on and off the field.

- Practice healthy self-care, attending to diet, sleep, rest, and spiritual life.
- Maintain perspective, but train like a warrior.
- Embrace that the essence of sport is to transcend self-limiting beliefs.
- Know that psychological victories lead to winning on the scoreboard.
- Be smart about recovery to minimize the risk of overtraining, under-recovery, burnout, and injury.
- Accept pain and fatigue as signals of growth and improvement.
- Know that all-or-nothing (black-and-white) thinking will wreak havoc on confidence.
- Recognize the blessings of injury.
- Avoid using alcohol and other mood-altering substances.
- Maintain a healthy relationship with coaches and consistently ask for feedback and help with goal setting.
- Focus consistently on how to improve the quality of practice time.
- Use time in the weight room to develop the ability to get into a zone-like state.
- Support the psychological development of teammates.
- Have fun and help others to have fun.
- Embrace all situations as opportunities to learn.
- Consistently work on becoming psychologically skilled.
- Enjoy developing a gold medal mind, and know it is a lifelong process.

Although you may not understand all of these characteristics now, as you continue to read you will not only come to understand them, you will learn how to strengthen them. They are skills that you can learn and develop. This is a "nurture" process, maybe with a small dose of nature. I am going to describe in detail the essence of these characteristics and explain how to develop them. But keep in mind that your journey to becoming a psychologically skilled athlete will be a function of your passion for the mental stuff. The ability to be still, look inside, practice the skills, get feedback from others, and ask yourself difficult questions are at the heart of the journey. My hope is that the process is one of the most rewarding and enjoyable you will ever undertake. But you will struggle at times. Consider these moments to be the growing pains involved in developing yourself as a psychologically skilled athlete. Approach these growing pains with fire in your belly. Attack the challenges head on, embrace the struggle, and know the dividends will exceed your investment, beyond all expectations.

Building Psychological Immunity

The process of developing immunity against disease provides a good analogy for the development of psychological skills. You might say that an athlete with a gold medal mind has a strong psychological immune system. As a result of hours of training to become psychologically skilled, an athlete becomes more resistant to "infection" caused by various psychologically challenging events or conditions. In life, viruses and bacteria can be found all over the place, on every door handle and countertop. Our bodies have natural defenses that guard us against infection, and we can ward off many illnesses without needing antibiotic or antiviral medications. But when we travel to foreign countries where we are likely to encounter unfamiliar pathogens, we may need to take steps to stimulate our immune system so we are protected against them.

In sport, there is a similar reality. Like our physiological immune system, our psychological immune system is generally strong. An athlete can typically shake off a bad performance in a short period of time. However, if you blow it in a major competition, the impact on your confidence can be severe. Think of an event like that as an antibiotic-resistant bacteria, for example, certain forms of *Clostridium difficile (*what the docs call *C. diff* for short). A tough pathogen like *C. diff* can make you very sick. Avoid it at all costs: I had it, and two weeks in the hospital only set me up for four more months to recover.

In the world of an athlete, a range of figurative viruses and bacteria exist. Having the psychological immunity to fight them off is essential to achieving and maintaining a gold medal mind. If ever you find yourself really struggling and unable to progress, consider seeing a sport psychologist, just as you would see a doctor for a serious illness.

In the world of sports, ordinary infections include:

- A bad practice
- Being tired
- Having a cold
- A diving board that is too stiff
- A crosswind in archery
- Icy conditions in alpine skiing
- Rain in a baseball game
- Going from sea level to altitude to compete in an endurance sport
- Playing outdoor soccer in 23°F weather
- A change in start time in track and field
- Really soft ice in speed skating

More resistant infections may include:

- A chronic injury
- Emotional abuse from a coach
- A season-ending injury
- Equipment failure at game time
- A series of bad performances
- Several weeks of consistently bad practice
- Conflict with teammates
- Financial issues
- Pressure from parents

Some of these factors will hurt you, but, like ordinary infections, will pass within a relatively short period of time. Plenty of rest, water, and good nutrition will typically resolve most physical infections. In sport psychology vernacular, setting daily goals, occasionally using visualization training, and having a friendly dialogue with yourself will typically take care of a minor ailment. However, for more resistant issues, a more potent treatment will be required. You will need a program of rigorous visualization training, extended periods of concentration training, and close attention to goal setting—all techniques explained in this book.

In any case, you must have a strong dose of determination and be willing to go to any length to achieve your dreams. And you must be willing to embrace emotional as well as physical pain, because you may experience both along the path to a gold medal mind. Why? You will become more in tune with your thoughts and feelings. I know this sounds a bit New Age, and is certainly not part of the typical vocabulary in the athletic world. But increasing your awareness of how you think and *feel* is essential to the process of change and to performance enhancement. Basically, the process of becoming psychologically skilled and internalizing the characteristics I describe in this chapter requires you to know yourself better not only as an athlete, but also as a person. And you will probably come to know yourself better through sport than you could have ever imagined. If you do not believe this yet, just trust me on it for now and keep reading with the same intensity you apply to your physical training.

Here's a suggestion: consider allowing yourself to become mentally prepared before you pick up this book each time you read it. Yep, do something, anything, that helps you create a state of mind, heart, and soul that ensures your "practice time" will be of the highest quality. Again, this stuff really applies to all that you do. That is one of the aspects that make it so much fun!

CHAPTER 3

Taken Hostage by Your Mind

A book that has long been near and dear to my heart is W. Timothy Gallwey's *The Inner Game of Tennis,* first published in 1974. I still refer to this book as the bible of sport psychology. I can't remember how I stumbled across it, but I first read it in 1979. It not only turned my tennis game around, it improved my performance in all other sports as well. The first result of reading the book was that I stopped breaking racquets, which makes me think my parents gave me the book. It had gotten to the point where I had to stop breaking racquets or retire from tennis. The book brought my tirades to an end, and at the same time allowed me to enjoy the game more than I could have ever imagined. And this enjoyment was reflected in my scores. Over the last two decades, I have had many athletes read *The Inner Game of Tennis* and take notes on what they thought would help them win their own inner game.

Gallwey's theory is based upon the idea that our toughest opponent is the self. The "inner game" is the one we play in our own minds. Gallwey divides the self into entities he calls Self 1 and Self 2. Self 1 is "the thinker" and Self 2 "the doer." Self 1 is the source of fears, worries, doubts, concerns, lapses in concentration, and other inner demons. Self 2 is muscle memory, based in the motor cortex, where the memory of all complex movements is stored after thousands of hours of practice. The premise is that if we just let go, Self 2 will perform like poetry in motion. Without interference from Self 1, Self 2 will steal the show every time.

When I began working with Apolo Ohno, the great Olympic speed skating medalist, the first book among many I suggested he read was *The Inner Game of Tennis*. He read it and took notes, and we discussed the material in depth. In his autobiography, *Zero Regrets*, he writes about my work with him, and describes how we began the journey by exploring the inner game concept. Apolo writes:

> "Read this," Doug said to me one day, handing me *The Inner Game of Tennis*, the 1974 classic by Tim Gallwey, mindful that I had a lot of time in the sauna, or back in my dorm room, to think. "Here's what you're looking for in this book," Doug said. "Gallwey talks about 'Self 1,' the thinker, who is constantly telling 'Self 2,' a silent doer, what to do: bend the knees, watch the ball, follow through. Gallwey says that when you master the inner game—you confront fear, doubt, lapses of concentration, dealing with negative thought and low confidence—the scoreboard, the outer game, will take care of itself. To do that, you have to learn to control Self 1. (Ohno 2010, 101)

The goal, as you are probably beginning to see, is to not let Self 1 hijack your brain. Self 1 is powerful. It is seated in the prefrontal cortex, which is filled with billions and billions of brain cells that constantly generate thoughts. In the world of sport, thinking can lead to setting world records—and can also lead to disasters. Typically, in sport psychology, thinking is seen as detrimental to high-level performance. As you may have experienced, when you are in the zone, there usually is an absence of or very little thought.

In the psychology literature, Self 1 might be referred to as "negative self-talk." You know, the little voice inside that says things like, "Why did you do that?" "I can't believe it, not again!" "You idiot." "Coach is going to be pissed!" "Ahhhhh, you dummy!" These are just some of the G-rated things people say to themselves after making an error, losing a game, missing a shot, three-putting, and the like. For some, the self-talk is R-rated. We have all been there. Our internal voice can be ruthless and attack us without mercy. You may know the great Allman Brothers song "Whipping Post." My friend Beth used to say, "I don't have a whip in my hand, I have a whip in each hand." Athletes I have worked with can tell you I sometimes say, "Gosh, you've really taken yourself to the whipping post!" I have taken myself there many times while playing ice hockey. What I would say to myself on those occasions would easily be classified as R-rated.

In the world of applied clinical psychology, this voice is often called the inner critic, or, in some circles within psychology, the internal saboteur. The voice of the internal saboteur leads straight to self-defeating behavior. We become our own worst enemy. While getting attacked by the internal saboteur, or Self 1, we make decisions and perform in ways we would not have were we in a zone-like state. Self 1, the source of destructive, negative self-talk, is like SEAL Team 6 going in for the kill: skilled, powerful, and as fierce as it gets. Self 1 is focused and on point to take Self 2 hostage. Even a minor attack from Self 1 can derail all the muscle memory in the world. The basal ganglia, cerebellum, and motor cortex of the brain can be bursting at the seams with talent, but simply fail to produce once Self 1 takes the helm. In chapter 8, you will learn more about how even subtle shifts in thinking can take a person out of a zone-like state, even if the thoughts are not negative.

To think about it another way, Self 1 leads to what is called "bondage of self" in Twelve-Step circles. Bondage of self refers to situations in which we put ourselves in prisons of our own making and manufacture our own miseries. Merely because of the way you choose to think, your life or your sport can be more or less difficult. Based upon what theory in positive psychology says, our happiness, effectiveness, and ability to be in a zone-like state are functions of what we choose and choose not to think. For example, if you are an alpine skier and have always had difficulty with icy conditions, winning the inner game will be more difficult when the conditions are more like a bobsled run than a ski slope. Self 1 will have a field day, and if you are not able to control the onslaught of vicious thinking, you will manufacture your own miseries and put yourself in prison. While locked up in your internal prison, and if you are by yourself for an extended period of time, you will forget you have the key to get out. This is the worst place to be, either on the field or in life. The phrase "by yourself" is particularly critical here, because unless you are mentally skilled, it can be close to impossible to set yourself free from that prison. This is the reason I place so much emphasis on love and hugs.

I played third singles in high school tennis because I could not seem to beat the first and second singles players, Randy Sabett and Dick Moscati. A few of my brain cells believed I could beat them because of the way I hit the ball in practice, but when it came to challenge matches, I would get hijacked by Self 1—the thinker. Self 1 would take me captive, and from there I became the poster child of my own worst enemy. Self 1 generated internal chatter that fueled self-doubt and led to my pushing the ball around and playing not to lose, as opposed to playing to win.

After reading *The Inner Game of Tennis* the spring of my junior year, about halfway through the tennis season, my game changed. I learned how to deal with the torment of Self 1 in order to let Self 2 work its magic. So that summer, after the official season was over, I began beating Randy and Dick on a consistent basis. Yep, it got to a point where Dick would hang a tiki doll on the net in an attempt to jinx me, which did not work. It did not get into my head.

Dick also launched an attack that could have been taken right out of Gallwey's book, though I don't think he knew that. He tried to get me to think too much. When my serve was hot, he would ask me if I was inhaling or exhaling during my toss, a classic attempt to fire up Self 1. With the insight I had gained reading the book, I saw right through his sabotage attempt and resisted the temptation to analyze. The moral of the story: thinking is the archenemy of the zone-like state, the state of flow during which Self 2 will perform beyond expectations.

Self 1: Villain or Ally?

Up to this point, I have talked in terms that support Gallwey's premise that the negative-self-talk generated by Self 1 is bad news. But is Self 1 really an utter villain, waiting to take you hostage whenever it can? I do not believe in generalizations, and I do not have a crystal ball. I do not know, and no expert can tell you, when Self 1 is going to hijack your motor system. Only you will know when your thoughts and feelings get in the way—the point at which you become your own worst enemy.

In working with golfers, I have seen some on the verge of breaking a club after a bad shot, only to regroup and hit the next shot incredibly well—maybe even better than if they had not blown a gasket. And then there are the golfers who, upon experiencing the least amount of frustration, will blow the next shot and potentially the rest of the round. I have seen cyclists, swimmers, and runners who take themselves to the whipping post for slowing down when pain and fatigue strike, and then turn it on—accelerate—with renewed vigor in response to the Self 1 attack. And then there are those endurance athletes who start to feel more tired and more self-critical and lose confidence when an opponent passes them. In other words, the effect of an attack from Self 1 all depends on the individual athlete, something we call "individual differences" in the psychology world. Being mindful of individual differences decreases the probability we sport psychologists will generalize.

Self 1 gets a bad rap, in my mind. But it inhabits an area in which the strength and versatility of the human spirit is alive and well. We are all motivated in different ways. If taking yourself to the whipping post helps you work harder and train with fire in your belly, then ride that wave. I am not going to say that filling your head with nothing but unicorns and rainbows is the one and only key to unlocking the door to optimal performance. It may be, it may not. And depending on the day, time and situation, what works for you may change. This is where mental flexibility is important, and it is crucial to maintaining emotional composure, an essential feature of the gold medal mind. While you may not be able to control all negative thoughts or feelings, emotional composure will keep you from becoming *attached* to the type of thinking that goes right for the jugular.

Here is a story that illustrates my off-the-beaten-path perspective on this inner game stuff. I was working with a 15-year-old competitive tennis player who trained 20 hours a week outside of school. She had participated in competitive dance until she was 13, at which time she got into tennis. So she had limited on-court and match-play experience, particularly compared with her opponents. Thus, based upon her lack of history of winning during match play, her confidence was weak when it came to tournaments. She was in agreement that Self 2, although highly talented, was vulnerable to the vicious nature of Self 1.

A great deal of our early work together was focused on how she could win the inner game. She liked Gallwey's book and resonated with the concept. So she was open to participating in a little exercise to shed light on her experience with Self 1. We created a format through which she could conduct a dialogue between Self 1 and Self

2. Self 1 was addicted to scoreboard results. Self 2, however, wanted to be in the moment, play the game, play one point at a time, and have fun.

The following is an example of a typical internal dialogue this athlete would have prior to and during every tournament, playing both roles. Act I reflects a conventional wisdom perspective on Self 1, and Act II illustrates an alternative view. You will see that I refer to Self 1 as "friend." I do so because ultimately, this part of your mind is a friend. Self 1 wants you to do well. It wants you to win. However, it can create a problem of good intentions gone bad, similar to a parent who says to a kid, "You will win this time. Focus on winning this game." The parent has good intentions and makes the suggestion out of love. But in reality, the advice is entirely outcome oriented and will trigger Self 1 to run riot.

Keep in mind that in reality Self 2 does not have a "voice," because it is completely movement-oriented and based in muscle memory, not conscious thought. But for the purposes of this exercise, which is focused on training Self 1 to be an ally, it was necessary to give Self 2 a voice in the dialogue.

Act I

Self 1: You'd better do well. Don't screw this up.

Self 2: You are sabotaging my mind.

Self 1: You spend so much time, effort, and money on this... don't screw this up!

Self 2: You are not helping.

Self 1: This happens every tournament. Stop being so nervous, just get over it. You can't screw up anymore.

Self 2: It doesn't matter how I do as long as I am growing. You are making this harder. I'm done fighting with you.

Self 1: I won't leave you alone. You need me.

Self 2: I am frustrated, angry, and upset. You are gone forever.

Self 1: Nope, I'm still here. I'll always be here. You'll never get rid of me.

Self 2: You are a terrible friend. You just hurt me and bring me down. You make life harder than it should be. I can train and work hard without your help.

Self 1: You wouldn't be where you are without me.

Self 2: I hear you won't leave me alone, but I am asking that you give me some space. I get you want to be my friend, but there are times I need to be alone, like the morning of a match and during a match. You need to leave me alone at those times.

Self 1: I promise I won't leave you alone all the time. But I promise I will leave you alone in the morning before a match and during a match as best I can.

Self 2: Thank you for your word and being able to give me some space. You have to trust me on this one. It will help. Do you believe me?

Self 1: Well, there are only a few matches where you have done well without me. I really think you need me. But I will leave you alone for the next tournament.

Self 2: Thank you. I will talk to you soon.

Although Self 1 did ultimately agree to honor the request for space from Self 2, there was an antagonistic quality to this interaction. Tension and a bit of a fight characterized the discussion in the athlete's mind. She realized she lost the inner game time and time again because, in the end, Self 1 did not *trust* Self 2. So I had her entertain an alternative approach to dealing with Self 1. Act II is based upon her request to learn a different way to respond to Self 1. So I took on the role of Self 2 while she played Self 1.

Act II

Self 1: You better win this time. You better not screw up.

Self 2: Hey friend, good to hear from you. I am glad you are reminding me that it is time to win, to do well.

Self 1: Yes, I will lead you to victory, to this breakthrough all your coaches are talking about.

Self 2: I hear you. You motivate me during the week in practice to work hard, but before and during matches I need to let go of the score and stay in the moment.

Self 1: No, I think you have it all wrong; I am here to push you to do well.

Self 2: Friend, you know I am motivated. Trust me on this one. Maybe I even care too much and push too hard. This makes me tighten up and push the ball around. You have seen me do this.

Self 1: Well, I know you are motivated, but my concern is that when you start losing in a match you will give up.

Self 2: No, that's not going to happen, I have never given up. Have you ever seen me give up?

Self 1: No, you haven't. So what do you need from me?

Self 2: To trust me that staying in the moment, in the zone, playing one point at a time, will lead to my playing well and ultimately winning. Just trust me...

Self 1: But has that worked?

Self 2: Yes, remember the first match at my last tournament? That was the best I have ever played in a tournament. I was absorbed in the moment, remember?

Self 1: Yes, you were. I remember. I could just sit back and watch and not worry about you losing intensity.

Self 2: Yes, I was more intense than I am when you are pushing me and making me think about losing and having to try harder.

Self 1: It did work. So you want me to do that again?

Self 2: Yes, my friend, just trust that I know what I need to do to have fun and play my best.

Self 1: Okay, just know I am here in case you need me.

Self 2: I know you are there. I appreciate that and I will let you know if I need your help.

Self 1: Glad we could talk; I am much more at ease now and I trust you. Have a blast!

Self 2: Thanks, I am ready! I am feeling the passion. I know I can just let go, enjoy being in the zone, and play one point at a time.

Was this not a more friendly interaction? In many ways, this kind of inner dialogue is no different from working through a conflict with a friend. Remember, the friend probably wants to win, to be right, just like Self 1. Understanding that, you can respond in ways that will build trust and collaboration. It may take time, especially if you have been losing both the inner and outer games for a while. It may seem futile to try to make friends with Self 1, to get to the point at which Self 1 actually trusts you and is willing to do whatever it can to help you stay in a zone-like state. But you can help the process by embracing the idea that this is where the real game takes place: in your mind. You against you—that is where the fun lies. Become amused with how viciously you can treat yourself, but at the same time be amazed at how powerful your mind can be when Self 1 and Self 2 are in sync. Accept this as the place where you will ultimately win or lose on the scoreboard. Approach this with a sense of curiosity. You are gaining a life skill in every sense of the word.

I am proposing that the primary purpose of Self 1 is not to hijack or imprison Self 2. This is an area in which my opinion differs from Gallwey's and others in sport psychology. I believe Self 1 plays a functional role in the establishment of a gold medal mind. I understand negative self-talk because I get lots of it from my own Self 1. Up until about three years ago, shortly after getting to know me, a person would usually say, "Gosh, you are hard on yourself." After implementing many of the techniques I share in this book, I have been relieved of the "bondage of self" I experienced at the hands of Self 1. Now I know he is truly a friend, and I enjoyed the process of working through this long-standing demon. The taste of the psychological victory was as sweet as any victory I have ever experienced on the scoreboard. That is what I am hoping for you!

Having shared that, if you have made an agreement with yourself that being self-critical is just the way you are, I am going to suggest that you also learn to turn your mind into an ally. I suspect that you, like me, have at least a few brain cells that know your tendency toward negative self-talk is self-destructive. Engaging in the adventure of turning your mind into an ally will give you the key to letting yourself out of your self-imposed prison at any point in time. It will give you the ability to put yourself back into the zone-like state at will, the state of mind that leads you to perform beyond your expectations. Turning your mind into an ally will help you become a warrior in every sense of the word.

Just hold onto this idea for now. But from this point forward, make mental and even written notes when your inner saboteur speaks. It will give you clues that will help you learn how to channel that energy into the development of a gold medal mind. Yes, take written notes. Write down exactly what Self 1 is saying to you. Think of yourself as a scientist, collecting data and testing hypotheses just as Einstein did all the time, even when he was sleeping! The hypothesis you are testing is that Self 1 is not as ugly as you originally thought. This is part of the journey toward self-discovery I have been talking about. You are going to embrace, at least for several months, that this self-discovery stuff is the real sport you are playing right now.

Making the choice to practice these skills over and over again will allow you to truly become a student of the inner game. Before becoming a student of the inner game, a figure skater, for example, can tell me in great detail all the biomechanics involved in having an outstanding program. But she struggles with explaining the "biomechanics" of achieving and maintaining a zone-like state. My hope is that as a result of practicing the skills I teach in this book, you will be as proficient in describing how your mind works as you are in explaining your body mechanics. You may be surprised at what a thrill this can be! But be aware of your tendency to think in win and lose terms when it comes to psychological development. There is no scoreboard here. Your goal right now is to simply experience the process of reading this book one word at a time and indulging in the suggestions I provide. And again, I suggest that you take time to mentally prepare each time you sit down to read this book, practicing what you already know works to create a mental state that lends itself to the highest levels of comprehension, information processing, and retention.

CHAPTER 4

Gummy Bears Sticking Together

It was one of the most humid days of the year, and the air conditioning was down for the count. Stepping into the athletic department at Virginia Commonwealth University reminded me of entering a sweat lodge, but there was no way I could reschedule the meeting. Coach "Guzz" was a busy man, busier than most division I coaches, so I wanted to respect his time. Also, I had heard he was not a big fan of this psychology stuff, and I did not want to confirm any potentially preconceived notions about flaky psychologists. Other than talking with Guzz on the phone for about three minutes to set up the appointment, we had never met.

Upon entering his office, I thought to myself, "He is a mad scientist." There was stuff everywhere—books, equipment, a large white board covered with statistics, and much more. Guzz was a big man with a Fu Manchu mustache. I was slightly intimidated. "Doc, I am a perfectionist," he said. "I am a perfectionist with everything I do. If I am going to buy gummy bears, I am going to get the best gummy bears out there. And I want my players to be perfectionists too."

I responded, "I'm a perfectionist too. Glad to be in good company. But what about being human?" He said, "I don't think that way. I want my team to be a working machine and perfect in every sense of the word." I said, "Let's go for it," but wondered secretly if this working machine idea might not be the Achilles heel of the team. I believe in striving for progress, not perfection, as they say in Twelve-Step programs. But I thought I'd best let it be for now, and that maybe, just maybe, we could have another discussion down the road.

That experience was many moons ago; I do not even like to remember how long ago I had the honor of working with Coach Guzz, his staff, and his team. But I will never forget it, largely because of his reference to gummy bears. I started to use the term gummy bears to refer to factors that have the potential to become an athlete's Achilles heel. Are tendencies like perfectionism really that bad? I have learned that while they may seem positive at the outset, "gummies" are not consistent with a gold medal mind.

We all have our fair share of gummy bears that can wreak havoc in our lives, and athletes are no exception. Typically, an athlete I am working with will identify some of his or her gummy bears prior to my even asking. But at some point during our first few meetings, I will review with the athlete a variety of personality characteristics that are common even to competitive six-year-olds, and all too often seen among highly talented people. Some of these gummy bear personality traits are listed below. To make gummy bear pie, combine any five, stir, and bake under pressure.

- Extremely high standards
- Unrealistic expectations
- Continually raising the bar, even after failure
- Inability to feel satisfied
- Focusing on what went wrong, rather than what went right
- Taking good performances for granted
- High levels of self-criticism
- Habitual self-doubt
- Thinking (in the mind) but not believing (feeling in one's

heart) that one is truly talented

- A demanding nature
- Sense of urgency, lack of patience
- Fragile confidence
- Incredible intensity
- Fear of losing, making errors, saying the wrong thing
- Doubting one's ability to achieve goals
- Taking losing very hard
- Compulsivity (unhealthy repetitive behaviors)
- Obsessiveness (negative ruminations)
- Easy to anger
- And yes, perfectionism

Many of the traits listed above describe me too, and I know I learned them through my involvement in competitive sport over the years. From a nature-versus-nurture perspective, there is clearly an environmental factor at work. Sport and gummy bears go hand in hand. It is just part of the deal, and most coaches will nurture the development of these tendencies. When you add parents to the equation, with their own collection of gummy bears, look out. You end up with a bag full of gummy bears all trying to be perfect, and failing because they are getting hot, sweaty, and sticky.

Gummy Bears: Villains, or Friends in Disguise?

Are gummy bears really that bad, you might ask? I ask myself all the time. It is true they can serve as fuel, the juice that drives a person and sustains the gumption to power through adversity. In fact, they worked for me in certain situations, but then backfired. Years ago, while I was hospitalized for a variety of reasons, including being toast (a.k.a. burned out), a doc looked me in the eye and said, "You don't know how to just *be*. You are a human *doing*. You may know something about being human because of your profession, but you aren't living it." In response, I shouted, "But you are not an athlete. What do you know about competitiveness and pushing the envelope? Have you ever beat the shit out of yourself in a weight room only to do it all over again the next day? Have you?" As any brilliant healer would, he asked, "Really, is your method working for you? Look where you are. Was it part of your plan to end up here, having this conversation?"

I clearly remember sitting in that very small room with the attending physician, a resident, and a medical student all sitting in front of me with their clipboards. I was in a chair against the wall in my hospital gown, having not showered in three days. As the attending physician delivered this message, I recall lightly banging my head against the wall as tears streamed down my face. I was terrified—terrified of who I would become if I could not be competitive, intense, and on fire. I might become a blob, slothful. Or maybe even worse, I might become a New Age freak just wanting to *be*. However, a few humility-driven brain cells knew my gummy bears were going to kill me if I did not at least learn to keep them from sticking together and making a mess. In Twelve-Step terms, it looked as if it might be time for a little ego deflation. It was time for me to let go of some old beliefs and train my humility muscle. At last, I could embrace the line heard frequently in Twelve-Step programs: "Look where your best thinking got you!" Yes, it was time for a different approach, an approach I came to call the gold medal mind.

Part of the problem for driven athletes is that *doing* is what sport is all about. After all, a person cannot just meditate on a yoga mat and expect to increase physical strength. (Only the stupendous Phil Jackson could find a way to pull that off.) But as you will recall, the gold medal mind is largely a state of being in the present, being in a zone-like state—just being. The gold medal mind is about being aware, absorbed in the moment, free of all distractions, either internal (like thoughts) or external (the crowd, judges, or the weather). And gummy bears are often at the root of distracting thoughts. For example, after a poor performance, thoughts such as "I can't believe I did that again. Idiot! I will never get this right. Why don't I just quit," are driven by the gummies of perfectionism, harsh self-criticism, and unrealistic standards. Taken all together, they leave no room for error or experiencing what I call "random moments of being human." If the athlete makes an error, wham, it's off to the whipping post. Gummy bears may not agree, but according to gold medal mind ideology, if an athlete does not mess up, they do not learn or grow.

But are gummy bears all bad? The long and short of it is this: it depends on how many gummy bears you have in your mouth at one time. Think about it. Having high standards is not a bad thing in and of itself. Say high standards are a yellow gummy bear and you have only one. No problem, you eat it and down it goes—yummy. But if you have a yellow high-standards gummy bear in your mouth with an orange (unrealistic expectations) gummy bear, a green (demanding nature) one, a black (never satisfied) one, a red (perfectionist) one, and a purple (sense of urgency) one in your mouth all at the same time—ugh, you have a recipe for disaster. The gummy bears stick together, and you risk getting terribly sick. I have worked with loads of athletes who, after repeatedly getting sick on their gummy bears, start to hear thoughts of quitting rattling around in their brains.

In statistical terms, the way combinations of factors react to each other is called an interaction effect. Interaction effects can be significant or not significant. If they are not significant, nothing happens. But if they are significant, something is going to happen, even if we do not know what, or if it will be good or bad. And it is difficult, if not impossible, to say how many factors you can juggle (or, in our gummy bear analogy, eat) at one time. You may be highly self-critical, compulsive, and perfectionist, and notice only the mistakes you make versus what you do right, but that may work well for you. For you, this combo may be associated with a gold medal mind. But if you add one or two more factors, such as being extremely intense and taking losing incredibly hard, you may get a bad interaction effect, followed by absolute disruption of your gold medal mind.

Part of developing a gold medal mind is challenging yourself to look inside, into all the rooms and closets in your house, to identify all of your gummy bears. Then you have to go a step further to identify which ones work for you and which work against you. Remember, an essential aspect of having a gold medal mind is the ability to achieve and maintain a zone-like state of mind. A combination of an orange and a yellow and a green gummy bear might just be the perfect mix to get you into the zone. You need to investigate and find out what works for you. It may not be easy, because gummy bears can be subtle, and at face value a destructive trait may at first look good. Take pride, for example. In the wide world of sports, pride is an honorable characteristic. But there is another side to this coin. A person with pride may be arrogant, judgmental, self-centered, selfish, and generally impatient with others. These are not characteristics of a good team player, not at all. There is more to pride than meets the eye. It can be a good quality, but it has a dark side, like most gummy bears.

Here is another way to think about it. There is a time and place for gummies. Typically, there are fewer right times than wrong times. But imagine if you had the ability to turn your gummy bears on and off when you wanted to. For example, if you have had a bad performance and are incredibly frustrated, you may want to push yourself extra hard in practice to ensure you will not flop again. It may sound like a good idea, but be mindful that your intense-and-competitive gummy bear has a dark side. That dark side may lead to overtraining, overreaching, inadequate recovery, and even injury if you cannot turn it off when you need to. After a bad performance you may need to rest—and I mean passive, not active, rest. Being compulsive types, we competitive athletes have a hard time sitting still, let alone turning off potentially damaging traits that we think work well for us.

So what is the verdict on gummy bears? Ally or villain? On the downside, they take your focus off the journey—playing the game—and can lead to obsession with the scoreboard. Gummy bears can bust even the most mentally tough athlete out of a zone-like state. However, in the final hour I will insist that gummy bears are actually parts of us that are friends in disguise. They mean well. They are truly loving aspects of our personalities that are trying to help in the only way they know how. The fact is, without the help of our gummy bears we may not have accomplished many great things—maybe, but probably not. The trick is being able to regulate your gummies so they work for you, not against you. In the meantime, if you hear of a cure for perfectionism, please let me know.

CHAPTER 5

The Philosophy of Extremes

Aristotle, as you may know, was a big man on campus among philosophers. Among other words of wisdom, the saying "All things in moderation" was an important concept in his philosophy. Moderation makes sense, doesn't it? It sounds healthy in many ways. But it made no sense to me and my friends who ran around Weston Avenue, where I grew up in Niagara Falls, New York. Moderation was synonymous with boredom in our neighborhood. We liked to modify the old saying to, "Why do things in moderation when you can do them to excess?" That is what we were about. In a perverse way, we prided ourselves on going to extremes in our pursuit of sport, on pushing the envelope. After all, isn't that what athletics is all about? Maybe, maybe not. Around here, in the Boulder area, the practice of pushing the envelope still reigns supreme. No judgment—just a fact.

For me, the philosophy of extremes was ingrained by the time I was 11 years old, and for better or worse, it is still alive and well within me. You might think that as an athlete and coach I would subscribe wholeheartedly to the healthy moderation idea. But still, even as a psychologist, the concept of moderation has the same negative connotation for me that it did all those years ago—flat and boring. The conventional wisdom would suggest a psychologist would have a healthier outlook on life. In most arenas, I do, but when it comes to sport I feel a fire burning inside, an intensity in which the maxims "more is better" and "no pain, no gain" are guiding forces.

Rest assured, if we worked together I would not entertain forcing this philosophy on you. I already suspect, based upon the fact you are reading this book, that these maxims resonate with you. Part of the art of developing a gold medal mind is to avoid extremes. It also involves integrating all aspects of yourself so that your mind and body work in sync. If we had the opportunity to work together, I would nurture your tendency to push the envelope while at the same time, avoiding the trap of going to extremes. In other words, my goal is to help you find that sweet spot between pushing the envelope and avoiding the crash and burn. That is the gold medal mind in action. Simple stuff, but not easy. Consistent practice is required to change a "psychological operating system" that is not serving you well, in much the same way you have become outrageously physically skilled as a result of thousands of hours of rehearsal and correct repetition.

If I were to be rigorously honest, in general, I do not feel most athletes work hard enough. I mean in a smart hard way, not in the reckless way we used to train. Do I tell them this? I do not, because that is part of the coach's job description, not mine. But I certainly will tell an athlete when they are not working hard enough on his or her psychological training. It is honest and the right thing to do. Do I have to do this often? No, but as I have said, sport is just a microcosm of society. I can see how athletes interact with the world based upon how they approach practice, games, winning, losing, and mental training.

As you will learn later in this book, I believe that in order to "go to heaven," you must first "die" (the subject of chapter 14). My belief in this philosophy came from my work with Coach Philips, a division I soccer coach who shared the concept with me. This was precisely my father's philosophy as well. My belief came out raging at one particular point in my professional career. I laugh about it now. Shortly after I started working for the US speed skating team, the short-track team had a World Cup competition in Sheffield, England. I had been attending their practices for a couple of weeks, and spent most of my time on the ice talking with the athletes. There was a day, and then another day, and yet another day when the coach gave the athletes the afternoon off prior to this massive event. In fact, these afternoons off were written into the training program. And it made sense, a few weeks before a major competition, and in the spirit of "periodization," that she wanted the athletes to peak by the time they were at the starting line. (A training program designed according to periodization involves phases of training that vary widely in intensity. In the phase just preceding competition, the athletes will be peaking physiologically.) But I was going crazy. In the deep recesses of my mind, I was thinking, "Sue, are you kidding? They need to be pushing the envelope, feeling the pain and getting hungry. Why are you allowing them to play computer games in the afternoon?" Now I never said any of this to the coach, but boy, I wanted to. It made me nuts to see them having time for what she called regeneration. Regeneration, I thought—I will show you what regeneration is and is not. And it is not about playing computer games.

As I said, I kept my mouth shut and worked with the athletes who were willing, during their down time. I met with them individually and as a group on how to develop a gold medal mind. This allowed me to at least feel they were accomplishing something useful. Even back when I was studying exercise physiology, I hadn't believed all the drivel about active rest, passive rest (what some call sofa training), and periodization. In my day, the process was plain and simple: train hard and then some, until you were puking. This approach was confirmed for me when I started taking guitar lessons and came across a quotation by Ted Nugent (a musician popular in the 1970s). In this particular guitar book, he was quoted as saying, "I play the guitar. And I continue to play. At the point my fingers are bleeding

I know I am starting to get somewhere." Adrenaline surged through my veins after reading this. But it was not enough to inspire me to learn barre chords. At some point I decided my Seagull (a pretty good guitar) was made to be a piece of decor in my living room, not to play.

With the speed skating team, I took another step to ease my scientific mind (which in fact had not studied exercise physiology for many years). I met with the senior physiologist, Randy Wilber, PhD, to ask him about what I thought was a witchcraft-oriented training program. He gave me a detailed explanation of the science behind the idea of regeneration time, the decades of research supporting the fact that pacing was essential. Shaking my head, I said, "Okay, the coach is always preaching that rest is part of the training program." He assured me that given all that he knew about the skaters, their aerobic this and anaerobic that and power output and white blood cell count, the coach was spot on. And a visit to the library at the Olympic Training Center confirmed what the physiologist told me.

Years ago, when working with the long-track Olympic speed skating team, I met with each of the athletes early in the season to discuss their training goals. One athlete in particular wanted to narrow things down to weekly goals, rather than focus on her overall goal. And one of her weekly goals was to not go dancing. I asked why, what happened? She told me that the other night, several of the athletes had gone out to dance, and against her better judgment, she went along. Well, they had such a blast they closed the club down, and she went home and danced some more. I thought it sounded like fun, a good break, and I shared that with her. But she did not see it that way. "Outside of workouts, I need to stay off my feet. It is part of my recovery program. I can't afford to ask any more from my body than I do in practice. It is only preseason, and we have a long way to go. I plan to be on the podium this year." In fact, she did end up on the podium.

I have never seen an athlete use active and passive rest so well in my life. "Dancing" became our buzzword that helped her with pacing, rest, and regeneration during that season. She learned when she could "dance" and when she could not. And there were times when dancing actually became part of her training program. She had a heart-to-heart conversation with the coach about her need for rest. The exercise physiologist supported her and also talked with the coach. Yes, there were times the coach would come to me and ask if she really needed rest. It was not for me to say, so I suggested he speak with her directly. And she would be clear and direct with him about needing the morning or afternoon off. This takes a great deal of courage. Since that time, I have used the expression "dance the night away," to help athletes understand and surrender to their need to rest in order to avoid pushing the envelope in an unhealthy way.

In my experience, an athlete advocating for his or her own rest rarely happens. I can share story after story in which an athlete has had a bacterial infection, fever, and dehydration, and still refused to tell the coach, "No, I can't train today." There are days to push the envelope, and as you have learned, I am all about pushing the envelope. But there is a point at which it is plain, simple, and clear that rest is an essential part of the training program. On the extreme side, I have seen athletes just returning to play after an injury who push themselves beyond what is medically indicated. You may have done it yourself. In cases like this, I am very conservative and feel the risk of reinjury and setback is not worth the extra 2,000 meters a swimmer may try to do. This is a big deal in the world of competitive sport, and I see it at the youth level as well. My intention here is not to get into what is right, wrong, or in between. I am merely giving examples of what can happen when an athlete trains too much and incorporates too little rest.

I was interviewed by a writer from ESPN Women's Magazine once for an article on post-race letdown. I did not know there was such a thing, so I did a bit of research on the topic. Yes, it seemed post-race letdown was a real animal with sharp teeth and a vicious roar. Basically, it is an experience an endurance athlete may have after completing an extreme competition—an ultra marathon, for example. The athlete may experience a letdown, manifested by a little sadness, a sense of loss, and fatigue that sets in after months and months of training and then running 100 miles. For some, there is a restlessness and desire to get after it again, and to do it too soon. The brain may want to get back to training, but the body is not able to respond to the call to action. The body cannot respond for physiological reasons—depletion of glycogen stores and micro-tears in muscles, to name a few.

In the world of physiology and psychology, we have additional words to describe the result of pushing the envelope without recharging, including burnout, stale, overtraining, under-recovery, overreaching, flat—even toasted. (I got that word from a friend we call Captain, who used it to identify how we felt when we had been rock climbing all day and our bodies could not handle another move.) It is far too tempting to push. At times it is easier to push than it is to rest. But rest you must. I am not necessarily talking about sofa training, but I do advocate walking, spinning on a bike, short and slow runs, swimming a bit, and other activities we might call active rest. Post-race letdown calls for both active rest and passive rest.

So how do you find the sweet spot when it comes to training hard? There is no easy answer to this question. You may intuitively know when it is time to take a day off, but your coach often may not agree. If you are a person vulnerable to breaking the laws of periodization, you might want to consult with an exercise physiologist who can monitor you for signs of overtraining and under-recovery. Better yet, meet with a sport psychologist to watch for psychological signs of pushing too hard, because those signs appear long before the physiological signs do. Use common sense and take care of yourself, even if you risk your coach blowing a gasket when you say you need a day or two off. I cannot tell you how often swimmers come to me bleeding emotionally because they are toast physically. They have been swimming twice a day quite frequently throughout the week. By the time they come to see me, they are dreading hard workouts. Rest is typically not an option until they are injured. Then they are forced to rest, and usually come back flying because they have had time to recover not only physically, but also psychologically.

Ultimately, how and when to rest is up to you, and this is one of the challenging aspects of having a gold medal mind. When you are true to yourself, you run the risk of pissing people off. And that, my friends, is the subject of a long list of self-help books, as it applies to the game of life as much as anything else. Being encouraged to have a voice is rarely nurtured in sport or even school. A coach who is able to put his or her ego aside and welcomes what you have to say is helping with the development of a gold medal mind. However, many coaches have a "my way or the highway" mentality. Not good. A dose of humility and an ability to welcome feedback can go a long, long way when it comes to developing psychological mindfulness in athletes. Much of my work with female athletes, in particular, is helping them find their voice—their truth—and expressing it. This is a tremendously important quality to have in the game of life, for males and females alike.

CHAPTER 6

Connective Tissue and Mortality

> Sometimes our lives have to be completely shaken up, changed and rearranged to relocate us to the place we were meant to be.
>
> — Anonymous

I was incredibly blessed during my competitive career as an ice hockey player to have never been injured seriously enough to be out for more than a game or two. But when I was playing purely for the love of the game, disaster struck. It was April 1998 when I found myself lying face down on the ice with both legs numb, unable to get up. It was the type of thing that is not *supposed* to happen in a non-checking, no-slap-shot adult recreational hockey league. Without going into the details, the injury was a result of my innate competitiveness, which led me to put myself in a precarious position. I played to win and paid the price. But even though it took away my ability to play ice hockey—something that had drug-like qualities for me—that injury turned out to be a source of many blessings. And this is one reason I talk with athletes (and non-athletes) about what I call the gift of injury.

My hockey accident damaged a disc in my lumbar spine, causing an annular tear, which radically changed my level of physical activity. I was limited to walking about 30 minutes a day, and depending on my status, swimming for about 20 minutes. Lots of stretching and boring physical therapy exercises rounded out my exercise program. That is all I could do for about 12 years. For me, it felt like death. When an orthopedic surgeon advised me to stop everything and stick with walking and swimming, I replied, “Can you give me some Prozac?” Oh, I was angry. For nearly a decade, my back dictated how I lived my life. My back would say things like, “No, Doug, you are not going out to dinner tonight.” “Doug, you can only sit for an hour at a time today.” “Leave the movie now or you will pay the price.” “Forget about the gym unless you’re going to just sit in the whirlpool.” For someone who generally likes being in control, this has been one of the most humbling experiences I have ever had. But I was given what they call in Twelve-Step programs “the gift of desperation.” This resulted in my inviting a Higher Power into my soul to help make sense of the horror movie my life seemed to have become.

My physical limitations are humbling largely because they put me face-to-face with my mortality. After the injury, I felt my body had betrayed me. For all the years before that, I had only to think “move” and my body would respond, consistent with my brain’s request. For the first time in my life, this was not the case. I used to rock climb, trail run, mountain bike, road bike, water and snow ski, and play tennis, squash, racquetball, basketball, soccer, ultimate Frisbee, ice hockey, and volleyball. After the injury, the weekend would roll around and I got to decide between walking, swimming, and playing backgammon. (I actually made a bit of money playing backgammon.) On a good weekend, I could do all three in the same day. In Boulder, where super athletes reign, this could be seen as a pathetic activity level. And there have been times over the years when I contemplated moving from Boulder just to mitigate the psychological torture of living in a place like this.

I am sure I sound as if I am on the pity pot—and, at times I still am, even after all these years. But the one thing that keeps me dedicated to healing is *believing* I will pursue ice hockey, tennis, and rock climbing again. I will be back, in spite of what the health care providers recommend. Probably not running 5k races in 17:34 and 10ks in 37:12, but at least running two or three miles at an 8-minute pace. I have hockey sticks in both my office and living room to remind me every day to do something, anything that will get me closer to getting back on the ice again. Insane? Probably, and when the time comes that I can step back onto the ice, I am not sure I will do it. Because over this period of time, I have been gifted with more than a few brain cells that finally embrace the idea of regeneration—and finding meaning in other areas of life than athletics.

The Emotional Injury

The emotional trauma that accompanies physical injury can take a grave toll. And that is where I try to help. Emotional injury occurs as a result of the physical trauma and all the manifestations that may come with it, including physical pain, missing several games, the end of a season, the end of a career, failing to make progress in rehab, making progress but having setbacks. They can include repeated surgeries with no improvement, time spent going to appointments and dealing with insurance companies, out-of-pocket costs for treatments not covered by insurance, lost contact with the team, pressure from the coach, and even the fear of returning to play. This is the short list. (I mention out-of-pocket expenses because I have probably spent around $62,000 over the last 12 years to get to where I am now.)

The psychological features of the emotional injury can include frustration, irritability, anger, impatience, regret, embarrassment, shame, self-pity, fear, doubt, despair, rage, hopelessness, helplessness, and a whole host of other emotions that can turn the climate of the heart and mind into something resembling a Category 4 hurricane. While sitting across from an athlete sharing an injury story with tears streaming down his or her face, I typically say something like, "You are bleeding emotionally, and this is the aspect of your rehabilitation that I can help you with. We are going to treat the injury to your heart, because you might find that the emotional pain is worse than the physical pain. It really stinks. I hate that this happened to you. But if we put our heads together, I think you might find there's an enormous amount you can learn from this disaster. We will find out how this injury is a teacher in disguise."

While dealing with emotional injury, the climate in our hearts and minds can fluctuate like the mood of a person with bipolar disorder experiencing rapid cycling (meaning the person swings between manic and depressive episodes very quickly, sometimes every few hours). This is living hell for a person who struggles with this mental illness. And right after an injury, it is not unusual to experience rapidly cycling thoughts and emotions. If you have had such an injury, you may recall sitting in the emergency room after your injury or lying on the field feeling like a knife is going through your knee. Within 30 seconds, you can go from thinking you will never compete again to preparing yourself to play the remainder of the game. You are riding an emotional roller-coaster. One minute you are in tears, and a few minutes later have high hopes.

I am on the faculty at the University of Colorado Hospital in Denver, in the department of orthopedics. I often get the question, "What is a psychologist doing in the department of orthopedics?" The answer is that I get referrals from the orthopedic surgeons to help people heal from emotional injury. I have received many calls over the years from parents of athletes as young as eight years old who want me to help their son or daughter with an emotional disruption.

It is so sad to hear a dedicated parent say over the phone, "Dr. Jowdy, she just isn't the same since the injury. She sleeps all the time and doesn't really care about much at all. Her friends call, but she doesn't feel like going out. If I don't insist, she won't eat. The coach has invited her to come to practice and participate however she can, but she wants to sit at home playing computer games. I guess it is her escape. She was such a happy kid. I don't hear her laugh much anymore. I am worried things could get worse. The doctor is not sure she will play again. The chances are not good, but you never know, right?"

The type of heartbreak caused by injury can feel intolerable at times. I have worked with injured athletes who have suicidal thoughts or have even made a suicide attempt. As a psychologist, it is not my place to talk about returning to play, at least not until the physical verdict has come in. But it is within my scope of practice to help the athlete heal from the emotional trauma and manage all the feelings he or she experiences when returning to play. The decision to return to play involves collecting all the data necessary to make an informed decision. This decision is typically made in conjunction with physical health care providers.

There is another issue here as well, the fact that the emotional injury may not be limited to the athlete. Parents, teammates, coaches, trainers, and friends also can experience an emotional injury as a result of the athlete getting hurt. I will never forget a father sobbing uncontrollably as his daughter shared with me her experience of getting a concussion. She was a freshman in high school, playing varsity basketball, and identified as one of the best in the state. Her mother held her hand as the girl told me how she hit her head on the court, traumatizing her brain stem. Still crying, the dad made it clear the neurologist was adamant she would never again play a sport that might put her at risk for a closed head injury. At that point, tears began to emerge in the athlete's eyes. Mom hugged her, and tears filled my eyes too.

Even now, as I reflect on my time spent with that family, tears come to my eyes. This kind of situation is painful for everyone. The loved ones' hopes may be shattered right along with the athlete's dreams. It is not quite like getting a cancer diagnosis, but the emotions can be similar. I share a poem about cancer with some athletes whose emotional injury has become chronic, to the point that severe clinical depression has developed (what I call emotional scar tissue and a restricted range of motion around feelings). The poem, which I have hanging in my office, reads:

What Cancer Can't Do

Cancer is so limited

It cannot cripple love

It cannot shatter hope

It cannot corrode faith

It cannot destroy peace

It cannot kill friendship

It cannot suppress memories

It cannot silence courage

It cannot invade the soul

It cannot steal eternal life

It cannot conquer the spirit

— Anonymous

My father despised sport and thought it was a waste of time, so he did not understand my pain and whining after the injury that changed my life. His response was, "Now you can focus on your work." But he also sent me the poem I now have hanging on my office wall. And there you have it: years later I am writing about the issue and including the poem in a discussion about emotional injury. It is fascinating how life takes its own direction, whether or not it is consistent with our master plan.

The cancer poem brings to mind my days spent working at Denver Health Medical Center with people who had cancer. The courage they exhibited was inspiring, and again, a testimony to the strength of the human spirit. I have seen that same strength in athletes who have had career-ending injuries a year prior to Olympic trials. Compared with cancer, the lyrics are different, but the music is the same. The physical condition may be different, but the emotional injury can run just as deep.

In the spirit of suggestion, I am going to ask you to keep poems and quotations that you like in an athletic journal, even though they may not make sense at the time. Keeping an athletic journal—or "warrior journal"—is something I recommend to all athletes I work with. I encourage them to write about things such as how they get in their own way, for example, and in turn, how they can make their mind into an ally instead. For an athlete who is injured, I typically suggest that he or she reflect on a daily basis about life lessons learned as a result of being injured. I ask them to answer some of the following questions in their journal: How did your thoughts and general attitude today make your life harder? What did you do to refocus in order to nurture your gold medal mind? How often did you feel hopeless and want to give up? What did you do when that happened? What are you learning about yourself? What was the most beautiful thing you witnessed today? Did you tell someone you love them today? And many, many other questions geared toward nurturing a warrior spirit—one filled with strength, courage, determination, fierceness, and love. Your athletic journal may be something you cherish the rest of your life. It is not until we slow down that we contemplate questions such as the ones I described. Ideally, you will begin to keep such a journal now, today, even if you are not injured or have no reason to slow down. (For detailed instructions on creating and using a warrior journal, see appendix 5.)

Self-knowledge does not happen automatically in a culture that typically discourages self-exploration and the development of a personal identity. In sport, the athletic identity reigns supreme because of the spell the scoreboard casts on an athlete. Living in the world of sport, he or she does not have time to ask questions like, "Who am I? What do I want? Why am I here?" Reflecting on the mystery of life can seem useless, especially for those who have not experienced adversity. But being injured can slow the pace down to the point where the difficult questions beg to be asked, and can be answered during the healing of the heart that follows. In my mind, this is when the true healing really happens, and where the gold medal mind begins to flourish. This is the gift of injury.

Some years ago I was blessed to work with an amazingly competitive and wonderful young man. After being out with a torn labrum his entire sophomore year, he came back his junior year and finished second in the state wrestling championships. His senior year, he was expected to go undefeated and win state. However, at the beginning of his senior year, he reinjured his shoulder and later was diagnosed as having a damaged ulnar nerve. He would be out his senior year. There was a chance he would be back in time for the state championships, but in the end, he did not compete. He had another surgery and planned to use the time off to prepare for college—because during his senior year, even while injured, he had earned a full scholarship to a university that was one of the top 10 in the country for wrestling.

He went to the university and decided to "grayshirt" and work on healing. I know he was doing everything imaginable to get better, from being 100 percent compliant with physical rehab to training mentally. Toward the end of his first semester, he sent me an e-mail to catch up. He wrote,

"Within the last couple of months, I have been feeling a lack of passion for continuing wrestling at this level, not because I don't love it anymore, but because I am not sure the stresses that are carried with it are worth it to me anymore. My wrestling career has been shadowed with injury, and although I can overcome my constant struggles, I feel as though injuries are always looming in my future, and perhaps it is time for me to move on. I feel like the best thing for me to do is transition from wrestling to something else that I can do that will challenge my mind and body (probably bodybuilding). I am not totally sure about making the decision to give up on wrestling yet, and I have time to keep thinking about it. I have been keeping up with my mental training and adding to my warrior journal. This has greatly helped me stay grounded and warrior-like, which I have been proud of."

Reading this reminds me of a saying I like: "If you want to make the Universe laugh, tell her your plans." If he hadn't been injured, this exceptional young man would have gone far in his sport, really far, because he had what it takes physically, mentally, and spiritually. But the Great Pumpkin had another plan. And for me, he has been a source of inspiration, like so many other athletes I have worked with. I know that if I were in his shoes, my first instinct would be to become absolutely furious that the Universe had messed with my plans. But he took what he and I called the path of the warrior. He chose to see his injury as a teacher and embraced the life lessons. This led him to come to terms and actually find peace with the circumstances. He became a warrior in every sense of the word, in a way that would never have happened had he not experienced the gift of injury. As a result, he taught me lessons not only about healing from emotional injury, but also about embracing life. During one of our most recent conversations I said to him, "You have become an emotional Jedi knight and a spiritual warrior. Thank you for allowing me to walk by your side during this journey."

Injury: A Teacher in Disguise

The lessons injury teaches can be broken into two categories. The first category includes lessons that may seem more obvious at first glance than the deeper and more subtle lessons in the second category. The second category is made up of lessons that we typically learn through adversity, which is unfortunate, because they are fundamental to the development of a gold medal mind. I believe these lessons should be taught to athletes at the high school level, if not before.

Category 1: Lessons Learned

1. There are no guarantees you will return to play after an injury.
2. The healing process may involve one step forward and two back, or two steps forward and one back. All you can count on is the dance.
3. Injury to connective tissue (tendons and ligaments) can be brutal.
4. If you injure your back, become a warrior in every sense of the word. Be willing to go to any length to recover, with the hope of returning with a back stronger than it was before the injury.
5. Learning to embrace uncertainty can go a long way. Sometimes, no matter how good your questions are, your health care provider cannot give you the answers.
6. No pain means no pain. It does not mean full recovery. Even without pain, there may still be inflammation. This is why merely listening to your body can be a dangerous thing.

7. Returning to play can involve fear, frustration, and a sense of failure. In other words, you may get reinjured emotionally when you return to play. I encourage you to read the story of David and Goliath for inspiration on how to embrace fear when stepping back into the ring.

Category 2: Injury and Life

1. Life has little or no regard for our feelings.
2. We have much less control over the events in our lives than we think we do. “If you want to make the Universe laugh, tell her your plans” pretty much sums it up.
3. Sport is a microscopic part of life. If you want to gain some perspective, hike up to the top of Mt. Elbert, the highest mountain in Colorado. Standing at the apex of a mountain, 14,439 feet above sea level, can really bring this point home.
4. The quickest way to feel better is to volunteer your time. Walk dogs, volunteer at a homeless shelter, visit kids who have cancer at a local hospital—it does not matter what you do, as long as you immerse yourself in caring about the well-being of someone other than yourself.
5. Painting and guitar lessons may not be reasonable substitutes for your sport. This is primarily based upon personal experience; they may work for you. Just keep an open mind, explore, and play, and you might find an activity that leads you to experience an inner peace you never thought possible. Believe it or not, I know of one athlete who found such a path through knitting. After suffering a horrible concussion in a ski race, she started knitting with her grandmother every day after school. This allowed her to develop a powerful, emotionally intimate relationship with her grandmother. What could be more important than this?

6. Be careful about what you expect from others—family members, for example—and accept at face value what they can or cannot offer you and your healing. In general, non-athletes do not understand what a nightmare a sport injury can be.

7. Loneliness is hard. If you are a collegiate athlete, those first few weekends you spend on campus when the team is traveling can be gut wrenching.

8. You will learn to appreciate friendship more than ever. Be present if a person in line at the grocery store wants to chitchat. It may be the only conversation they will have all day. That brief moment in time will leave you both feeling better.

9. You cannot do it alone. We need each other. This is one of the all-time great lessons, but is easier said than done for us competitive and independent types who are driven by a need for self-reliance. You need to take your armor off and put the sword in the ground, surrender, and share your pain.

10. Learn to say these three most difficult words: "I need help." This can be a hard lesson, especially for men. And try to remember, you do not need to be bleeding emotionally to ask for help.

11. A higher power—the Great Pumpkin or whatever else may speak to you—can be strong medicine. I am not trying to get all spiritual or New Age on you, but I am suggesting that some reliance on a power greater than yourself can give you hope, as well as an ability to adopt an attitude of letting go that will help you navigate the never-ending challenges life has to offer.

12. Learn to forgive. Here's an "f-word" we would actually benefit from using more. You may feel your body has betrayed you, but you will be betrayed in life in many other, possibly even more difficult ways. Have I forgiven the health

> care providers who did not diagnose the real issue with my back for five years? Not yet, not completely. But the experience has been teaching me how to forgive, more than anything else that has ever happened to me.

Ask the "what" and not the "why" questions if you want to heal your heart. Instead of asking, "Why me?" ask, "What can I learn from this?" Searching for the gifts, lessons, and blessings in adversity is consistent with developing a gold medal mind. Asking why just leads to self-pity and feeling like a victim. And you have no time for that. At their best, injury and adversity teach us how powerful gratitude and appreciation can be. Despite all the research in the area of positive psychology about the benefits of keeping a gratitude list, few of us do this. But after a serious injury, a gratitude list can become a lifeline, potentially better than any antidepressant out there.

At the end of each day, list five items—people, places, or things—you appreciate. You can use your warrior journal for this purpose. For example, an athlete who had a career-ending injury listed the following five items in his journal one day:

1. My uncle
2. My former coach
3. A place in the campus library where I feel peace
4. The poet Rumi
5. Today's sunrise

To help you get started, go someplace where you find it easy to reflect, and write down every possible thing you can think of that you are grateful for. This will serve as a warm-up for your gratitude muscle and making this practice a regular part of your routine.

It should be coming clear to you by now: as a result of injury, or any form of adversity for that matter, you can change in ways you never imagined. Existential thinkers would call an experience of severe adversity, such as a career-ending injury, a "boundary experience." An experience like that wakes us out of the trance we sometimes live in, allowing us to "give birth to a dancing star," according to Nietzsche. From a Buddhist perspective, that trance may be considered part of the realm of "hungry ghosts," a state in which we suffer from what some call "the disease of more." In this state, we can never feel emotionally full, no matter how many matches we win, how many medals we earn. There remains a void, what some call the abyss. We want more, and may continue training for years when everything else points in the direction of retirement. For example, logic and reason may say, "No, don't run today!" But in order to fill the emptiness, a person may override reason and logic and run, because if they did not run, the emptiness would be too painful. The disease of more is the basis of workaholism, the silent epidemic that leads to emotional injury not only for the workaholic, but also for kids whose parents suffer from this addiction.

Successfully dealing with emotional injury is one of the few ways to wake yourself up from the trance, so you can find satisfaction and meaning regardless of whether you finish on the podium or not. This is a cardinal feature of having a gold medal mind. So for those of you blessed with injury, please let yourself cry, scream, laugh, and ask for help. Remember that during the test, the teacher is quiet—the teacher being life, and injury the test.

In the spirit of the psychological victories I emphasize in this book, I would like to suggest that rehabilitation from injury can be as rewarding as being on the podium, if not even more rewarding. Sounds nuts, right? Maybe it is, but let us try not to quit before the miracle happens, as they say in Alcoholics Anonymous. For an injured athlete, the miracle can be finding out who he or she truly is. And knowing oneself is the essence of a gold medal mind, on and off the field.

CHAPTER 7

Making Your North Star a Reality

What is it that keeps us going in sport, against all odds? What gets us through a grueling cardio workout when we have no desire to be at the gym in the first place? What drives us back onto the court after a discouraging series of bad performances? All winning athletes have some kind of vision, a magnetic force, a burning desire deep inside that allows them to keep going and excel in spite of frustrations and setbacks. This is what I call the North Star. It is an athlete's ultimate goal—for example, to win a gold medal or be a national champion, or, for a kid, to become a professional athlete. If you prefer, you could call the North Star a desire, a wish, a dream, the fire, aim, fantasy, or bull's-eye—you get the idea.

The North Star—also known as the Pole Star or Polaris—has always served as a guidepost for explorers so they would not lose their way. For more details, I turned to my 12-year-old niece. Over a FaceTime session, Elaina explained, "It is like a magnetic force. You know, a star that had so much power the people followed it, and it helped them not get lost. The North Star gave them a compass to stay on their mission. We all need a North Star, don't we?" Exactly.

For an athlete, having a magnetic force is as important as it was for the explorers back in the day. Having something to keep your eye on will make all the difference in your ability to stay the course. A poster I saw hanging in an advisor's office stated, "Obstacles are what you see when you take your eyes off your goals." That is it in a nutshell. Keeping your sights set on the North Star will ensure you do not get derailed by the obstacles you are bound to encounter.

You may ask, what obstacles? They can take many forms: an argument with a teammate, a conflict with a coach, a strained hamstring, equipment problems, failure to make a team, making a mental error and losing at a World Cup, a season-ending injury, vicious attacks from fans and sports writers. Any of these might be enough to cause you to lose sight of Polaris momentarily, or make you forget you ever had a North Star.

Think of these occurrences as natural events of varying severity: wind, rain, snow, sleet, hurricanes, tornados, and earthquakes. The kind of upsets Mother Nature gifts us with to make the journey toward any destination more exciting. I have experienced bad weather in sport and the game of life. Without question, I have experienced earthquakes that rate at least a 6.0 on the Richter Scale, to the degree that I almost left my career as a psychologist over 20 years ago. I am sure you have as well. And what keeps us going? Plain and simple—the power of the North Star.

An example of a North Star I will never forget was shown to me by the competitive pole vaulter Pat Manson, a national record-holder in collegiate pole vaulting. Pat's North Star was represented by a piece of pole he hung over his bed, labeled with the height he was training to soar over. Waking up every morning and looking at the pole stimulated his brain. The goal became ingrained, so when it came time for practice, Pat was already engaged. No distractions, no excuses, no whining, no self-pity, no justifications—just pure focus on the North Star.

Find your North Star and allow it to be your guide. When "bad weather" distracts you, set your sights back onto your North Star, again and again and again. I have worked with many athletes who start a season fired up, focused, and determined to realize their dream for the season. Then some bad weather sucks them into a spiral of doubt. Sure, losing a little confidence is normal after a series of bad performances. A field goal kicker who misses a high percentage of kicks will become discouraged. But if he keeps the goal of playing in the pros in the forefront of his mind and learns from the missed kicks, he can keep the fire alive to train hard physically and mentally.

Having a North Star keeps an athlete's attention in the present moment, so that in the face of discouragement or even hopelessness, he or she will ask, "What can I do to improve myself today?" This question will lead to action. Action allows a person to detach from the inner critic. An athlete may hear the inner critic say, "You will never kick in the pros." But the athlete does not have to believe it. The voice may be strong, but actions are stronger. You will realize your North Star if you take specific steps, outlined below, like a warrior.

Setting Daily Goals

The key to achieving your North Star is to start with daily goals. For example, you might set a daily goal of getting mentally prepared for practice, each and every day. Your daily goals will serve as pieces of the puzzle, and with every piece you will get closer to achieving the complete picture, your North Star. In the sport psychology world, the North Star would be called an outcome goal, and daily goals—the steps you take along the way to the North Star—are process goals. If it helps you to use these terms, go for it.

The ability to set and achieve daily goals is a key characteristic of the gold medal mind. Writing down these goals is helpful, but is sometimes easier said than done. Writing down a goal means you are making a commitment to putting forth the effort to make it happen, which adds accountability to the mix. Informal studies with Olympic athletes show that many do not set short-term goals because of the fear of failure. For competitive people who are typically highly self-critical, it can be threatening to create yet another performance situation by setting goals. But one of the larger benefits of being consistent about setting goals is it helps you deal better with your inner critic. Avoiding setting goals will simply further strengthen the inner critic's muscle. Give what I am going to suggest at least a six-month trial before drawing a conclusion about whether or not goal setting works for you. The gold medal mind is about trying, experimenting and learning. (In appendix 3 you will find a goal-setting form I designed to help make this process easier.)

I am going to share with you a method for setting goals that will improve the likelihood that you and your North Star come face-to-face. But before getting into the how, here are some of the benefits of setting daily goals:

- Teaches you how to deal with success and failure
- Increases commitment, discipline, persistence, determination, and accountability
- Helps when you are feeling tired or bored in practice
- Improves concentration
- Enhances communication with your coach and teammates
- Fosters recovery from injury
- Assists you in pushing through self-limiting beliefs
- Boosts enjoyment
- Facilitates the process of learning who you truly are (and what you *want*, versus what you must or should do)

Having a daily goal(s) to focus on can help you bring your attention back to your overall outcome goal when you start to wander from the present moment. Setting daily goals is one of many ways to sharpen your ability to go consciously into a zone-like state, and to come back to this state when your thoughts or emotions have momentarily booted you out. Your daily goals become your focal point to ensure you stay in the present, one moment at a time. The objective is to make consistent strides in developing yourself as a physically and psychologically skilled athlete. Consistency is essential, so you can avoid or minimize the time you spend in a slump or at plateaus. These times are a natural part of the learning process, but I would like you to move through them quickly. In a sport like gymnastics this may seem unrealistic, but I have seen athletes break through such episodes more quickly by setting clear daily goals.

Setting daily goals requires you to focus on specifics. For example, when lifting weights:

- "Focus, stay with the movement, one rep at a time."
- "Be absorbed in the movement of the weight, on both the positive (concentric contraction) and negative (eccentric contraction) phases of the exercise."
- "Breathe in sync with the movement, breathing in on the positive phase and out on the negative."
- "Connect to the relaxation and contraction of each muscle group, feeling the lengthening and shortening."
- "Enjoy the burn, the pain."
- "Nothing less than precision."
- "Fatigue is a reminder to lock into the mechanics and my breath."

Yes, I just listed seven distinct goals for how to focus while doing seated leg press, for example. For just this one exercise in the weight room, there may be that many different opportunities to allow absorption to be your guide. You may not have to break down your goals like this all the time, or for every aspect of your sport, but this kind of focus on the specifics will not only help you reach your daily goals, but also improve your ability to stay in the present moment and cultivate a zone-like state.

Your footwork, the position of your head, your follow-through, maintaining good form when you are getting tired or bored—any of these can serve as a specific daily goal. Channel your energy into specifics. The more specific, the better. I am hammering away on this point, because you will soon realize there are many forces trying to pull you in the opposite direction. Your own inner critic is probably the most powerful of these forces. Remember, Self 1 will attack when you start to doubt your goals and abilities. Having a specific focal point or target on which to refocus when Self 1 comes knocking is essential.

In short, daily targets allow you to get absorbed in the present moment. With every set and every repetition, no matter how boring the exercise, you will become absorbed and enter a zone-like state, just as if you were competing. Your brain will love this. You will start having fun, and you will see performance gains occur much faster than if you went into practice simply thinking about working hard. Follow-through is the key to success with daily targets, so enlisting others to practice with you can be very helpful. The idea of teamwork is as applicable to sticking with mental training as it is to playing defense well.

My hope is that setting and pursuing daily goals becomes an aspect of your training you come to love. I encourage you to talk with your coaches and teammates about your practice targets for the day. You might even want to meet with your coach on a regular basis to help you set daily goals. Your coach will then be able to focus on specific aspects of your development to help you increase your learning curve. Over time, you will realize you are developing as an athlete faster than you would have if you had not set daily goals.

Six Ingredients for Success With Daily Goals

I have identified six core factors that I call the "active ingredients" for setting and attaining daily goals. As much as possible, the goals you set for yourself should be:

1. Specific
2. Realistic
3. Measurable
4. Positive
5. Believable
6. Fun

I want to emphasize two particular ingredients: Be sure your goals are stated in positive terms and are believable. Keep your eye and heart on the direction in which you want to travel, not on the road you want to avoid. For example, think, "I will maintain composure," as opposed to "I won't lose my temper." And it is crucial that your goal is believable—a factor not often emphasized in the sport psychology literature. You need to believe that your goals are achievable and that you have what it takes to realize them. Having a little doubt about achieving your daily goals is okay. But if in your heart your reaction to your daily goal is, "What? No way," revise it so you can believe it is within reach. This way, as you are able to achieve goal(s) on a consistent basis, your confidence will increase, and your overall belief that you can achieve your goals will soar.

Knowing that with the right amount of effort and precision you can achieve your goal will keep your motivation high. A season can be long and grueling, so it is paramount to maintain a high level of motivation. Believing your goals are within reach will make working toward them fun, because you can look forward to experiencing that sweet taste of victory when you get there. And even if you don't achieve a certain goal, merely having set and pursued it is a psychological victory in its own right. The sensation of working your butt off to accomplish the goal will be incredible. The important thing is the process, the proactive and aggressive steps you take to work toward your daily targets.

Be mindful that setting these goals will require commitment and accountability. Establishing a goal is a call to action, as they say in business, and simple, but not easy, as they say in the Twelve-Step world. It is a lot like setting up a mini-competition in which your toughest opponent is...? Yes, you guessed it, yourself. But that is exactly what you want. You are actually doing some simulation training. You are setting up a boxing ring in which, in corner #1, there you are standing at 5'11", 217 pounds, and in corner #2, there you are again, standing at 5'11", 217 pounds. This scenario—your mind facing off against your mind—is exactly what you want. You are trying to create a place and time to embrace the doubts that may emerge when you hold your feet to the fire. Or the worry you experience when your coach knows what you are working on, but you do not feel you have what it will take. It is all part of the process. My hope is that you learn to love the process, because loving the journey is another integral aspect of developing a gold medal mind.

The Process of Setting and Achieving Daily Goals

Step 1. As soon as you can after practice is over, identify the degree to which you achieved your goals on a 1 to 7 scale—with 7 meaning that you totally achieved the goal and 1 indicating you think you would have been better off staying home. List what you did well in that practice session, whether it was related to your goals or not. Identify areas in which you could improve, items that could serve as your goals for the next day.

Then pick two or three that actually will be your goals for the next day. They can even be goals that you had set for today that still need work. (Using the goal-setting form in appendix 3 may help you be accountable to yourself.)

Step 2. That evening, take time to visualize yourself achieving these goals.

Step 3. Write the two or three goals down and take them with you to practice the next day. You might want to dedicate a small notebook to your goals, or put them in your phone so you can look at them prior to practice.

Step 4. Spend some time before practice visualizing yourself achieving the goals you set. Again, you might want to make a teammate(s) or coach aware of your goals for that day to help with accountability and commitment.

Step 5. Go back and repeat steps 1 through 4, every day.

Every so often, take time to celebrate the achievement of goals. Treat yourself to a neuromuscular massage or acupuncture session to help with recovery. This kind of treatment is not necessarily a luxury or reward, but it is easy to unconsciously deny oneself this kind of self-care.

Daily Physical Targets of Successful Athletes

Here are some examples of effective daily targets from athletes with whom I have worked. These are process-oriented goals, the kind of daily goals you will identify when following step 1 in the goal-setting process outlined above. They are focused on physical skill development—the mechanics. Note how specific the goals are. They are the ones individual athletes and I discovered would result in their performing close to perfectly for particular aspects of their sport. I provide them as examples, because left to a more conventional approach to goal setting, you might set a less specific goal, such as "hustle more in practice" or "make 70 percent of my shots."

Swimmer (backstroke): "Head still, neck relaxed."

Track and field (hurdles): "Stay tall, arm in front, driving after the fourth hurdle."

Ice hockey (goaltender): "Square, now, connect."

Baseball (hitting): "Keep arms up, chest up, head on ball."

Baseball (pitching): "Straight up, soft leg."

Basketball (jump shot): "Elbow in, use legs."

Gymnastics (vault): "Aggressive and block."

Daily Psychological Goals

Like Pat Manson, the pole vaulter who wrote the height he wanted to jump on a piece of pole above his bed, you may want to put a sign in your locker or on your bedroom wall that says something like "State Champion." This is your outcome goal, your North Star. But you also need focused psychological targets to pursue on a daily basis. These are pieces of the puzzle that increase the probability you will realize your ultimate dream, wish, or desire. Below are some examples of goals that help increase psychological fitness by sharpening your focus on specific psychological targets. (Again, consider using the goal-setting form provided in appendix 3 for help in setting and achieving specific daily goals.)

Developing confidence: "When I get frustrated, I will immediately shift my attention to my breath and say to myself, 'Now, present.'"

Developing motivation: "If I feel lazy in practice, I will indulge in thoughts and images of my daily goals and North Star."

Developing concentration: "When I get distracted, I will focus on breathing in deeply, saying 'ease' to myself as I breathe in and 'zone' as I exhale slowly."

Developing more effective communication: "When I don't understand my coach, I will ask him or her to clarify immediately."

Or, “When I am angry and feel like chewing out a teammate, I will take two deep complete breaths, bounce a little on my toes, and think, ‘Let it go, let it go.’”

Developing emotional composure: “If I get overwhelmed with worry and doubt, I will indulge in thinking about what I know is true. I will bask in that heartfelt sense and feel my passion grow.”

Developing the ability to inspire: “Whenever the time seems right, I will look my teammate in the eye and say, ‘You’ve got this!’ (Or some other short, specific phrase.)

Developing the belief factor: “Upon awakening, I will breathe in deeply and breathe out slowly, allowing images and sensations of myself performing at my best to become vivid and as real as possible. As I see myself performing beyond my expectations, I will silently repeat to myself what I know is true about my skills, gifts, abilities, and talents, and let those words and feelings soak in deeply.”

Getting back into a zone-like state: “When I slip out of the zone, I will say, ‘Ease, slow’ to myself, using a soft gaze and feeling immersed in my body.” Or, “I will breathe in deeply and breathe out slowly, telling myself, ‘Let go’ on the out breath. I will make a gentle fist with each hand, raising my shoulders easily on the in breath and releasing my hands and letting my shoulders drop as I breathe out.” Another option: “I will lock into an image like powerful waves crashing onto the shore of a beach to help me slip back into a zone-like state.”

Improving the ability to cope with Leroy (pain and fatigue): “When I feel like slowing down, I will shift my attention to feeling my body move and maintaining perfect mechanics.” Or, “I will welcome Leroy by saying, ‘Bring it on, my friend, you are here to help take me to another level. Stay with me, stay with me—we’ve got this, my friend.’ I will allow myself to enjoy the sensation of the burn, the sweat, the surge of energy.”

> *Improving self-acceptance*: "When I feel bad about myself or think I've let everyone down, I will share this with a friend who will not try to change my mind or give advice, but will just listen."
>
> *Developing mental toughness:* "When I get overwhelmed with worry and feel weak, I will visualize and feel my inner strength and passion grow."

What do these mental goals have in common with the physical goals? Yes, a high level of specificity. Identify some specific psychological goals for yourself, write them down, and put them on your locker or on a card in your equipment bag (or use the goal-setting form in appendix 3). At first you will need to consistently remind yourself to change patterns of thinking. For example, if you are used to doubting yourself after a mistake, this may have become a habit. Breaking the mental habit requires you to make a conscious choice to reprogram the way you think by refocusing to performance-enhancing thoughts over and over again. And as you begin to think differently and become more psychologically fit, your North Star will become more of a reality. Remember, the many pieces of the puzzle are what create the gorgeous picture of a mountain range or horses galloping across a field against an amazing sunset. The finished product, the picture, is your North Star.

The Effort is the Psychological Victory

Following a North Star teaches and reinforces one of the most important aspects of developing a gold medal mind: learning. Think about it. Is not pursuing your dreams, wishes, desires, hopes, and daily goals all about learning? And what else is there? To me, this idea is a guiding principle and a truth, and much of my work with athletes revolves around helping them explore that truth.

For most athletes, sport is all about winning and losing, good and bad, success and failure. My response to this kind of thinking is, "Yes...but no." When it comes to goal setting, sport is all about effort and learning. You learn what you need to know to succeed as you put the effort into achieving your goals. And you learn when you fail to achieve your goals. With a goal medal mind, when your "ship begins to heel," you will know exactly what to do. When you win, you will learn what worked, and when you lose, you will learn what happened so you can right the ship to minimize the probability it will happen again. This is when being an athlete becomes really fun.

Once you understand goal setting is all about effort and learning, the threat of commitment and fear of failure are neutralized. Yes, outcome is important, but the truth is when the effort and focus are there, the outcome will take care of itself. Imagine you are a swimmer extra worried about achieving a daily goal of maintaining correct biomechanics on Friday because the week has not gone well. If you are focused on the doubt, your anxiety over accomplishing the goal will soar. So what to do? Focus instead on the effort, on "playing the game"—breathing, visualizing, staying in your body (not your mind), and engaging your heart. The effort is the psychological victory. It is a win just because you set the goal and put forth the effort. Doing so increases the likelihood that you will focus on the essential ingredients that will lead to achieving the desired outcome, rather than give top billing in your mind to emotions, such as worry. Understanding and owning this brings you one step closer to becoming a psychologically skilled athlete, and ultimately one step closer to realizing your North Star.

In my experience, upon reaching the end of a book, I feel as if I have crossed the finish line, and often I do not bother with the appendixes. Should this be your approach as well, please reconsider and check out the tools I offer in the appendixes. In addition to the goal-setting form I've mentioned, I've included a practice and competition reflection form that will help you target the physical and psychological factors most important to improving your performance. In the spirit of the gold medal mind, I encourage you to not wait until the end, but to take a look at these tools now (or when you next pick up the book), before reading on.

CHAPTER 8

Thinking Less: A Psychological Lobotomy

I was with the long-track speed skating team in Helsinki, training for an upcoming World Cup. We were on a grueling European tour that involved competitions in four different countries in one month. We stayed a week in each country—Finland, the Netherlands, Hungary, and Germany—with our travel days considered our time off. To say the least, it was intense. After one morning ice-training session, I was sitting in the locker room with the athletes. Informal chatter about the upcoming World Cup filled the room. Out of the blue, one of the athletes asked me, "Can you give me a psychological lobotomy for the races?" In response to my questioning look, he added, "I just think too much. If you could get my brain to stay in the locker room, I would do much better."

This made sense to me, so I said, "Let's do it! It will take some work, but it will happen." "So what are we going to do?" he asked. "Oh, just sit still, and then sit some more," I responded. The skater looked at me like I was a bit left of center. But I knew what I was talking about. Those of you who were fans of the original Star Trek might recall Spock saying, "Pain is a thing of the mind, and the mind can be controlled." And that is what this chapter is all about: learning to control the mind. Yes, it is about sitting still and then some—sitting and sitting and then sitting some more. This is the most profound way to learn how to achieve and maintain a zone-like state. You will get the most "bang for your buck" by allowing yourself to become a student of what I am about to explain.

A zone-like state requires you to control your thinking, most of the time thinking less versus more. Controlling your thinking and quieting your mind allows you to get absorbed in the moment. Absorption is a word commonly used in the hypnosis literature, and it is everything and more when it comes to the zone-like state. Being absorbed in the moment is the equivalent of being in a mild trance. I will not get into the details of hypnosis, but I know you have experienced the feeling of being absorbed in the moment, perhaps when staring into a fire pit, watching a great movie, or reading a wonderful book. Absorbed in the moment, immersed in the present—it is a bit of a blissful and euphoric feeling. And it seems to happen randomly and without explanation. However, by following the suggestions in this chapter you will be better able to consciously create this state of consciousness. Being able to create a zone-like state is one of the most significant characteristics of a gold medal mind.

From a statistical perspective, being able to get into a zone-like state may be the most important factor in winning the race. If we were to run a simultaneous multiple regression correlation (a rigorous statistical test to determine the significance of different variables) to find out what ingredients of the gold medal mind are most potent, we would throw in all the ingredients we believe are correlated with the gold medal mind. These would include confidence, dealing with distractions, handling pain and fatigue, staying motivated, coping with pressure, and other psychological skills. I would bet that the ability to achieve and maintain a zone-like state would account for most of the variance—meaning that achieving and maintaining a zone-like state is most statistically significantly associated with a gold medal mind and, ultimately, an athlete's ability to set personal records.

Earlier I talked about my introduction to sport psychology at the age of 13. As you will recall, after I tried visualization training and found it helpful, I began to read every book I could find on the psychology of sport. That did not take long, because only a handful of such books existed at the time. One of the gold standards was the first edition of *In Pursuit of Excellence* by Terry Orlick (1980). Orlick discusses the use of relaxation training as a means of enhancing performance. Basically, relaxation training teaches a way to control the hypothalamic-pituitary axis, the good old HPA. In simple terms, this means learning to control your nervous system. Given the fact that anxiety is at the top of the list of athletes' struggles, relaxation training is essential to practice. I too struggled with anxiety before games, and because my parents would not let me pop Valium, Xanax, Klonopin, or Ativan, I decided to try the natural "anti-anxiety medication" described in Orlick's book.

The specific technique Orlick described was called progressive muscle relaxation (PMR), which was discovered by Edmund Jacobson in the 1960s. (As a side note, Jacobson was the pioneer who studied the physiological basis of imagery training. Ahead of his time, this guy was.) PMR is a technique that involves tensing and relaxing every muscle group in turn, from the forehead to the muscles in the feet. It is a surefire way to get in touch with the body, and allows you to tune into subtle tensions that might interfere with performance. Long story short, in tenth grade, when I came home from school, I would put on my yellow tracksuit with black stripes (ugly but appropriate for a young fan of the Boston Bruins and Pittsburg Steelers). And then, surrounded by posters of Bruce Jenner, the American who won the gold in decathlon in the 1976 Olympics, I would lie there and practice the relaxation exercise for 30 minutes. I recorded the script from the book onto a cassette tape (yep, that was the state of the technology then). I would listen to it every day, typically skipping weekends. Listening to the recording helped me experience the relaxation in a more powerful way, because a recording allows the listener to let go and get absorbed, eliminating the thinking needed to guide oneself through the exercise. For this reason, I have made audio recordings for PMR practice and concentration training available for purchase on my website (www.goldmedalmind.com).

My experience with PMR made me even more a believer in sport psychology because I found myself increasingly in sync with my body and able to handle the jitters that came with performing in big games. And maintaining the composure of the body, one's physiology, is essential to high-level performance. Learning to be still had everything to do with peak performance, so I stuck with it, even though it was downright boring much of the time. The practice enabled me to "have the butterflies fly in formation," as Orlick said many years ago—a perfect description of how this technique works. But it was only as effective as the amount of practice I put into it. Looking back, I can honestly say that after that year of consistent practice, I still today can recall the feeling produced by the exercise and generate a relaxation response very quickly by breathing a certain way and bringing my attention down into my body. The technique is that powerful.

Mental Control Through Concentration Training

The exercise I am about to describe, what I call concentration training, is the foundational technique for developing a gold medal mind. Understanding and mastering it will help you with just about all of the other mental training methods I describe in this book. This is a life skill. Sitting still and focusing the mind is something I believe we should learn in kindergarten or sooner, before the mind turns into "monkey mind" as a result of all the worries it takes on. (In fact, there have been several articles in the magazine *Mindful* describing experts going into schools and teaching kids to be still and focus on the present moment.) The monkey mind, a Buddhist term, is what interferes with the zone-like state, and pure awareness and absorption are the cornerstones for overcoming monkey mind. This is why sitting, sitting, and then sitting some more is so important. And yes, it can be boring, but soon you will not care about that.

What I am calling concentration training bears some similarities to the practice commonly known as mindfulness training or even meditation. But it is different and, I believe, more effective for athletes. The ultimate goal is to arrive at a time and place at which you disconnect from your fixed mind and experience "pure awareness." This may sound somewhat Buddhist in nature, and in some ways, it is. After all, who knows how to focus attention better than those Buddhist masters of concentration? Before you become intimidated, read on to see how simple the practice really is.

Concentration Training—The Formal Practice

In the following pages, I am going to describe a formal technique for an effective concentration practice. Before you try to make the practice part of your routine, I suggest you work up to it gradually, taking small steps that will allow you to truly enjoy the process. You can think of this technique as a way to strengthen your mind, much as resistance training strengthens your body. You take small steps to increase weight when lifting, and the same holds true for concentration training. Start by sitting for just 10 minutes a day, listening to instrumental music (some suggestions: Peter Kater, Jim Brickman, Jean-Luc Ponty, George Winston, Andreas Vollenweider, In Credo, Emancipator, Sayama, Lazybatusu, and R. Carlos Nakai). The music will serve as your focal point. Every time your mind wanders, go back to the music. Do this daily for two weeks. Next, practice the concentration exercise described below for 5 minutes a day. Every two weeks, increase your sitting time by 5 minutes until you get up to 20 minutes a day (although I have known some athletes to practice for 30 to 45 minutes a day). Believe you can do that and go for it, challenging your critical inner voice that says, "No way, that's too long for me!" Allow the slogan, "Easy Does It" to be a guiding principle. No scoreboard here!

If you allow yourself to get up to about 20 minutes a day, you will be blown away by the mental control you will have. (I would not hesitate at all to practice twice a day.) And this mental control is what will allow you to get into and maintain a zone-like state. It is the only way I know. There is no substitute for sitting your butt down, day after day. Sound like work? Maybe. I encourage you to consider that this type of training can be more challenging than any practice you can have on the field, course, court, or ice rink. But also, I encourage you to have fun with it. Observe the random thoughts you have and be amused by the way your mind dances around and resists being in the present moment. Adopt an attitude of curiosity as you watch your mind fight to remain in control. The instructions are as follows:

1. Sit in a chair with your feet flat on the floor. There should be 90 degrees between your upper and lower legs (at the knees), and 90 degrees between your upper and lower body. Rest your hands on your upper legs with your shoulders back and down, as if you were moving them to tuck them into your back pockets or doing the weight-training exercise known as rows. Be sure your shoulders are not stiff or rigid and there is no excess tension in your neck and shoulders. No forcing, trying, pushing, or working at it. Let it happen. The point is to sit upright in a correct posture to ensure your mind is sharp and ready to work. Slightly tuck your chin, again, not so your neck is tense or stiff, but just so your airway is as clear as possible. It helps some people to imagine a helium balloon attached to the crown of the head: as you imagine the balloon rising, the chin tucks in slightly, neck straightens somewhat, and shoulders drop a

little and relax. The reason for all this detail about posture is that it is the foundation, where it all starts. In some traditions, this is formally called taking your seat. I call it sitting with purpose or discipline, because it resonates more with athletes. When you have taken your seat with attention to detail, you will feel that something is about to happen—something that is not in your usual repertoire.

2. Now, feel yourself sitting. Notice the position of your head in space; feel your shoulders, your arms, your hands resting on your legs, your back against the chair, your butt in the seat, your upper legs, the bend at your knees, your lower legs and feet on the floor, your shoes on your feet. Wiggle around a bit and settle into a position in which you feel comfortable, not rigid or tense, but as if you are "riding the wave" of these guidelines. Enjoy sitting still, being quiet and calm, as you settle in.

3. Look straight ahead and pick a spot on the wall that will become your focal point. In my office, I have people look at a colorful picture on the wall and ask them to pick one spot in the picture to gaze at. Now, as you sit still, quiet, and calm, place your attention on this focal point. Do not stare at it intensely, but instead let the focal point come to you, adopting a soft gaze. With a soft gaze, with soft eyes, get absorbed in this focal point. At the same time, with a soft gaze, let your attention settle on your breath—the air entering and leaving your body through your nose. Breathe in and breathe out, at the same time getting more and more absorbed in the focal point. As you breathe in, you may feel your rib cage expand to some degree, and on the out breath, you will feel your rib cage contract—breathing in, breathing out, in and out. Breathe in deeply and exhale slowly, in and out, feeling yourself get more and more comfortable as you sit still, quiet, and calm. You may find yourself getting into a zone-like state. You may notice that your peripheral vision has narrowed. If

someone were to wave a hand in front of your eyes, you would see the hand, but it would not break your attention. Breathing in, breathing out—in and out. Enjoy being still, quiet, and calm. Let it happen, versus trying or forcing it to happen. There is no pushing or striving here. Just allow yourself to be absorbed in the moment with no judgments and no scoreboard. Just be still, quiet, and calm.

4. On your next out breath, let your eyes close gently and focus inward. Take a few moments to check in on the position of your body and make adjustments to maintain your seat, because as we relax we can get sloppy with posture.

5. Beginning at the top of your head, become aware of the muscles throughout your scalp, forehead, sides of your face, eyes, and around your mouth, letting your teeth part slightly. Now focus on the muscles in your neck, back, front, and sides. Let your attention drift to the muscles in your upper arms; feel them. Become aware of the bend at your elbows and shift your attention to your forearms. Feel your hands and become aware of each finger, one at a time. Feel the air make contact with your skin, each finger, and the back of your hands. Notice the temperature of the air against your skin. Just become aware of it, and enjoy the sensation. Check in with yourself and your posture, and make any adjustments that seem necessary to remain upright and comfortable. You should have a sense of determination, but not intensity—this is about letting go.

6. Now bring your attention to your upper back, the muscles around your shoulder blades, along your spine, and in your lower back. Simply observe these areas. Feel your back making contact with the chair. Shift your attention to the muscles in your chest and be aware of the slight movement of your rib cage as you breathe in and breathe out. Notice the small but powerful muscles between your ribs, feel them, and let your abdomen soften.

7. Shift your attention to your butt, feeling your seat supported by the chair. Feel the weight of your body supported by the chair, your back supported by the chair, the bend at your knees, your shoes on your feet, and your feet on the floor. Allow your attention to focus on the muscles in your upper legs, your quads and hamstrings, and just observe those muscles. Notice the bend at your knees and the muscles in your lower legs, the front and back of your lower leg. Let your attention drift into your ankles and feet, feeling your shoes on your feet and your feet on the floor. Enjoy sitting still, being still, quiet, and calm.

8. Take a moment to feel your entire body, the top of your head through your neck, arms, hands, back, chest, upper legs, lower legs, and your feet on the floor. Make adjustments to your posture so that you are comfortable, but sitting with determination, without being rigid. Letting go.

9. Shift your attention to your breath, the air entering and leaving your body through your nose. Allow your attention to settle in on your breath cycle, breathing in and breathing out, enjoying being still, quiet, and calm. Think of a word you find relaxing, peaceful, and meaningful. Now, each time you breathe out, say this word quietly to yourself. Let your attention stay with your breath and the word. Breathe in, breathe out, and with every out breath, say the word silently to yourself. You can change the word in time, but for now just take the first one that comes to mind. Some call this their sacred word, not in a religious sense, but to indicate that the word is special, meaningful, and a source of strength. Stay with your breath and the word, feeling your body supported by the chair, feeling the position of your body.

10. When (not if) your mind dances off (which it will), gently bring it back to your breath and the word, over and over again. Stay in the moment, the present, one breath at a time, by staying with your breath and your special word.

When (not if) your mind wanders, gently bring it back again to the present moment. The mind gets bored easily. It wants stimulation. It will get caught up in the future or the past, because being in the moment is not too exciting for the brain. Simply bring yourself back to your breath and the word. You may allow yourself to be amused by the stories your mind tells and all the directions it goes, some meaningful and some stupid, but always come back to your breath. As they say in some traditions, bring yourself back to your breath a thousand times.

11. Continue to enjoy the experience of sitting still, breathing in and breathing out, one breath at a time…one breath at a time. Occasionally, allow your body to be your focal point. Let go of the word, and as you breathe in and breathe out, focus on your neck, shoulders, arms, hands, back, the movement of your rib cage, your legs, the bend at your knees, and your feet on the floor. Allow yourself to be "down in your body." Become absorbed in being in your body for a period of time, and when your mind wanders, bring your attention back to your body, over and over again. And then shift your focus back to your breath and your word, staying with your breath over and over again.

12. When time is up, feel your body once again: the top of your head, neck, arms, hands, back, chest, legs, shoes on your feet, and feet on the floor. Begin to take deeper breaths, so as you inhale you feel the fresh air entering your body. Breathe in deeply through your nose and exhale slowly through your mouth. Feel your rib cage expand on the in breath and contract on the out breath, breathing in and breathing out. While taking these deep breaths, make a gentle fist with each hand and then stretch your fingers out. Move your feet around and point and flex your feet, extend one leg at a time, left and then right, to get the blood flowing into your upper legs. As you continue to take deep breaths, move your shoulders by rolling them

backward easily and slowly. Now turn your head from side to side, easily and slowly. Continue to take deep breaths, and when you are comfortable and ready, slowly open your eyes and readjust to the room, the light, and all that is around you.

13. Remain seated for a minute or so. Then get up slowly, have a few sips of water, and continue with your day, feeling good about having invested this time into your athletic and personal development.

Overcoming Obstacles

When you practice concentration training, it is normal to experience internal distractions due to the stream of activity in your mind: thoughts, ongoing chatter, memories that pass through or decide to take up residence. Your mind just does not like the idea that you are sitting still, in a non-striving state, being in the present. Chatter or memories will come in and try to kick the focal point (your breath and the word) out of the ring. Thoughts will fight as hard as they can for your attention, and they do not like to lose.

The distractions can also come in the form of feelings, either pleasant or uncomfortable. Having feelings come to the surface when sitting still is normal. When in "doing mode," we can put up a fortress around our hearts and minds to keep feelings at bay. But do not be surprised, after you have settled in and quelled the thoughts and memories vying for your attention, if feelings start to emerge. The goal here, if there is a goal, is to not judge the thoughts, memories, or feelings that appear. Just observe them, watch them, and they will ride into the sunset. They are merely players out on the field; your goal is to dispassionately watch them go by and gently bring your attention back to your focal point. The exercise is about you and your focal point, the same way it is about you and the ball when you are at practice.

You can think of all distractions—thoughts, memories, feelings, sounds, a tight muscle or itch—as factors that make the water murky. With these factors dancing around in your mind, it is difficult to see the focal point because the visibility is so poor. But as you breathe and continue to be still, and gently—I emphasize gently—bring your attention back to the focal point time and again, you will find the visibility is improving. You will experience what the monk Thomas Keating calls "interior silence," a state in which you feel still, comfortable, quiet, centered, connected, peaceful, and relaxed. This is an incredible feeling, and it happens without effort. That is the paradoxical nature of concentration training and the zone-like state. Simply by directing your attention to the focal point, you allow transformation to happen. By letting go, and not trying, you allow yourself to be absorbed in the present moment. That is where you will perform at your best and truly enjoy yourself.

The word that serves as your focal point during concentration training is not something to get attached to. The word and your breath merely provide a place to retrain your focus when you are distracted, so you can experience the state of interior silence, also known as the gap. The gap, a state of pure awareness, is at the heart of the zone-like state.

Concentration Training—Informal Practice

Sticking with a program of formal concentration training is highly challenging. If you miss a day, do not judge yourself. Make up for it with informal practice by incorporating some of the following brief focusing techniques:

- Before getting out of bed, take five deep, complete breaths.
- When you get into bed at night, after settling in, take five deep, complete breaths.
- Before starting the car, take two deep, complete breaths.

- Before getting out of the car, take two deep, complete breaths.
- Before making a call or sending a text, take one deep, complete breath.
- Before answering the phone or reading a text, take one deep, complete breath.
- When at a red light or four-way stop, take one deep, complete breath.
- On the hour, every hour, take four deep, complete breaths.

In addition, turn your cell phone off for at least two hours a day. This will provide you the opportunity to truly be in the present moment, in real time. (I have more to say about this suggestion in the workbook I wrote to accompany this book.)

Informal practice can keep you engaged with the idea of learning to focus your attention. As I mentioned, sticking with regular practice will be challenging. I share the following story not to suggest you do the same thing, but rather to identify the level of commitment it can take to reap the rewards of concentration training. I was working with a 15-year-old athlete to whom I introduced concentration training. This is a kid who was competing at the international level in his sport. The next week I met with him to ask how the concentration training was going. He shared the following, "I did it every day except for one. So I did it twice the next day to make up for it." Wow, I thought. I had never known an athlete to do that in the more than 30 years I have been involved in this work.

This is what I am talking about when I say commitment is required. And you have what it takes, so believe it and start right now. Set this book down right now, and sit still, enjoying being quiet and calm, absorbed in the moment. When you get back to the book you will more likely be in a zone-like state and focused on the reading. I encourage people I work with in school, college student athletes for example, to practice for 5 minutes prior to hitting the books. Doing so will eliminate the warm up—the 20 minutes or so it takes to get locked into the coursework.

Why This Sitting Thing Works

Just as sport is a microcosm of life (an expression I learned at the age of 18 from the sport psychologist Shana Bendix), practicing concentration training is a microcosm of sport. Concentration training poses both mental and physical challenges, much the way physically practicing and competing does. What you do during concentration training reflects exactly what goes on when you are practicing and competing:

- Taking your seat is the equivalent to the process of warming up.
- The soft gaze is like getting mentally prepared for the practice or game.
- Attending to your posture during the exercise is equivalent to using the right technique during your physical performance.
- Staying with the breath is no different from being absorbed in the moment—a cardinal feature of the zone-like state. And being absorbed in the moment is what all coaches want you to do at all times.
- Practicing concentration training on a consistent basis involves motivation, commitment, and discipline. You know very well how these factors apply to achieving physical excellence.
- Keeping from falling into the trap of merely going through the motions during physical performance requires intensity and focus. The same intensity is required during concentration training to regain your focus when your thoughts start bouncing all over the place.

- Moving out of the exercise is like cooling down.
- "No judgment" speaks for itself. Judging yourself during physical performance will take you out of the zone-like state more quickly than any distraction out there. Judgment is a distraction produced by your brain, and because of that, you can eliminate it. Much like the judgments sport writers or other athletes compulsively tweet about you and your team, you can choose to read or not read the thoughts your mind generates. With concentration training you can chose not to judge yourself or think in win-or-lose terms, no matter how many times your mind wanders.

With concentration training, there is no winning or losing, success or failure, good or bad. There is only the present and returning to the present when the boats come sailing through (an analogy I sometimes use when explaining how to let thoughts and feelings pass by). When following up with an athlete about his or her experience with the exercise, the first thing I typically hear is, "I couldn't do it. I'm bad at it. I could not quiet my mind." Patiently, I explain, "There's no good or bad, it's all about allowing yourself to come back to the present when your mind drifts. If there is anything that could be called 'bad' here, it would be getting aboard one of the passing boats—that is, indulging in the story being projected on the screen of your mind. But all you have to do is come back to where you really are, sitting there enjoying being in the present." The present—isn't this what you hear coaches screaming all the time? "Focus, focus! Stay in the present. Keep your head in the game." Just another example of how concentration training is a microcosm of what goes on during practice or a game.

Let patience and amusement be your guide during the practice, because you will be put to the test. Some days, within minutes you will be at war with the boats, trying to sink all of them instead of simply going back to your focal point. Remember the boats are just fighting for your attention and will do anything to distract you from the present moment. This is where you have a choice. You get to decide where you will focus your attention. It is the same choice you have during practice when you are bored or in a game feeling nervous. Choose to stay with the focal point, and a zone-like state will follow. The rest will take care of itself. Even if you do not win on the scoreboard, you will experience a psychological victory by choosing to focus your mind when it would be easier to indulge in worries, doubts, or fears (all the territory of Self 1). Let go, with no judgments, no win or lose, just absorption in the present moment.

The following might sound extreme, but if you want to get an idea of the level of precision or attention to detail you can bring to concentration practice, read chapter 6 in *The Art of Doing Nothing* by Veronique Vienne. This chapter, entitled "The Art of Napping," outlines steps you can take to make your naptime most productive. Yes, instructions on how to nap! To help bring this extra attention to detail to your practice, you can purchase an audio recording for concentration training on my website, www.goldmedalmind.com.

Neurofeedback: A Dose of Technology

Since the time I started to work with the US speed skating team, I have used concentration training in the way I have just described. While in Colorado Springs, Milwaukee, or Park City, I offered a drop-in concentration training group that all athletes were welcome to attend. When we were on the road, I offered a group in the evening that combined concentration and visualization training (the subject of chapter 9). The amount of time we spent varied and depended on the amount of chatting we did afterward.

But shortly after I started working with the Olympic Committee, they acquired the equipment to conduct neurofeedback training, a form of biofeedback. Biofeedback training involves placing sensors on the body to measure body functions like blood pressure, heart-rate variability, electrodermal activity (a.k.a. sweaty palms), brainwave activity, muscle tension, and so on. While connected to the sensors, a person can see on a computer screen how tense, relaxed, or in between they are based upon these measurements of physiological systems.

Neurofeedback specifically measures brainwave activity, tracking the degree to which an athlete is in the zone—a nonthinking state of consciousness—at any given second. And the equipment we had allowed us to detect how ever-so-slight changes in thinking impacted concentration. Basically, an athlete could learn to control the degree to which he or she could get into the zone by adjusting breathing and thought. It was the most profound way to teach the ability to focus and to refocus when distracted. I used this technology with Apolo Ohno more than any of the other skaters. We would meet, connect the sensors, and then go to war (war being the fight against the self—you against your own brain, or Self 1, as we have discussed). It took a while to convince the athletes that they were not competing against the machine; the machine was merely reflecting back what was going on in the brain. In his autobiography, *Zero Regrets*, Apolo writes about the neurofeedback work we did together.

> I got hooked up. I took a breath. The display looked like one of those old-fashioned Pong video games, with peaks and valleys all over the screen. I couldn't stay focused on anything for more than two seconds, it seemed. I tried counting. *Eee-boop, eee-boop,* the machine would grunt, a soundtrack of sorts to the Pong-style up-and-down on the video.
>
> "Calm," Doug said. "Work at being calm. This machine will give you immediate feedback. When you learn how to control this, it's probably one of the most powerful ways you can go to control your thinking. And when

> you can do that, you're putting your mind in the state most conducive to peak performance. *When* you learn—not *if* you can learn." (Ohno 2010, 102)

We met on a regular basis so Apolo could learn how subtle changes in his mental state would impact a relaxed state of concentration—being in the zone. Over time, we increased the challenge by playing the sound he heard at the start during the biofeedback training: "Ready…go to the start…and BAM," the gun would go off. We would also play crowd noise as he worked to remain in a zone-like state. On a large video screen, we would show footage from past World Cups or other championships to simulate the competitive environment as best we could. I believe this form of simulation training worked well. It was the next best thing to being there, while simultaneously providing direct feedback on the degree to which he maintained the zone-like state in spite of distractions. If you have access to biofeedback technology, I recommend the experience. You will be surprised at the sensitivity of the equipment and how humbling it can be to learn to control your own mind and body.

Bottom line—the ability to focus and come back to the present when distracted is the mother lode when it comes to having a gold medal mind. There is no substitute for learning to achieve and maintain a zone-like state, and there is nothing better than concentration training for learning how to turn your mind into an ally. The exercise I've described here can be boring and drive you nuts, but the practice will teach you patience, a skill as important in life as it is in sport. And believe it or not, it can actually be fun to embrace every aspect of the practice as you develop your ability to concentrate. All you need is time and desire. Every one of the characteristics you need to develop a gold medal mind—and all of the suggestions I will make in the following chapters of this book—depend on you being able to focus your attention to achieve specific goals. With all the distractions we face, both external and internal, there is no way to overestimate the power of not only being able to focus, but to refocus over and over again.

CHAPTER 9

Juggling, Electromyography, and Your Mind's Eye

My interest in sport psychology was sparked in 1979, when my high school ice hockey coach introduced us to mental practice (a.k.a. visualization training). Before games, Dickie Nolan would say something like, "Boys, what I want you to do is close your eyes and *see* yourself passing, scoring, and kicking ass." That was the extent of his instructions. Now, after decades of research dating back to the 1960s, we know there is more to it than just *seeing* yourself perform. However, Dickie was way ahead of his time.

The team's response to Dickie's advice was mixed. About half the guys thought he was nuts. It is possible they were nonbelievers, because at the same time Dickie was talking about visualization, the assistant coach Timmy Ryan was telling us about karma. (Timmy was a California boy who had gotten a dose of the New Age movement long before it hit western New York. Even today, the word karma does not float around western New York the way it does here in Boulder or in California.) But a handful of us were believers, including V.J., Crazy Legs, Speed, Shack, Whitey, and me. We would sit together after practice and picture in our mind's eye what we did well and what we wanted to improve on. I found it helped immensely, so for me it became an after-school ritual. Even the believers thought I was a little crazy for taking it that far.

The books I was reading at the time supported my interest in visualization training. One in particular was *Sports Psyching: Playing Your Best Game All of the Time* by Thomas Tutko and Umbero Tosi (1980). The authors wrote about using one's imagination to improve performance and enhance consistency. They encouraged readers to take photos of themselves performing, line them up on a table, scan them, and then, with eyes closed, visualize themselves performing well. Sounds easy, right? The toughest part was getting the photos, for at that time you had to have the roll of film developed, which sometimes took days. So if pictures were taken at a game on Sunday, the photos would not be ready for review until midweek, not leaving much time to update the mental images for the next weekend. But aside from the film-developing issue, the practice was simple. The biggest challenges were unclear images, getting distracted by random thoughts, or seeing bad performances. And these are still some of the most common problems athletes have with visualization training. I will address these issues later in this chapter.

I used visualization training for years as an athlete and also as a coach with my players. As a student, I took this form of training into the lab for closer examination. While earning my undergraduate degree, I did an honors thesis that looked at the impact of mental practice on performance—beanbag toss, of all things. And then, while I was working on my first master's degree at Penn State, I examined the physiological processes of mental practice for my thesis. In brief, my research involved measuring muscle activity by electromyography (EMG) while people visualized themselves juggling. The goal was to see if muscles at rest were activated during mental practice. Sure enough, they were. In several pilot studies, a group of us also measured heart rate, galvanic skin response (sweaty palms), brainwave activity, and respiration during visualization. And again, we found these physiological systems were all activated during mental practice. This research was later published in the *Journal of Sport and Exercise Psychology* and then in a book chapter I coauthored with Shane Murphy, entitled "Imagery and Mental Practice," for the book *Advances in Sport Psychology*. I had immersed myself into the study of mental practice just as I had athletics. In some ways, it became my new sport after my competitive career ended.

When I was at Penn State, our ability to measure physiological activity was limited by the equipment we had. I can remember us sitting around and guessing what we might find if we had more sophisticated ways to measure what was going on in the body and, more specifically, the brain. Then, about 10 years ago, I learned about a book entirely dedicated to mental practice. It is called *Imagery in Sport,* by Tony Morris, Michael Spittle, and Anthony Watt (2005). I was thrilled to open up this book and find a chapter entitled "Psychophysiological Research on Imagery." The mother lode: an entire chapter devoted to what was going on in the central (brain) and peripheral (body) nervous systems during mental practice. The chapter cites loads of studies conducted in several labs using brain studies such as magnetic resonance imaging (MRI), functional MRI (fMRI), and computed tomography (CT) scans to look at the brain during mental practice.

Back in the day, we could only wonder what was going on in the brain. But here it was, right in front of me, the facts. I will not try to describe the results of the research here, but in short, while one is at rest and visualizing, specific parts of the brain are activated in the same way they are when one is physically practicing a skill. This is an oversimplification, but the bottom line is that the research is showing that visualization is a profound way to enhance performance. We have believed this to be true for a long, long time, but the science provides support, leaving no room for doubt. If I were to take it a step further, new research in neuroscience is showing that mental activity like visualization can actually change specific areas of the brain. This type of mental workout has benefits far beyond what Clark, Corbin, and Jacobson, back in the 60s, could have ever imagined (no pun intended). These three were pioneers in studying the effects of mental practice on performance. If you are interested in the technical stuff, I would encourage you to read *Imagery in Sport*. For the basic how-to, read on to learn what steps will make the time you devote to mental practice most productive.

Using Mental Practice as a Form of Training

The first step in developing an effective visualization practice is for you to *believe* that it is a powerful way to train. You may recognize that when you even casually think or daydream about performing well, you tend to do better. You also know that when you watch a great athletic event on television you get pumped to go out and play. And if you do, you find yourself engaged and generally performing really well. These are just examples of how engaging your brain in a goal-directed manner helps your performance. So think of mental practice as enlisting the power of your mind in ways you never imagined. Engaging your mind, multiplied by one thousand! You can consciously create what you want to have happen on the field in specific ways, guided by the elements I describe next.

Use All of Your Senses

By nature, visualization involves visual images, but there is more to it than just "seeing" yourself perform. You will get the best results by incorporating all of your senses into your mental practice, not only vision but also hearing, taste, feeling, touch, and smell. (I even advocate using the so-called sixth sense, intuition, which I will discuss a little later.) For example, in the case of running, during visualization you want to *feel* your shoes hit and leave the pavement, *hear* the sound of the gun at the start, *taste* the sweat, and *feel* the movement of your body, the contraction and relaxation of your hamstrings and quads. In swimming, for example, there is not a whole lot to see. Primary for a swimmer using visualization training is hearing the sound of the water, seeing the bottom of the pool, and, most important, feeling the precise rhythm and timing when moving at top speed through the water. This is new territory for many athletes, because seeing oneself perform is what happens naturally in the mind. With practice, however, you will develop the ability to include of all your senses.

Repetition

Like physical practice, visualization involves repetition. With practice, your ability to focus will improve. Think of the process as developing your visualization muscle. Break your visualization sessions into sets and reps, just as you do when lifting weights. Do not try to visualize for long, uninterrupted periods of time, especially in the beginning; it will only lead to frustration. Can you imagine sitting and visualizing yourself running an entire 3,000 meters? Instead, break your mental practice into manageable sets. For example, with tennis, visualize yourself serving five times (i.e., first serves), then simply breathe and let your mind rest, then visualize five more serves (second serves), followed by a rest, and so on. In the case of running the 3,000 meters, visualize different parts of the race for each set, making each last about 60 seconds. For example, in your first set visualize the start, in the second set visualize maintaining perfect mechanics when feeling tired, and in the third set see yourself surging at the 200-meter mark. The number of sets per session will depend on your ability to concentrate. This is why I always have an athlete practice concentration training (explained in chapter 8) for a few weeks prior to starting visualization training.

Internal Versus External Perspectives

An internal perspective involves visualizing yourself from a first-person perspective, with you in your own body looking out through your own eyes. An external point of view is called a third-person perspective, and involves visualizing yourself as if you were watching yourself on a video. You may want to use an internal perspective when you are working on getting the feel of your sport, the kinesthetic aspect of your performance—for example, taking a shot on net in ice hockey, taking a penalty kick in soccer, being on the beam in gymnastics. In contrast, an external perspective will allow you to see the positioning of your body—how you are holding your arms and whether your toes are pointed during a dive, for example. In basketball, an external perspective will allow you to see yourself playing defense in order to get a sense of where you are on the court in relation to your teammates. In golf, you can watch yourself to be sure your mechanics are spot-on when putting. You should experiment with each perspective in different situations to determine what is most helpful for you. This is where working with a professional can help, or with your coach if he or she is knowledgeable about using this skill.

Emotions

To make visualization training most effective, you want it to be as lifelike as possible. No matter what the level, sport is emotional for athletes and even spectators. It is about passion. "Feel the passion" is how one athlete described his visualization process. He was a speed skater who skated the 500 and 1,000 meters, both sprint events that require explosiveness and high energy for optimal performance. This silver medal winner found that generating strong positive emotions like passion made visualization most effective for him.

Listening to music that generates specific emotions helps some athletes. For others, putting on crowd noise while visualizing gets excitement, hunger, thrill, and passion raging through every cell in the body. Be creative and have fun experimenting to find out what creates the exact emotions needed to get your blood flowing so you are at your best.

For example, you may find that watching video prior to visualizing can cause excitement and passion to surge through your bloodstream. Just think of how strongly we want to go out and play after watching a great game on TV. I can still vividly remember watching the US men's ice hockey team beat the USSR in the semi-finals in the 1980 Winter Games before going on to win the gold medal. After that game, we all rushed out into the street to play hockey until we were on the verge of hypothermia.

When

Another key element of visualization is knowing when to practice. Some of the best times to use this skill are before, during, or after practice and before, during, or after a competition. Before practice, visualization can help you get mentally prepared. During a workout, it can help you make the most of feedback you receive from a coach, because after receiving the feedback you can review in your mind's eye what changes you will make (in your stroke, for example). And after practice is a great time because you can review, rehearse, and internalize or consolidate what you learned. Visualizing what you have learned and how your skill level is developing will improve your confidence. Look for opportunities during the day to take a few minutes to practice, for example, when traveling by airplane, train, or bus, or during a study break. If you are in the library studying, go outside for 5 minutes and visualize. The practice itself is easy; having the discipline to make the time is the challenge.

When it comes to using visualization in a competition, you may first want to ask yourself this important question: "Will my visualizing before or during a game make me think too much?" Remember, the zone is about being absorbed in the moment, with little or no thought. For some athletes, visualization before or during competition may lead to thinking too much. On the other hand, it can serve to help you concentrate on the task at hand instead of dwelling on worries, doubts, fears, or concerns. It is up to you to experiment and see how visualization works best for you on game day.

Speed

The speed of your mental practice can be altered to achieve different goals. If you are a figure skater working on a new skill that has been difficult to master, try visualizing in slow motion. On a 1 to 10 scale, in which 10 is real-time speed and 1 represents being still, visualize yourself at a 4, then a 6, and so on, gradually increasing the speed of your mental practice until you are comfortable visualizing at real-time speed. From an internal perspective, slow motion will allow you to really get the feel of the movement, and an external perspective will help you see the movement of your body. This is similar to watching yourself on video in slow motion to clearly see the subtle mechanics that make a difference in the eyes of the judges.

Changing the speed of your visualization can be impactful in sports like swimming or running. For example, a swimmer struggling with his or her backstroke times may benefit from visualizing swimming at a slightly faster speed than normal. One way to do this is to time your mental practice of the 200 meters, for example, so that your performance during visualization training is at the same speed you know you can swim the event in a meet. What is most important is to get a sense of moving through the water at a faster pace, with the emphasis on timing, rhythm, and stroke rate. In a case like this, when the stroke rate you are visualizing is a little faster than normal, talk with your coach so you can be sure you are visualizing the mechanics of your stroke correctly.

Self-Instruction and Cues

Before actually visualizing, it can help to give yourself some cues, key words that support the execution of the skill. Think of a cue or key word as something that, when said to yourself, brings everything together. A psychological cue word for many athletes is "breathe." When an athlete says breathe, it serves as a reminder to stay in the present moment. And as we know, being in the present is at the heart of being in a zone-like state. To help a gymnast stay in the present and get absorbed in the execution of the skill, we identify words she can say to herself prior to visualizing. For example, one gymnast would say, "calm, salute, powerful hurdle, aggressive and block, tight shape, and stick landing." Specific to the vault, these words triggered vivid images for the athlete so her attention to detail was strong. When I am guiding a visualization session, I will give the cue words right before the set of mental practice, and then shut my mouth and let the athlete visualize.

The idea is to find the right cue words, so that when you hear them, everything comes together mechanically. Before beginning visualization training with an athlete, we spend time together identifying cue words that seem to resonate most with that athlete. One athlete who specialized in the 400-meter hurdles would say to himself when approaching the sixth and seventh hurdle: "arms, explode." Two words were all he needed for everything to come together. During his visualization training he would do the same thing: as he approached the sixth hurdle in his mind, he said those words to himself and visualized the result. Experiment with different cue words until you find the ones that work best for you. You might want to ask your coach for help with this.

Intuition

I assume you have an idea what intuition is. In a nutshell, it is your gut feeling, an inner sense that you know exactly what to do in a given situation. When you are in a game, say ice hockey, the defense sometimes makes unexpected adjustments. Within tenths of a second, you need to make a decision to exploit that defense, and that decision may not be based upon what was rehearsed in practice. It is your call in the moment to act. And what you do does not require thought. You do not have time to think. The decision you make is based upon a heartfelt sense, an inner knowing devoid of any thinking.

During your visualization training, use your intuition muscle. Get used to trusting your inner sense of what to do. This is where visualization training gets fun, because you are not following a script. It is time for improvisation, for reacting immediately without thought. Practice it in your mind's eye to become more comfortable trusting your body's wisdom, that you have exactly what it takes to meet the challenge. Nurture this in yourself, because there is no greater place to operate than from a place of trust. As you incorporate intuition in your mental practice, you will start to surprise yourself out on the ice, court, field, course, and even in the game of life.

Other Helpful Techniques

Listening to music while visualizing can get the blood flowing, helping you really get absorbed in the experience. Just think about how it feels to watch people backcountry skiing on massive slopes with high-energy music in the background. Doesn't it get you pumped? Try wearing your football helmet or holding the volleyball in your hands while visualizing to give yourself some tactile cues. It can be helpful to record a description of what you want to visualize (or record someone else describing it, like your coach) and listen to it during your mental practice. This will allow you the opportunity to not have to think too much about what you are doing and whether you are doing it right or not. The recording will guide you. I find many athletes have more vivid and controllable images when listening to my voice or a recording at home. In the case of a team sport—field hockey, for example—it is easy to set up a group visualization during which someone (maybe a coach) provides instructions to attack in a specific way. There are no hard and fast rules here. Be creative and have fun with this method of training. (On my website—www.goldmedalmind.com—I offer a visualization training recording that you can purchase to help with your practice.)

Potential Challenges During Mental Practice

As with any practice, there are a few challenges you may experience when using visualization training. Sitting still and concentrating on visualizing your performance may seem simple. It may come easily to some of you, some of the time. But in general, I have found that athletes struggle with various issues when visualizing. Especially when you first start the practice, frustration may occur. Here are some suggestions for overcoming specific challenges.

Negative Images

You may find yourself imagining negative outcomes, messing up—striking out, missing the putt, or crashing the bike in downhill mountain bike racing. Have patience, give it time, and start with simple images. For example, in basketball, at first restrict your mental training to visualizing yourself dribbling the ball at practice. Then gradually work up to more challenging situations, such as drills in practice, scrimmaging in practice, and then various game situations. Before visualizing, give yourself brief instructions that serve as a guide to your training, just as your coach might. These instructions should serve as an anchor to ground you in your mental practice. If the negative images continue, see a sport psychologist.

The Blurry Screen

Having trouble concentrating is a common problem among athletes beginning visualization training. You may find your mind jumping all over the place like a monkey swinging from one tree branch to the next. Be mindful that visualization training is a concentration exercise in disguise. Reread chapter 8 several times and practice the concentration exercise daily for a few weeks prior to starting visualization practice. Try opening your eyes in between visualization sets and use cue words more frequently. Keep your sets short, and practice when you are feeling most alert and mentally sharp. Experiment with using mental practice right after a workout, when your nervous system is activated and you are already in a zone-like state.

Trouble With Control or Speed

My first suggestion is to be patient with your practice. However, one particular strategy seems to help most if not all folks who struggle with the control or speed of their visualization. I learned this from a friend of mine who was a professional ballet dancer. The exercise involves standing with your arm straight and extended over your head. Your arm should be at a 90-degree angle to the floor, with your hand touching your ear and your palm facing outward. Think of your arm as the second hand on a clock. The objective is to move your hand from 12 o'clock, the starting position, to 6 o'clock, ending with your arm down at your side, palm facing your leg and arm perpendicular to the floor. Set a timer for 30 seconds, and from the "starting line" move your arm from top to bottom so that you are in sync with real time, taking 30 seconds to go from top to bottom. Ideally, you will move your arm at a speed consistent with real time, instead of moving it too slow or too fast. You may find the movement is choppy, just as your visualization can be. Be patient. Start with your eyes closed, and then graduate to practicing with your eyes open. Starting with your eyes closed (as you do when beginning to visualize) will allow you to tune into the pace at which you move your arm. After mastering the 30-second time interval, you can move to the next level by setting the timer for 60 seconds and bringing your arm from 12 o'clock to 6 o'clock and then back to 12 o'clock. Be patient, let go, trust yourself, and be mindful to not try too hard.

Time Management

No time for visualization training? I don't buy it. If winning is important to you, you will find the time. You will recall the story of how my friend Pat Manson, who held the national record in pole vaulting, wrote the height he was planning to master on a piece of pole hung over his bed. Just before going to sleep, and again as soon as he woke up, he spent 5 or 10 minutes visualizing jumping. Think about where in your day you can squeeze in a few minutes of mental training. Practice in the car on your way to a workout (unless you are the one who is driving, that is). Use time spent traveling on a plane or bus or waiting in the airport as a valuable opportunity for mental practice. Take 30 seconds to visualize during practice, while on a water break or between drills. Or ask your coach to give you time during practice to visualize. To the pro athletes out there, you know you have plenty of time.

Not Feeling It

Sometimes you just will not be able to feel the movement. This is the time to use what is called body rehearsal. While standing, close your eyes and actually move your body as if you were performing the movement you want to practice: hitting a forehand in tennis, for example. Physically swing the racquet as if you were on the court, and then visualize the movement without moving your body. Alternate between body rehearsal and mental rehearsal. Some athletes find that closing their eyes during body rehearsal helps with visualizing. You can even work on this during practice. During ice hockey practice, while scrimmaging, for example, close your eyes while you are on the bench and feel the movement of your body while the memory is fresh in your nervous system. Another option is to stretch for a bit and watch yourself on video prior to visualizing. For some, stretching gets the body and mind warmed up so the feeling during mental practice is more intense. One last suggestion is to wear or hold your equipment during your mental practice. If you are a lacrosse player, for example, wear your helmet, gloves, and cleats. If you are a tennis player, wear your shoes and hold your racquet. If you are a skier, put your skis and gloves on and hold your poles. As you experiment with these suggestions, you will get the feel.

Like so many other psychological skills I have shared thus far, visualization is not just a sport technique, but also a life skill. Writing this chapter, I learned just how true this is. For some reason, my perfectionism kicked in on this chapter, to the point I struggled and procrastinated like crazy. So what helped? One day I decided to stop fighting with myself. I put my feet up on a chair, rested my head against the wall, locked into some good music, closed my eyes, and visualized myself writing. I could feel my fingers dancing on the keyboard, sentences emerging on the computer screen while allowing images of inspiring moments in my life to rattle around in my consciousness. Letting go of the idea of making the chapter perfect and putting trust in my mind and heart allowed me to be aware of what I was writing, but not think too much about it. It enabled me to access that blissful feeling of being aware but not thinking—a.k.a. being in a zone-like state. I let ease, comfort, passion, and fun be my guides, and the strategy proved highly effective (and fun).

What You Can Expect

Visualization is a practice that has virtually no downside. Yes, mental training will take time out of your day and can be frustrating because of the potential challenges I have identified. But the reality is that this is a way to practice your sport with no risk of injury. You can practice all you want without overtraining or under-recovering. Once you master the technique, you can look forward to learning new physical skills much more quickly, having easy access to the zone-like state, engaging in effective mental preparation for practice and competition, and generally performing beyond your expectations. Consistent practice of this skill may even lead you to make adjustments to your North Star, because you may find yourself believing in possibilities you would never have considered before learning to use your mind as an ally.

CHAPTER 10

Learning to Love Leroy

It was a very cold winter day in Colorado Springs, and for me, what might have been just another day at the office. The athletes of the US short-track speed skating team were caroming across the ice first thing in the morning at the World Arena in the south part of town. I had picked up my cranberry-walnut bagel and hot Earl Grey tea from Wooglin's Deli and found the warmest spot I could in the players' box. But in fact, this was not a typical day at the office, because we had guests: the exercise physiologists from the department of coaching and sport science at the Olympic training center. They were equipped with needles and test strips. This was destined to be one of those days the athletes would come to both hate and love. I could already see how they would hate it. I was the person who could help them love it, or at least embrace it.

On this cold winter morning, the goal was to measure blood lactate. In plain terms, the athletes were participating in a test that would shed light on what they were made of. At maximum athletic intensity, our bodies draw on anaerobic capacity, the energy system responsible for the ability to dig down deep. This type of cardiovascular fitness is what keeps an athlete going when his or her legs feel like they are going to fall off and the heart is about to burst at the seams. The question is, "Does this athlete have the ability to move lactate and maintain the pace, or will he or she decelerate?" At the Olympic level, having this ability is typically what makes the difference between a gold and silver medal, a difference than can come down to .001 of a second. People believe that most, if not all, athletes are on the same playing field when it comes to physical skills at the Olympic level. The differences among them are psychological. In speed skating, like other endurance sports, the psychological aspect applies to how well athletes handle pain and fatigue. Yes, there is a physiological aspect to handling lactate (or lactic acid, as most athletes call it, though they are not the same thing). When it comes down to the last 100 meters or so, it is all grit.

When things get intense, we use lactate as fast fuel for the muscles, heart, and brain. To utilize lactate, the body splits lactic acid into a fuel part (lactate) and an acid part (hydrogen ions). The acid part, a waste product, interferes with muscle recruitment and with the blood's ability to circulate oxygen to the muscles. That is the downside of lactate, the reason it feels like the wheels will fall off. The oxygen debt and the body's increasing inability to pay it back during the brief rest periods between reps can lead to nausea and light-headedness.

This test day was the day blood lactate—what you probably know as lactic acid—would be squirting out of the athletes' ears. At various intervals during practice, the athletes' fingers were pricked and blood samples drawn. The blood would be checked for the level of lactate at any given level of intensity. At some point during the testing (I am guessing toward the end, because some of the athletes were starting to vomit), one of the skaters came to the bench to have his blood drawn. He was struggling, holding onto the boards for dear life while holding out a finger to be punctured. If nothing else, a split second of rest can give the illusion the pain will disappear. But it is merely an illusion, and the sense of relief lasts only a few seconds.

A surge of mental and physical pain is just around the corner, ready to attack.

This skater looked up at me and asked, "How am I going to make it?" I smiled, hoping this nonverbal communication would suffice as an answer. He did not buy it. My style is sometimes less than conventional; I am not always the warm and fuzzy psychologist I might be. The skater asked again, this time with more intensity, "How am I going to frickin' make it?" Again I smiled, and said, "Make what?" By this time he was getting quite annoyed and exclaimed, "Why don't you try it?" I said, "Try what?" At this point he turned his head away in disgust. After waiting a few seconds, I yelled, "You mean Leroy!" He turned his head, looking utterly confused, and replied, "Leroy? What are you talking about?" Reaching for a piece of white tape from the trainer, I said, "Leroy—pain." And then, while he was looking at me as if I were the one losing it, I wrote "NO LEROY" on the tape and plastered it on the front of his helmet.

Before he had a chance to say anything I yelled, "No Leroy, young man! Now is your time. Leroy is your friend, my man. Welcome him. This is what you train for every day. To come face-to-face with the very thing that will put you on the podium!" Oh boy, I thought to myself, this is either going to go really well or explode! I continued, "The better you are able to make friends with Leroy, the faster you will go at the end of the race. It is plain and simple. No Leroy."

The athlete did not respond to me directly, but once his blood was drawn, he put his head down and muttered, "No Leroy." I smiled and watched him do the mental gymnastics necessary to enter an altered state of consciousness to finish the test while maintaining good mechanics. The mechanics thing is crucial, because when Leroy comes knocking at the door, the skater's tendency is to want to straighten up. Lifting one's center of gravity just a few millimeters will greatly impact the force the athlete is able to create. The formula, as coaches and skaters know it, is: Leroy + standing up = going slower.

That equals getting beaten, and getting beaten was not in our vocabulary. Once they completely understood the formula, most, if not all, of the skaters learned to welcome Leroy and even came to love Leroy. But learning to love Leroy only happened with hours of training in the classroom and on the ice with the techniques I will describe later in this chapter.

I want to be clear that "No Leroy" does not mean absence of pain. No Leroy means embracing the pain and learning to love it. We used the simple phrase "No Leroy" because it was short and powerful, and it stimulated the brain to embrace the idea of making friends with Leroy. From my perspective, Leroy is just another reason to love playing the game. It is part of the challenge inherent in developing a gold medal mind. For endurance athletes, this is the cornerstone of going faster and faster and faster—loving Leroy versus the dread that is common among these athletes.

Leroy does not only show up for lactate testing. In fact, most of you probably have not experienced the pleasure of lactate testing, but know Leroy all too well. Leroy, in the form of physical pain, can come calling in any of the following situations:

- Lifting weights
- Performing core exercises
- Doing plyometrics
- Running hills or sprints
- At the end of the race in endurance sports (e.g., running, swimming, biking, Nordic skiing)
- At certain points during practice and games (e.g., in basketball, lacrosse, ice hockey, soccer, tennis, badminton, squash, racquetball)
- In the acute phase of an injury

And what about emotional pain? Although this situation is often overlooked in sport, Leroy can take a psychological as well as a physical form. Leroy may come out after any of these events:

- A bad performance (discouragement)
- Criticism from a coach (rejection)
- Negative press from sports writers or fans (feeling criticized)
- Making a mental error (sense of failure)
- Letting a teammate down (embarrassment)

Overload and Adaptation

Okay, so what is there to like about Leroy? Everything. Embracing Leroy makes us stronger in a number of ways. Let us look at the principles of exercise physiology, overload and adaptation. Strengthening a muscle requires resistance (e.g., lifting weights). As a result of the resistance—a form of overload—a chemical reaction occurs. Then, with the proper rest, the muscle grows and strengthens. The muscle adapts by growing larger and stronger.

The same principle applies to cardiovascular fitness and to the aerobic and anaerobic energy systems. The same applies to flexibility, and to learning motor skills. We rehearse skills, our motor system adapts, and we learn to execute complex movements without having to think about them. And the same applies to psychological fitness. With overload—challenging the brain with visualization training, for example—adaptation will occur, improving the brain's ability to create images, sensations, and emotions. From a neurological perspective, the brain will physically change in various ways as a result of visualization or concentration training.

Therefore, I encourage you to see Leroy as something that will lead to physical and psychological overload. Through the suggestions I provide, adaptation will take place, leaving you stronger than you were prior to coming to terms with the need for Leroy. Specifically, as a result of embracing Leroy, your strength and endurance will increase. Consider the fact that without Leroy, you in fact will not become more psychologically or physically skilled. That will make it easier to embrace the pain and fatigue that comes with overload.

Making Friends With Leroy

The bottom line is we cannot improve without Leroy. I know it sounds fairy-tale-like, but Leroy is our friend. And what do friends want for us? They want us to be happy. Whether athlete or non-athlete, we cannot win, let alone be happy, without Leroy. When doing interval training, loving Leroy is the last thing most of us think about because interval training is ridiculously painful. Some days it can seem intolerable! But developing a friendship with Leroy is what will lessen the sting. It may not completely eliminate the sting, but it will certainly lessen it so you can maintain the proper mechanics to skate, run, or swim fast when Leroy crashes the party.

Great, you might say—I understand the concept, but how do I push through Leroy? This is the challenge all athletes face, especially endurance athletes. I will tell you what I shared with a group of running coaches a while back. The coaches were in a certification-training program sponsored by the Lydiard Foundation, an organization that teaches the principles and practice of the late and great running coach of New Zealand, Arthur Lydiard. Lydiard was known for the pyramid structure of his training, which is based on developing an aerobic foundation before introducing other aspects of training. I work with the president of the Lydiard Foundation, Lorraine Moller, a former Olympic bronze medal winner in the women's marathon.

During the course, I told the coaches, "When Leroy comes knocking at the door, welcome him in. Sit down at the table and break bread together. You need to get to know Leroy, because he is fascinating.

He is simple but complicated. Offer him dessert and an after-dinner drink. And after that, go sit in the living room for more casual conversation and perhaps a cup of tea. Yes, tea; Leroy loves tea. Ask him questions, anything you can think of. It can be, 'Where did you get your name?' or 'Can you still do your job and inflict less pain than you do?' 'How do you make me hurt so bad?' 'Are you a masochist?' 'What makes you laugh?' 'What do you do for fun?' 'Is there a secret to making friends with you?' The possibilities are endless. Maybe you want to go for a run with Leroy to see if Leroy experiences Leroy. Use your imagination."

Yep, that is what I said to a large group of elite-level running coaches from all over the country. Did I get some strange looks? You bet I did. And did that cause emotional pain for me? No, because I already knew my story about making friends with Leroy was a bit left of center. And several coaches approached me after the presentation to learn more about how to take the idea of making friends with Leroy back to their athletes.

Now for the bottom line: what you can do to learn to love Leroy. I know many of you already hate him, but there is still time for a fairy-tale ending. Here are some suggestions that have been tested in real live laboratories—that is, at the tracks, pools, and ice rinks where I work with athletes during practice.

Get into your body. A mantra I used with the skaters was "down in your body." Leroy will, by his very nature, get you up into your head. It is not your body that registers Leroy as downright brutal—it is your brain, which senses the pain. Therefore, if you are able to stay out of your head, you will at least minimize the feelings of pain. It is a distraction technique, to some degree. Whether the source of the pain is inability to process enough lactate fast enough to keep your muscles from shutting down or some other biochemical process, work on focusing your attention down in your body. For example, if you are a skater, focusing on correct biomechanics of your stride, relaxation of the neck and shoulders, and proper arm swing will ensure your center of gravity stays where it should be so you do not decelerate. Experiment by focusing on your body in different ways to find the sweet spot, the place where you do not feel the pain as much and your mechanics are close to perfect.

Take deep breaths. Breathe, and breathe some more. If you tune into your body when experiencing pain, you will notice that your breathing becomes labored and shallow, which makes the problem worse. Pain causes muscles to tighten up, impeding oxygen flow and leading to the build up of even more acid waste products. You don't have to worry about getting too relaxed or "loosey goosey," as Coach Guzz called it. Your objective is to facilitate what the body does naturally—move huge amounts of lactate.

You can use this breathing technique for strength and conditioning, too. You know how after running an interval you want to just bend over and put your hands on your knees to catch your breath? Just say no! This is your time to repay oxygen debt, replenish your energy stores, get rid of acid wastes, and so on. Stand up, no matter how uncomfortable it is, and breathe—slow, deep breaths. Put your hands on top of your head if that helps. The method even has a fancy name these days: excess post-exercise oxygen consumption, or EPOC. It is the opposite of what your body reflexively will want to do, but a gold medal mind does what is most powerful, not necessarily what is most comfortable.

Focus on your breath. This is a little different from breathing deeply and slowly. Just as you can focus on your body to distract your mind from pain, you can use your breath as a cue when Leroy strikes. In some sports, the pain can be episodic, not constant. Take the last several miles in a marathon: the pain comes and goes, ebbs and flows. The tide comes in and the tide goes out. It is a dance of sorts. And staying with the breath is like keeping the beat. From a musical perspective, when pain strikes you are in essence playing polyrhythms. That is, there are several different "sounds" going on, including pain, but through it all, you keep the beat. This keeps your brain from giving Leroy the lead guitar role in your mind. If you focus on your breath, Leroy will be playing rhythm guitar instead of lead.

Visualize yourself performing with Leroy in the house. As you will recall, visualization training involves feeling all the sensations that are part of your sport. Feeling the pain while visualizing will allow you to desensitize yourself, to get used to the pain. Try thinking of this technique from the perspective of overlearning motor skills. You practice over and over and over—shooting hundreds of free throws daily to get your nervous system used to the movement, in essence, strengthening Self 2. Visualizing yourself maintaining good mechanics and maintaining your pace with Leroy on board is a similar kind of practice. You are increasing your pain threshold by turning your mind into an ally, a cardinal feature of a gold medal mind.

Talk to yourself. Before you get to the point at which you feel like you have to slow down and vomit, use words to minimize the impact the pain is having on your mechanics and plain old enjoyment of the moment. After all, my hope for you is to enjoy this aspect of your performance. Yes, enjoy the pain. So what can you say? Some athletes say things like this *before* the pain is in full force: "Now is the time." "Bring it on." "Come on in, Leroy." "Burn, burn, and breathe." "Kick its ass." Experiment and find the words that actually energize you to transcend your pain.

Earlier, rather than later. In the area of stress management, we talk about doing something before a panic attack starts. Once you are in panic attack territory, there may be no turning back. At that point, perhaps nothing short of intravenous Valium will reverse the stress response and keep your sympathetic nervous system from running riot. The same applies to Leroy. Think of the Leroy scale as 1 to 10, where 10 is emergency room material and 1 is how you feel lying on a beach. For some of you, when the pain is a 4 on the Leroy scale is the time to do something to counteract it. Do not wait for the pain to soar. Inoculate yourself against it now. Use some of the suggestions listed here when you first perceive the pain, instead of waiting until the pain hijacks your brain.

Focus on mechanics. I have worked with swimmers whose primary goal is to keep Leroy to a minimum. For some, when Leroy is at about a 4, the athlete gets absorbed in relaxation of the neck, the rotation of the body in the water, the movement of the legs at the hips, or the movement of the shoulders—something that makes the entire stroke fall into place. It is a way to think, but not think. One swimmer would focus on the position of her head only. By doing that, she kept Leroy from passing a score of 6, and the mechanics of her stroke would not be compromised. Find out where you can focus to keep your mechanics precise and Leroy to a minimum.

Focus on cue words. Again, I'm suggesting that you talk to yourself. But this time, find a word—one word—to serve as your focal point. Some words athletes I know have used include fire, strong, explode, fly, power, zone, force, and ease. The word you choose can be any word that works to takes your mind off the pain. This technique is something like focusing on your breath, but for some, works better. So when the pain is a 4 on the Leroy scale, begin saying your word to yourself to create the mental and physical torque you need to power through the last miles, meters, or feet.

Train like a maniac. There is still no substitute for intense physical training. This way of improving your body on the physiological level increases its ability to consume, transport, and utilize oxygen and process lactate—by pushing it when it counts in practice. When you are doing sprints, for example, do not decelerate until it is time. I tell athletes that a cardinal reflection of a gold medal mind is accelerating through the finish line and not even entertaining the idea of slowing down for at least a few feet after that point. Crazy? Yes, but remember, a gold medal mind is not about comfort, either physical or mental. You are pushing your boundaries, allowing the process of overload and adaptation to occur.

Expect to have fun with pain. Your expectations are powerful. This is the power of positive thinking that Norman Vincent Peale wrote about in his book by the same name in 1952. To increase the likelihood of a positive outcome, expect a positive outcome. You may want to think of it as what is called a self-fulfilling prophecy. I am sure you have read about this on a tea-bag label at some point in your journey. Now you know it is directly related to loving Leroy. Take it on as part of your performance to have fun with Leroy, to play with him. It will be a psychological victory if you can maintain your speed and mechanics regardless of the outcome. And as you are coming to understand, the gold medal mind is all about psychological victories. Placing your attention on developing a friendship with Leroy is a psychological victory in its own right.

Start lifting weights, if you do not already. Use weight lifting as a training ground to make friends with pain. You will find that as the pain sets in during the last few repetitions of a set, you will want to sacrifice your form to reach the magic number. If you are doing curls, for example, you may begin to use your shoulders or back instead of isolating and letting your bicep muscles burn as if they are on fire. Compromising your form is a way to attempt to put out the fire. But this is just an illusion; it does not decrease the Leroy and will only put you at greater risk of injury. When your muscles are on fire, use that as a cue to deepen your focus on correct mechanics. You are using lifting as a training ground for what you will do in the pool, on the bike, on the track, or on the field. Refer to chapter 12 for tips on how to lift weights to maximize your time in the weight room. You will strengthen not only your body, but also your mental muscle.

Set a goal to make friends with Leroy. Yes, plain and simple, make a plan to develop your ability to better deal with pain. In more technical terms, your ultimate (outcome) goal here is to increase your pain threshold. That is, given a level of pain intensity, you will experience it less than you would have if you had not engaged in some mental gymnastics. For example, before you set a goal to increase your pain threshold, a 7 on the Leroy scale will seem like a 7. But after focusing your attention on making friends with Leroy, a 7 will feel the way a 5 did before the mental training. Embracing this challenge is a blast! Your confidence will soar as you take the opportunity to turn your mind into an ally. Instead of hearing your mind complain, "Ugh, it hurts too much! I can't stand it!" you will be saying, "Hunger, explode!" or "Feel it and surge!" This is gold-medal-mind material.

Reward yourself for embracing Leroy. Hey, after all, this is hard work. On a physiological level, your body will hurt. There is no way around it. By working like a maniac, pushing through the pain using these suggestions, your body will break down. This is part of the overload process. Some of you will not even have time to rest long enough to recover (adapt) before going into battle again. So reward yourself by getting a neuromuscular massage, a deep-tissue massage, acupuncture, sacro-occipital or craniosacral work, or even Rolfing. In reality, these modalities are not a luxury, but a necessity, depending on the intensity, frequency, and duration of your training. I would go as far as to say everyone, athletes and non-athletes alike, would benefit from an acupuncture treatment now and then. So reward yourself for your efforts to set goals to embrace Leroy and make him your friend.

There you have it: the formula for learning to embrace and love Leroy. Never again will you shy away from a speed workout or an extra set in the weight room. You can now have fun with the process, knowing the workouts you dread are actually something to be excited about. You have learned to be psychotic—out of touch with reality—in a healthy way. You will now be out of touch with the reality that you feel like dying during practice. Think of dealing with Leroy as a skill. It will take time and practice to internalize the skill, and you are now at the beginning of the learning curve. Some of you already have an incredibly high pain tolerance, but we are talking about gaining more, more, and more tolerance. When you have learned to really love Leroy, the pain you feel in competition will pale in comparison to what you have come to embrace in training.

CHAPTER 11

Oceanfront Property

Let's talk about real estate. Not because it is a great long-term investment, but because it applies to the gold medal mind in a significant way. If you have more interest in exchange-traded funds than real estate, you don't have to believe what I have to say. Just humor me by rolling with the metaphor for a paragraph or two.

My father taught me when I was very young about the fundamentals of real estate. He is from a small farming village in Lebanon north of Beirut, and from an early age heard from his own father about the value of land. One big lesson was that there is only so much land, and as the supply of land decreases, the demand goes up, along with prices. In the spirit of this fact, think of oceanfront property. There is only so much of it to be had, and much less in some parts of the country than others. This is the reason property on the ocean is so much more expensive than anywhere else. Even trailer parks on the Pacific Coast Highway (the famous Route 1) in Santa Monica are more expensive than those in Boulder.

In 1995, when I was living in Palo Alto, California, I took a little day trip down the coast. One place I stopped was Monterey Bay. I immediately fell in love with it and decided I needed to live there. As I was driving down Ocean View Boulevard, there it was: a for-sale sign in front of a fixer-upper. The house was right on the ocean, but the reality was that it was uninhabitable because it was in tatters. It looked as if no one had lived there for years. Basically, it was a shell that at best would have to be taken down. But the price? $999,000—yes, just for the land, a standard quarter-acre lot. Can you imagine what that would cost now, more than 20 years later? Bottom line, there is a lot of investment horsepower in oceanfront property. Remember, the point is that there is only so much land, and oceanfront property is expensive. And oceanfront property has a strong impact on us. After all, where do people want to vacation? On the oceanfront, because it is a powerful and lovely place to be. Time spent there is memorable. It has a strong impact on us, and we will tell stories about vacations by the sea for years to come.

Oceanfront Property and Your Mind

Now consider the "real estate" of your mind. Thoughts that live in the oceanfront property of our minds are more powerful than the thoughts lurking around in the suburbs. There is only so much land in the mind, and just as in the world, the oceanfront property there is costly. If worry, fear, doubt, concern, insecurity, and regret live on the oceanfront of our minds, it will damage our performance, and our health, for that matter. So the question we must ask ourselves is where we want to put thoughts such as, "I can't do this," "This is going to be too hard," "I am done, I don't have what it takes," "Oh sh*t, I can't miss this one," "It's over, we aren't going to win," "The coach hates me," and other vicious attacks on yourself. You know the kind of thoughts I am talking about—the ones that can hijack your mind and paralyze your motor system.

In all sport psychology literature, you will find it suggested and even recommended that thoughts classified as negative be placed out in the country in a shack. Not even in a trailer park on the plains of Kansas, but in a shack that is barely standing, as far from reality as you can imagine. Maybe in the deserted salt mines in Leadville,

Colorado. Certainly nowhere near the oceanfront. You may have heard something about a technique called "thought stopping." When you have a negative thought (a doubt, for example), you tell yourself, "Stop." In computer terminology, you simply block and delete the negative thought. Makes sense, right? It seems it might work, based upon conventional wisdom, but I cannot tell you the number of times during presentations and talks that athletes have asked me, "Well, how do I do that?" Or they tell me, "I tried that, and it does not work. As soon as I say 'stop,' the negative thought comes back." The key issue, often not addressed, is exactly how we evict negative thoughts from oceanfront property and move them out to a shack that is barely standing.

The Scoreboard and Your Unruly Tenants

Negative thoughts are typically driven by fear—fear of a horrible outcome. Some call this fear of failure. Thoughts like, "Oh no, not again!" "You idiot, I can't believe you did that!" "You will never get it right!" "This is a nightmare. I can't wait until it is over!" are all manifestations of one of the most powerful emotions—fear, or even terror. All of these thoughts are based upon worry, doubt, and concern about losing. In other words, they are entirely outcome oriented. When outcome-oriented thoughts occupy oceanfront property in your mind, it becomes close to impossible to get into and maintain a zone-like state. So what should you do?

If you recall from chapter 3, I identified Self 2 as focused on playing the game, being in the moment, and operating from a zone-like state. This is all based in process-oriented thinking. When your mind is in process-oriented mode, worry, fear, and doubt may not disappear completely, but you will turn down their volume. Process-oriented thoughts will occupy your oceanfront property, keeping fear-based, outcome-driven thoughts at bay. The response of the gold medal mind to unruly tenants in your property is to shift to a process-based state of mind.

No doubt you understand how the battle in your mind between outcome and process can be harder than playing the physical game. Mental fatigue is the enemy of the zone-like state. In chapter 3, I described a dialogue technique that can be used to foster a better working relationship between Self 1 (outcome) and Self 2 (process). In the heat of mental warfare during a game, you have no time to engage in a dialogue with yourself. Below I will share some different suggestions on how to get into process mode when you are under attack by an outcome-oriented tirade in your mind. These suggestions will allow you to quickly, within a matter of seconds, shift your focus of attention while staying right where you want to be—in the present moment.

Some Potential (Legal) Steps to Evict Tenants

1. The first step is to send, via certified mail with return receipt, a Pay or Quit Notice. Translated into gold-medal-mind language, the equivalent action would be to focus on your breathing. Plain and simple, breathe. Take slow, deep, complete breaths. This will shift your attention away from Self 1 (the thinker) and prevent your nervous system from getting too activated. As you know, when you get too nervous you start ruminating on negative chatter that will ultimately overpower your strongest attempts to shut it down. Having racing thoughts is a cardinal symptom of being nervous. So breathe.

2. Sit back and see if the tenants respond to the Pay or Quit Notice. They will have three business days to do so. The same applies to your thoughts, but give them maybe three seconds. Observe the unruly stuff going on in your ocean-front property. Just observe. The idea is to create space between you and the thoughts, to detach. This is a subject-object dance consistent with Eastern philosophical

perspectives. Your mind is the subject, and your thoughts are the object. Let the subject observe the object, the game being played. Detach from the negative thoughts swinging like monkeys from one vine to the next by simply watching them. Simply observe them in a very disinterested way.

3. Allow yourself to not judge the thoughts. In other words, keep your competitiveness out of it. No win, no lose, no good, no bad, no success, no failure—just you thinking about your thinking. In fancy terms, this is called meta-cognition. For example, imagine you have a thought like, "I am an idiot!" immediately followed by "Ahhh, don't think like that!" By judging your negative thought, you are getting into the ring and will end up fighting with yourself. And we know where that ends up. Judging your thinking and trying to fight negative thoughts is an act of indulging in them. The moment you indulge, you give them oceanfront property in your mind. Observe and watch in a disinterested way. I place emphasis on disinterested, because competitive people are intense and have a tendency to judge and want to fight. These tendencies may be effective on the squash court, but in the gym of your mind, they lead to disaster. (Let us thank the great J.H. Flavell for identifying this process of meta-cognition back in 1979, in a foundational article published in *American Psychologist.*)

4. Keep in mind that the tenants wreaking havoc in your oceanfront property are just thoughts—thoughts that are basically not true. They are a fiction, a horror story made up by your own mind. Again, don't identify with the thoughts. Take a step back by reminding yourself those unruly tenants are a lie—a myth, and not a fairy tale with a happy ending. Hold the book in your hand, but do not read it. Take satisfaction in knowing that once the sheriff delivers the eviction notice (that is, when you start focusing on your breath), you will be allowing yourself to move back into a zone-like state.

5. Gently, and I emphasize the word *gently,* shift your attention to something other than the wild parties being thrown in your oceanfront property. Where should I shift it? you might ask. Again I say, to your breath. Or you can focus on your body if you want—to your feet in the ski boots, hand on the racquet, water on your body, whatever fits the situation. Remember the saying we used when I was working with the US speed skating team: "down in your body," a simple reminder to move from the mind into the body, down into Self 2 (muscle memory). Down in your body, let trust wash over you. Feel that deep sense of trust and letting go, knowing your body will execute in the manner it has prepared many hours for. Let go, trust, and believe all the people who believe in you, perhaps more than you do yourself. Some athletes I have worked with describe it this way: "All I need to do is perform instinctively. No thinking." The word instinct seems to resonate in a powerful way, helping them stay in a zone-like state.

6. Remember, zone-like, zone-like state. Go back to the zone-like state, the foundation of the gold medal mind. Everything I have suggested here so far will bring you back to that state of mind if you just let it happen. Remember, you cannot force it. The more you force it, the more turbulent the water in your mind will become. That is why breathing, observing, going down in the body, are all ways to let go and get back into the zone. This should sound very familiar by now and reinforce what I suggested you consider when practicing concentration training.

7. If the thoughts are really stubborn, you can have a talk with them. This might sound nutty, but try something like, "Hey friend, I know you want to help, so let's go, inspire me! Let's enjoy this. Game on. I will become the other team's worst nightmare. Yep, we will make them regret they ever entered the building today. No fear, just courage, force, and power!" A football player I knew who sometimes got

> into a fear spiral when intimidated by other players would say words like this over and over to himself. With that kind of self-coaching, how could he fail to be fearless and put every cell in his body in the direction of performing beyond expectations? (See chapter 3 for more ideas on how to have a productive dialogue with negative thoughts.)

If you think these suggestions sound difficult, you are right; they will be difficult at first. They require you to be able to shift your attention and get absorbed in the present moment. Fear-based thoughts are typically rooted in the past or future. Thus, being in the present will allow you to transcend the negative thinking. In essence, the basis of all of these suggestions is being able to concentrate and be absorbed in the present moment. And because that can be challenging in the heat of the moment, these suggestions may be easier said than done. But they may not be as difficult as you might think. Try them throughout the day, even when off the court. *If you are really struggling, I encourage you to practice the concentration exercise in chapter 8 and work up to at least 20 minutes.* With consistent practice of the concentration exercise, shifting into a state of absorption will become second nature. There is no other substitute for learning to focus your attention. I cannot emphasize this enough. I know the exercise can be tedious, frustrating, and boring, but the results will be profound when it comes to this oceanfront-property idea.

So stop right now and sit still for 10 minutes, following the instructions I outlined in chapter 8. Or, in the spirit of going to extremes (the subject of chapter 5), sit for 45 minutes! Yes, I believe that extreme action must occur at times to achieve outlandishly profound results. I am not talking about winning on the scoreboard. I am referring to psychological victories and the development of a gold medal mind. (But see how easy it is to think of the scoreboard when I use the word results!)

They say in Twelve-Step programs, "If you have decided you want what we have and are willing to go to any length to get it, then you are ready to take certain steps" (Alcoholics Anonymous "Big Book," 58). People who desperately want to escape the throes of addiction embrace the idea that going to any length is the only way to "land on the podium"—in Twelve-Step terms, to achieve lasting sobriety. Those of us in recovery know we cannot treat a migraine headache with 200 mg of ibuprofen. In other words, you will not develop a gold medal mind by practicing these suggestions only when you feel like it. It will take discipline of the heart, mind, and soul to internalize the skills and be able to get into a zone-like state on command. Consider again what I suggested earlier: for at least the next six months, embrace the idea that developing a gold medal mind is your real sport. As you may have realized by now, the pull to go back to your default mode is ridiculously strong. That is one reason why lasting change is so challenging to achieve. Engage your heart, because it is the most powerful performance-enhancing drug you can get (something I will address in depth in chapter 15).

Outcome, Process, and the Moral of the Story

You may recall our discussion in chapter 1 about the association between outcome and what I have described as five-ring fever—an obsession with the scoreboard. But is outcome-oriented thinking really all that bad? Not always. A focus on outcome can help during practice when you are tired and getting sloppy. Outcome will remind you of the upcoming tournament so you can dig deeper and have a better workout. In this case, outcome can help you stay in a zone-like state. Outcome can be a great friend in the off-season when you really do not want to train. Motivation can wax and wane during this time, but if you think of the upcoming season and your North Star (that is, your ultimate outcome), you can get out of bed half an hour earlier to practice concentration training, watch videos, and visualize yourself achieving your goals. This is the gold medal mind in action!

If I were presenting this idea of oceanfront property to a group of athletes and coaches, I would stop at this point. I would give them about 15 minutes to think about the life and times of Outcome and Process and write a paragraph about what they think the moral of the story will be. After all this chatter about the story and characters, there must be a takeaway, right? So put down the book, get paper and pen (or your iPad, if you will), and spend 15 minutes writing about what you feel is the moral of the story. Don't overthink it!

(15 minutes and counting...)

Okay, what did you discover? What did you conclude? I wish I could hear your opinions, because I am sure there is truth in all of them, all pieces of a puzzle that create a beautiful picture. Outcome and Process walking down the beach at sunset hand in hand, celebrating their friendship. Outcome and Process, not ready to move in together, but getting along better than ever. As the late and hysterical Jackie Gleason would say, "How sweet it is!"

From my perspective, the moral of the story is that the real game is played in your head. Your mind is the court where Outcome and Process battle it out. It is you against you—two sides of you who at first glance appear to be enemies. On one side, there is Outcome, who seems to be a terrorist ready to hijack the brain at any turn. And on the other side is Process, a loving and supportive character who simply wants to play the game and have fun. Is it a match made in heaven, or psychological warfare? If you can embrace the truth that this field is where the game is played and won, you are well on your way to developing a gold medal mind, and subsequently seeing results on the scoreboard. You will have five-ring fever, but not be consumed by it. Outcome will know when to speak, where and how. Process will do what she does best—that is, keep you in the zone-like state that will lead you to perform beyond your expectations. And performing beyond your expectations is what it is all about, regardless of what the scoreboard or Outcome have to say. The zone-like state is the equivalent of a psychological gold medal.

As you work with these ideas, be mindful you will have both types of thoughts, outcome and process. It is normal. It is human nature. It occurs as a result of being put to the test, and I see it in sport more than any other area of life. There will be times you will be totally in the zone and not thinking at all—no process, no outcome. You will be in a state of relaxed concentration, absorbed in the moment. But there also will be times when outcome-oriented ways of thinking will start occupying oceanfront property and wham, you will be taken right out of the zone. Welcome to the human race. Do not fight this reality. Instead, incorporate on a regular basis the suggestions I have offered, even off the field. Allow process-oriented thoughts to occupy your oceanfront property and you will come ever closer to performing beyond your expectations—surprising yourself over and over again.

CHAPTER 12

Moving Steel

I will never forget that Christmas morning when my father led my brothers and me downstairs to the laundry room to present a special gift. Upon entering the room, we came face-to-face with a dream come true: a brand new bench press and room full of weights. I emphasize brand new, because my father was known for buying used stuff. This equipment was new, compliments of Sears, Roebuck & Company, my dad's employer. The bench was fancy, a thin piece of foam about half an inch thick covered in red and white vinyl. The bench inclined, so we could do incline bench and preacher curls. And it had the capability for leg curls and extensions. We felt the way I imagine the kid in the movie *A Christmas Story* felt when he got the bee bee gun he longed for. Later we made (yes, made) a squat rack, although my mother would use it as a clothes rack when she ran out of clothesline space in the basement. It was a bit of a battle keeping it clean and available for squats.

It was not long before the laundry room became known as "the dungeon" where we would move steel (cement covered by plastic, in the case of the Sears weights). And it did not take long for the dungeon to become a gathering place for the athletes in the neighborhood, in particular Jim Attfield and Dave, Chris, and Steve McGovern. Back in those days, we left the door open so the dungeon was available for use any time. My father was awakened one night at

11:00 p.m. by Atts (Jim Attfield) moving steel. He had performed at a less-than-ideal level on the football field that day, and was moving steel to blow off some steam—and probably punish himself. Back in the day, the act of punishing oneself seemed honorable and courageous. It was a miracle we were not injured more often. We still laugh about how the smell of Bengay analgesic permeated our bedrooms. Thankfully, today we know much more about healthy training based on science.

The dungeon was full of posters of Bruce Jenner, the US gold-medal winner of the decathlon in the 1976 Olympics in Montreal. There was a sign Dave McGovern painted that read, "This is the house of pain. Be ready to hurt, hurt bad." There was a poster showing every muscle of the human body, so we could develop the lingo and be specific with our lifts—lats, quads, tris, and so on. Of course, the decor included a few posters of the most attractive women of the time, Farrah Fawcett and Elle Macpherson. An old faded picture of Jimmy Page and the band Led Zeppelin were proudly displayed, because many of their songs shook the walls as we worked out. And it did not take long before duct tape became a part of the decorating scheme. Duct tape to keep the foam-rubber pads on the bench from falling apart. Duct tape to keep the cement from falling out of the weights after it crumbled inside because we dropped them so often. Two-by-fours were nailed in a random manner to the squat rack to keep it from tumbling down.

I tell this story and have dedicated a chapter to lifting weights because, like many coaches, I believe championships are won in the weight room. Moving steel is where it all starts, no matter what the sport. Spending time moving steel is one of the best ways to improve concentration skills and your ability to get into a zone-like state. So having your own version of the dungeon is yet another of my recommendations to help you develop a gold medal mind. It does not have to be in your laundry room. Your version of the dungeon can be the weight room at the rec center, a private gym, or the fitness center at a local college.

For any of you who might be in charge of a weight room dedicated to athletes, I suggest you paint one of the walls to convey the "house of pain" idea. Because whether the athlete moves the weight slow or fast, whether the weight is light or heavy, and whether the move is an eccentric or concentric contraction, there will be pain—pain the athlete must learn to love. Even if there is no physical pain, there will be the mental pain of boredom, which at times can make it easy to have sloppy form. Yes, to be honest, moving steel can be boring, but that is yet another point at which we can learn to grow.

Depending on your sport, you may think lifting weights need not apply. But consider the fact that Tiger Woods introduced lifting weights to the sport of golf. Who would have thought golfers would lift weights? The practice proved valuable, even if for no other reason than to prevent injury by strengthening all the muscles that are vulnerable to repetitive strain injuries. Another example that may come as a surprise dates back to 1989. At the time, I had just finished my master's degree at Penn State and was doing a research assistantship with the US Olympic Committee. I worked with both the junior national archery team and the national table tennis team, along with other sports. Can you imagine, archers and ping pong players lifting weights? But they did, typically three times per week. From the standpoint of the coaches, one reason for moving steel was that a stronger muscle endures longer. And in both of these sports, endurance is essential. From a psychological perspective, moving steel helped the players strengthen their minds.

Yes, moving steel increases your physical strength; there is no arguing with that. Perhaps more important, in my opinion, is how it increases your mental strength. You boost your psychological immune system by focusing during every rep and every set, one breath at a time, without music, with only the entertainment your mind provides. The more absorbed you become, the more you will be entertained by the dance of the mind. Eventually, the way your mind dances around may start to seem like a comedy show, a show you have already attended while practicing concentration training.

Here is how this works. You will reach a point at which fatigue and pain will want oceanfront property in your head. Just observe those sensations, focus in on the movement of the weight, and let the pain become background noise. If you can, enjoy the burn and let it serve as a cue to get even more absorbed in the experience, deeper into a zone-like state. Lifting is an ideal arena for practicing getting into a zone-like state. Embrace the moment and stay with the pace of the movement, the mechanics, and your breath. There is a lot going on, but at the same time, not much is going on at all. You are thinking, but not thinking, a hallmark of the zone-like state. Feel the sweat running down your face and back. Embrace the sensation of beads of sweat trickling north to south; experience the salty sensation as it drips into your mouth. And *push it, push it*! This is your time to give it everything you have got, just as you do every second of every minute of practice and when you are on the field.

How to Move Steel for Maximum Benefit

Learning how to lift weights was one of the first skills we tackled when I worked with Apolo Ohno. During one of our first meetings, we walked to the weight room at the Olympic training center to explore a sport psychology approach to lifting. Apolo showed me what his workout looked like. I did not even consider telling him what exercises to perform, how many sets or reps, or how much weight to use. Our focus was solely on where he should place his attention before, during, and after a set. The point was to use this time in the weight room as a way to develop mental control, that crucial characteristic of the gold medal mind. Apolo addresses this in his autobiography, *Zero Regrets*:

> Weight training was another perfect time, Doug said, to work on strengthening your mind, to use strength training as a form of meditation, and to focus your mind to achieve discrete goals. "These are just some of the techniques," he said, "that we're going to use to train your mind to transcend pain and fatigue." Before heading to the weight room, then, I would lock in. First I would focus on my breathing, to calm my mind and my heart rate, to center myself. In, out. No counting. Just focusing on the breaths themselves, allowing whatever distractions there might be to dissipate. (Ohno 2010, 96)

Here is the exact approach I went through with Apolo. You can begin to use the same steps today when you hit the weights:

1. Before touching the weights, while you are standing there, take three deep, complete breaths. At the same time, focus inwardly, on your body, feeling your shoes making contact with the floor. Feel a quiet fire burning deep within your soul, hungry for pain. Do this before every set.

2. Make an event of putting your body in the correct position. Attend to the placement of your feet, shoulders, and so on.

3. Feel your hands on the bar, the cool temperature of the metal, the texture of the bar.

4. Practice with precision. Pay attention to every set, every rep, every detail.

5. As you move the weight, tune into the quality of the movement, applying all the instructions on correct mechanics your strength and conditioning coach has given you (e.g., elbows secure at your side, head in a neutral position, and shoulder blades back and down, in the event you are doing external rotation of your arm to rehab after shoulder surgery).

6. When (not if) your mind wanders, gently bring your attention to the movement of your body, get in tune with the relaxation and contraction of the muscle groups (e.g., quadriceps, hamstrings, and glutes, in the case of seated leg press).
7. Move the weight at the pace you have been instructed to on the positive (concentric contraction) and negative (eccentric contraction) phases of the exercise—for example, a two count on the positive and a four count on the negative phase.
8. Focus on relaxing the parts of the body you are not using during the set (e.g., relaxing your neck when doing curls).
9. Breathe in sync with the movement of the weight in the way you have been instructed (e.g., inhale on the positive phase and exhale on the negative phase).
10. Stay focused on every rep, one by one, and when (not if) your mind wanders, bring it back to the movement of your body.
11. Then comes what you have been waiting for: pain and fatigue. This is the reason you are here. Overload leads to adaptation. This is the time for precision and moving with the grace of a dancer. The tendency at this stage of the set will be to get sloppy and sacrifice quality for quantity. Do not let it happen! Use the pain and fatigue as a cue to be conscious and mindful and to move the steel in a controlled manner, with precision. Feel the pain intensify—love it! Pain and fatigue are the cues, the voice that tells you to get more deeply absorbed in the movement.
12. Once the set is done, you can let your mind dance around and think about your grocery list. But instead, you may want to abide in the presence of the pump, the burn, and all the other sensations that go along with transcending the pain and using your mind as a weapon to move forward when your body wants to do otherwise. Get a sip of water,

> talk to someone briefly, shake your arms and legs out, and then, as you get closer to beginning the next set, begin to take deep breaths. Inhale deeply, exhale slowly, letting that quiet fire start to burn in your soul. With practice, this will happen more easily and quickly.

A few additional suggestions about the process: don't listen to music, and, if possible, ask the gym managers not to play music over the speakers. This is a time for you and the pain. It is your time to be with your mind and all the emotions that emerge as you think about how prepared you feel for the next game or worry that you are not ready. Remember, these thoughts are merely sources of information. They are not good or bad, just thoughts (in many cases not even true, so do not believe any of them). Stay neutral and in a zone-like state, the quiet fire burning in your belly. Trust you will be ready to soar when it is time.

Also, absolutely no phones in the weight room! The other day when moving steel I noticed people looking at their phones between sets. Initially, I thought they were changing songs. But as I got closer and zoomed in, I saw they were texting. One person was texting with one hand while doing a dumbbell curl with the other! Our need for constant stimulation is getting out of control. Yes, I have a strong opinion about this. The weight room offers you an invaluable opportunity to strengthen your mind, but the process requires your undivided attention. Think back on the suggestion I made in the chapter on concentration training: leave your phone off for two hours a day. Yes, two whole hours. Learn to be with your thoughts and emotions. This is the way to evict bad tenants from your mind and learn to focus your attention on what leads to psychological victory.

Making It Work for You

The gold-medal-mind approach to moving steel applies to every type of conditioning technique, not just weight lifting. I have shown athletes this focusing technique using flexibility training, core work, Pilates, yoga, Feldenkrais, the Alexander Technique, qigong, and tai chi. Many of these conditioning methods already encourage a targeted use of the mind, but even with yoga or qigong, there is room for improvement from a gold-medal-mind perspective.

Most of you should be able to incorporate this approach during the time you spend stretching. Allow yourself to be absorbed in the muscle group you are stretching. Feel the muscle fibers slowly lengthening as you breathe into that muscle group with a single-minded focus on your body. Immerse yourself in the pleasure of feeling your hip flexors lengthen. I can tell you it will greatly increase your enjoyment of stretching. You will also reap the benefits more quickly. Take it from me, the guy with the tightest hamstrings in the universe. Not until I became conscious of every rep, absorbed in a particular muscle group, one breath at a time, did I have the patience to hold a stretch for 30 seconds and do three or four reps. And it worked. (See appendix 6 for ideas on using methods other than weight training as forms of mental conditioning.)

Some athletes have told me they find the technique demanding, even mentally exhausting, but agreed that it strengthened them both physically and psychically. Ask yourself: "Am I ready to die in order to go to heaven?" If your answer is yes, you will at least give this approach a try. This question will probably make more sense when you read chapter 14. But in the meantime, have fun with it. And remember, no music.

CHAPTER 13

Listen to Your Mother

Back in the day when my mother would send me letters, she would end each one with, "And be sure to eat a green thing every day!" She got this from David Brenner, a comedian big in the 1980s, who joked his mother would tell him the same thing right before they got off the phone. My sister-in-law, in her own sarcastic way, used to try to get under my skin by quickly slipping in "eat a green thing" just before hanging up. Little did I know that many years later, I would include advice about eating green things in a sport psychology book.

This chapter is about following the kind of advice your mother might dish out on diet, sleep, water intake, alcohol use, and finances—about how fundamental lifestyle is to developing a gold medal mind. I remember a poster, maybe an ad for Nike, showing a cyclist with the following words: "Eat well, get plenty of rest, and go like hell." There you have it. Just what your mother would say (except, maybe, for "go like hell"). Doing nothing more than following the suggestions in this chapter will improve your confidence. When you know you have prepared in every way imaginable, your confidence will just naturally be higher.

In my first or second meeting with an athlete, I ask about his or her eating habits: protein consumption, use of supplements, water intake, and amount of fiber eaten, among other key factors related to athletic performance. At times, especially when working with a youngster whose parents are present, this can prove interesting. While I listen to the child telling me about breakfasts consisting of a bowl of cereal and a pop tart, the parents begin gazing at the floor and sometimes shake their heads. Once, I had a father ask, "What does this have to do with his confidence?" I cannot remember what I said, but I know I was thinking, "Everything."

The fact that half of my educational background is in exercise science contributes to my belief in the benefits of healthy lifestyle practices. I became a bit of a freak about dietary habits early on, after learning in a college nutrition class that eating at Burger King shrinks your blood vessels. (I am still not sure if that is true, but it scared me nonetheless.) I would not be at all surprised if some of you, especially in places like Boulder or Denver, think that what I am about to share is old news. If you already know the drill, you may decide to skip this chapter altogether. But why not read on, just for the heck of it. You never know when you might learn something new.

Dietary Habits

Developing a gold medal mind—being able to focus attention, process information, make good decisions, remember the coach's instructions, and the like—requires enlisting the brain's horsepower. The brain's source of power is food. And specific foods eaten at certain times will result in the brain working more effectively. I will share with you the basics here, and you will be off to a good start. But to learn the specifics, I highly recommend you consult a nutritionist specializing in athletics, who will be able to offer you a tailored nutritional program based upon your particular needs. For example, a sports nutritionist can explain what specific foods, eaten within 30 minutes after practice, will maximize the benefits of your workout and aid with the recovery process.

The right food is crucial if you want to have the kind of brain horsepower that leads to a gold-medal-mind level of cognitive functioning. Our bodies digest the food we eat by mixing it with fluids (acids and enzymes) in the stomach. When the stomach digests food, the carbohydrate (sugar and starch) in the food breaks down into another type of sugar, called glucose. The stomach and small intestine absorb the glucose and then release it into the bloodstream. Once in the bloodstream, glucose can be used immediately for energy or stored in the form of glycogen in the liver to be used later. The long and short of it is that the body operates on glucose. And it is essential to eat the right foods to maintain stable glucose levels. When levels of glucose in the bloodstream fall too much, we get lightheaded, feel weak and maybe dizzy, are unable to think clearly, and become less able to handle stress, among other detrimental states of mind and body. Again, learning to eat the right foods at the right time is essential to maintaining stable glucose levels and adequate glycogen stores. So before believing what you read online or see on the latest infomercial, consult an expert. It will be worth every penny!

The best way to build glycogen stores is to consume adequate protein, as opposed to relying on carbohydrates. Like water, we need much more protein than we think we do or even would like to eat. I rarely get all the protein I need, and I live on chicken, fish, and turkey. I even have chicken and salmon for breakfast at times. And I still come up short on the dietary requirements for protein. I keep soy nuts with me at all times, because one-quarter cup contains 11 grams of protein. (Note: peanut butter and tuna fish contain little protein unless you eat tons, which will tip the scales when it comes to caloric intake. Especially peanut butter.) Talk to your sport nutritionist about your protein requirements and then meet that demand as much as possible. You might also talk with a body builder, because those folks know more than many nutritionists about dietary requirements specific to the demands of athletes.

Your dietary habits not only impact brain function, but also how well and how fast you recover from workouts and heal from injury. Due to the overload we experience as a result of training, there is a continuous catabolic (breakdown) process at work in our bodies. This is not bad, because it leads the body to adapt to the workload, which is what we want in order to become faster, stronger, and more flexible. But that adaptation occurs as a result of taking in real, whole, nutrient-dense food—in other words, quality nutrients in the form of premium food. Let this be your guide.

Your post-workout meal is the most important meal of the day. Carbohydrate and muscle protein stores become depleted with high-intensity exercise. Without proper nutrition, the remolding and repletion process you want to encourage will come to a standstill, and while you may be training harder or lifting more, you may not be seeing the results. If you do not put adequate nutrients in the tank, you cannot expect to see the results you would like. The post-workout window is also a time where your muscles are insulin-sensitive and can use carbohydrates most efficiently. By fueling post-workout you not only help decrease inflammation and cortisol levels, but also foster much faster recovery. Cortisol, as you may know, is a chemical associated with stress. While necessary in many ways, it may also have adverse consequences, such as suppressing the immune system, for example. Decreasing cortisol levels post-workout is essential to healthy recovery.

How much carbohydrate and protein you need will vary widely depending on your sport, size, training intensity, length of workout, and goals. For the carbohydrate portion of the post-workout meal, many nutritionists prefer starchy vegetables, such as sweet potatoes, yams, squash, or pumpkin. Starchy vegetables provide antioxidants and are a nutritionally dense carbohydrate option. You should eat these foods in the first 30 minutes post-workout, but no longer than an hour afterwards. It takes discipline and planning to make this happen. However, consistent with the gold-medal-mind approach, you must go to any length to optimize your body's functioning.

If you are healing from injury, the demand for high-quality nutritional building blocks increases. During the rehabilitation process after injury, what you eat will have a profound impact on how you recover. Wrestlers use the term "eating clean" to refer to compliance with precise dietary requirements. If nothing else, eat clean while you are healing from an injury. Many foods have anti-inflammatory effects. The gut and liver prefer those to ibuprofen and Voltaren, two medications commonly used to decrease inflammation.

Learn a bit about the wide range of supplements available to assist with recovery. There are far too many to mention here, but it is worth the cost to consult with a professional who is competent in this area. Do not get lured into spending unnecessary amounts of money on fads when tried-and-true supplements may be all you need.

A word about protein and energy bars. The huge selection of these products has made them a grocery aisle in and of itself. With some protein bars, in two minutes you can eat as much protein as you would find in half a chicken. But attend to the fine print, particularly sugar content. Sugar is a subtle foe. Our daily intake should be limited to 32 grams on a 2,000 calorie per day diet. And a Clif Bar contains 23 grams of sugar! A high dose of sugar like this all at one time can put your blood sugar level on a roller-coaster ride, especially if you typically do not eat much sugar. The steep rise in blood sugar will wake up the pancreas to spit out insulin, which will bring the high levels of glucose down rapidly. After coming down from a sugar high, you will be tired and want more.

An ultra marathon runner I was working with cringed when he heard I considered Clif Bars a healthy option. He turned me on to Epic Bars, which are 100 percent sugar free and use only grass-fed cows in their beef bars. Since this runner was sponsored by Epic, he would bring the bars to our sessions. Typically, an Epic Bar contains

15 grams of protein and is gluten free. I keep my office stocked with them now and pass a few along to athletes I work with every chance I get, because lo and behold, I find many are eating high-sugar energy bars just as I had been.

And what about "eating a green thing?" I have struggled my entire adult life to get my minimum daily requirements of fruits and vegetables. Yet they are an undeniably important factor in good nutrition. If you, like me, do not naturally gravitate toward this food group, I am not sure what it will take for you. But do not deny yourself what is consistently advocated in just about all dietary regimens.

Here are a couple of my (perhaps successful) attempts to up my fruit and vegetable intake. Years ago I marched into Whole Foods and approached Kat, a rock star of the natural living aisle, where supplements, minerals, vitamins, and the like are sold. I asked, "What can I take to get my fruit and vegetable requirements?" Kat smiled as if she heard this question every day. She showed me a product called Green SuperFood, made by Amazing Grass. She said, "Although this is not a substitute for the real thing, it is by far the best supplement you can take if you are short on fruits and vegetables." Even though it is quite expensive, I always have a supply of Green SuperFood in my fridge, with the hope that the cells in my body that need green nutrients are relatively satisfied.

Here is another possible way to go. One day, while caught up watching a TV channel dominated by infomercials, I learned about the NutriBullet (a kind of high-tech blender) and how to make a NutriBlast smoothie out of fruits and vegetables. I shook my head as the dude selling the NutriBullet put it in a head-to-head competition with a regular blender. In spite of all the claims, I was not convinced this wonder machine was for me. Then something interesting occurred. Over the next several months, I crossed paths with three individuals, all of whom eat "cleaner" than any athlete I know. And they all talked about the NutriBullet. Holy smokes, I thought. I bought one, and most mornings now put the following into what becomes a NutriBlast smoothie: kale, Swiss chard, pineapple, blueberries, coconut milk, almonds, whey protein, chia seeds, quinoa, maca, cocoa, goji berries, and açai. (The last six ingredients are what some call "super foods." Do they make a difference? I don't know, but the foodies in Boulder swear they will.) The point is, this is where I hit pay dirt with greens and fruit. It is my latest and greatest way to eat a green thing and keep Mom happy.

Water

Although I discussed food first, good nutrition actually all starts with water. You have heard it before: adequate water intake is essential, especially in dry and hot climates. For athletes working out in the heat of the sun, it is even more crucial to hydrate adequately, and then some. For many, it is close to impossible to take in enough water, since the outflow is so extreme. I have heard many nutritionists say if your pee looks like chicken soup or even weak lemonade, you are in a state of dehydration. Ideally, your urine should be mostly clear. Using thirst as a barometer is misleading. Experts say that by the time we are thirsty, we are already dehydrated. We lose water every minute, regardless of whether we are working out or not. Even if we are not sweating, we are losing water. Just imagine the water loss that is occurring when you are doing dry-land training in the heat of the day with a 30-pound weight vest on. I have witnessed athletes doing a three-hour dry-land workout in 98ºF weather at altitude, and just watching the workout made me thirsty.

I cannot tell you exactly what to drink or how much and when, but I can tell you it is paramount that you drink enough. Most serious athletes I work with in Boulder and Denver carry around a water bottle at all times. It should be standard equipment, no different from carrying your phone around. For the *average* person, drinking at least half of one's body weight in ounces of water each day is recommended. But during training, taking good-sized gulps every 15 to 20 minutes, maybe half a cup at a time, is recommended. Talk to your nutritionist about a daily intake adequate for your sport and training demands.

I played football one year in high school for a coach we used to call "the Big Red Dick." The coach's name was Richard and the school's nickname was The Big Red. Putting these two names together for the coach shows what we thought of his personality. Some of his bottom-line rules were that we could not sit during a game, we had to wear our helmets strapped up the whole ride home if we lost a road game, and we could not drink water during practice. In August in Niagara Falls, New York, the temperature could be 90 degrees, with 85 percent humidity. It was brutally hot. And yes, we were allowed no water, even when we had double sessions. Times have changed since then; no coach would inflict this kind of torture on players. But it is still difficult to get as much water as you need to perform well.

In some sports, such as ultra marathon, it can be even more difficult to get enough water. It is not uncommon to see athletes collapsing from heat exhaustion. If your body is screaming for replacement of the water it has lost, all the mental gymnastics in the world will not get you into a zone-like state. The techniques I recommend to deal with old Leroy (pain and fatigue) might not work if you do not have enough water on board. The way to do your best in this department is to keep in mind that you need to drink even when you do not feel like drinking.

A brief sound bite about the current proliferation of sports drinks (e.g., Powerade or Gatorade). Many of these products are loaded with sugar and need to be cut with water. But you may want to explore some of the many low-sugar electrolyte replacement drinks available. Part of this process involves experimenting to find what works best for you. Know yourself, but again, it may be a good idea to talk with an expert about whether products like these are right for you.

Sleep

I have worked for teams for whom rest was written in as part of their training program. Yes, good old-fashioned rest was required—everything from a good night's sleep to a nap to just getting off one's feet and everything in between. This is what is called passive rest in the exercise science world. Just as it sounds, passive rest means doing nothing. Nada. Got it? If you have trouble with this concept, I encourage you to read the book *The Art of Doing Nothing* by Veronique Vienne, especially chapters 2, 3, 4, 6, and 7.

Sleep is an anabolic (building) process. You have heard of anabolic steroids. You know they can help a person become better, stronger, and faster. And you know they have dangerous short- and long-term side effects. Sleep works the same way, but without the side effects. As a result of our daily activities, especially the overload we experience in training, our bodies break down. And, as already noted, we recover and get stronger through adaptation, which is based upon sleep as well as dietary habits. There is no substitute for sleep. The word on the street is seven to nine hours for most of us. For those who are training on top of normal, everyday activities, your need for sleep will be even greater.

It is not enough to get a mere minimum daily requirement of sleep. We need quality sleep. Quality sleep is the deep, restorative sleep that allows for anabolic processes to occur. I will not bore you with too many details of sleep architecture, but you probably recall that there are a number of sleep stages, including rapid eye movement sleep (REM sleep, when you dream) and non-REM sleep. We need the deep, slow-wave, non-REM restorative sleep (stages 3 and 4) to recover as much as possible from the overload experienced during the day. However, I have seen many athletes (and non-athletes, for that matter) who have problems with sleep. Sleep issues can include difficulty falling asleep, waking during the night, trouble getting back to sleep, and waking much earlier than desired. Not good, any of them. If you are highly stressed or struggling with strong negative emotions, it is likely you will experience one or all of these difficulties with sleep. What can you do? Well, there are remedies such as Sleepy Time tea, valerian root and other herbs, and melatonin (taken sublingually), as well as conventional prescription drugs for sleep problems. Alcohol is the most disastrous insomnia remedy for many reasons, including the fact that it does not work very well.

In Colorado, there has been a surge in the use of cannabis to help with sleep. Based upon anecdotal experience, I can tell you that pot will help you fall asleep, but not stay asleep through the night. And in addition, in spite of what some believe (including some MDs who prescribe it), cannabis is highly addictive.

Whether or not you decide to take a sleep is aid is up to you and your health care provider. But if you want to try what are called behavioral techniques (nonpharmacologic methods) to help with sleep, here are my suggestions:

- Go to bed and wake up at the same time every day, or as much as possible. This includes weekends.
- Take time to prepare for sleep—maybe 30 or 45 minutes prior to getting into bed. Take a hot bath or shower, stretch, read, do guided imagery or a relaxation exercise. (On my website, www.goldmedalmind.com, I offer a recording of a guided relaxation exercise specifically designed to facilitate a good night's sleep.) Or try some combination of these. The idea is to not just jump into bed and expect to sleep, especially if you are feeling worried, frustrated, or irritable. You prepare for practice with a warm up, and getting ready for sleep is really no different. Sleep is a physical skill with a psychological component.
- Turn off electronic devices. For at least an hour before bedtime, do not watch TV, use a computer, or be on your phone. For some, this will be a challenge. It is for me.

- Try not to nap during the day, but if you do, keep it to about 20 to 30 minutes and before 3:00 p.m.
- Do not get into bed unless you are sleepy. Sleepy is a mental state; tired is a physical state. When you are sleepy you will fall asleep more quickly and easily than if you are just tired.
- If you do not fall asleep within 10 to 15 minutes, get out of bed and do something relaxing until you get sleepy. You can stretch, practice a relaxation technique, listen to music, read, or journal to get out whatever is rattling around in your head.
- Keep your room dark and cool, about 66 to 68 degrees or so. The idea is to not be too warm.
- Play some kind of pleasant background noise to block out any sounds particular to your living situation. For example, in a dorm or apartment building, people may be talking in the next room. Run a fan or play music. Smart phones offer all kinds of apps that might help with sleeping.
- Do not ingest caffeine or nicotine after a certain point in the day. For me, if I have caffeine after 1:00 p.m., I will be up all night. Occasionally, I allow myself to indulge in chewing tobacco. (Yes, it was a performance aid while in graduate school. Even now, when I need to really focus to write, I put a pinch between my cheek and gum.) If I chew after 6:00 p.m., my mind is off and running all night. Find your cutoff time and stick with it, even if you are tired and want a pick-me-up later in the day.
- Avoid sleeping longer the following night if you did not sleep well the night before.
- Remember to go to sleep and wake up the same time every day. I know that is painful if you get up at 7:00 a.m. and stay up until 3:00 a.m., but you are trying to develop a routine. There is a chemical basis for this, an enzyme in your body that builds up throughout the day to help you sleep at night.

Your primary care doctor can provide more information about this to help you appreciate the importance of a consistent schedule.

- If you are traveling internationally, prepare for the change in time zone. Your coach should make this part of your training program. If you are not sure how to do it, consult with a physician or exercise physiologist who is competent in the area of sleep architecture. Ideally, your coach will have a physician who is board certified in sleep medicine talk with the team about traveling internationally. When I worked with the US speed skating team, there were times I would be with the long-track team in Europe for four weeks, come back to Colorado Springs for a week, and then be off to Japan and Korea with the short-track team for two weeks. It would take a couple of weeks after that adventure to readjust to Mountain Standard Time.

Like diet and water intake, your sleep has everything to do with your function and performance, from recovering from workouts to cognitive processes, including attention, concentration, information processing, decision making, listening to feedback, and making adjustments. Remember, sleep is an anabolic process, like steroids. After a long day, the body, mind and spirit need "sleep steroids" to rebuild.

Alcohol and Drugs

Is there anything wrong with athletes wanting to put on an innocent little buzz and have a good time? What's the big deal? Well, I cannot even begin to tell you all the stories I hear about athletes getting in trouble as a result of using alcohol and drugs. Alcohol, pot, and prescription medications—namely opiates (pain killers) and benzodiazepines (anti-anxiety meds)—are the drugs most commonly used and abused by athletes, including high school and college athletes.

My bottom line on this: abstain and make the sacrifice in order to develop a gold medal mind as well as be a role model for other athletes.

The following story comes from a high school athlete I have worked with for some time on gold-medal-mind development. Some of her teammates took a walk on the wild side one night. Two seniors and one junior got caught using alcohol at a party. They were caught cold-handed by the police, but they denied it to the administration. If they confessed, the consequence would have been a two-game suspension. And if they denied drinking in the face of the evidence, they would be out for seven games. The crazy part was that they pleaded innocent, all three of them, even though the consequences for getting caught would be much more severe. Unbelievable, I thought, when I heard this story. My first question was, "Did the coach kick them off the team?" She said, "No, and the coach did not even tell us about it. We found out in school because everyone was talking about it." I do not know what the coach was thinking, but in my opinion, he was not thinking at all. I believe a coach's standards should be higher than those of the administration and the law. If I were the coach, the athletes would have been done for the season, because making the choice to drink was a purely selfish act, done with absolutely no consideration for the family (a.k.a. the team). And if it looked like that they were drinking in an addictive manner, I would have referred them to a treatment recovery program. (Elements Behavioral Health has rock-star options when it comes to treatment programs.)

Just read the news for more examples of the wreckage caused by the use of drugs and alcohol, among athletes and non-athletes alike. There is a saying in A.A.: "I wasn't drunk every time I got in trouble, but I got in trouble every time I was drunk." With all of the possible negative consequences, why do athletes chase altered states of consciousness? Plain and simple, it feels good. Alcohol and drugs light up specific parts of the brain in ways that a good meal, winning a game, or even great sex cannot come close to. Putting the right chemicals in the right amount into the body will lead to fireworks a person may never forget. Selective amnesia occurs for the hang-overs and time spent with one's head in the toilet. But the euphoric emotional memories are quite resilient and stubborn. I have heard dozens of people with more than 20 years clean and sober recall in vivid detail their glory days: where, when, who was there, and what they used at a specific tailgate party. They can recall the lively banter that went on while getting juiced up for the game. The positive emotional memories do not disappear. Therefore, regardless of the legal consequences, when someone leaves jail after an arrest for driving under the influence, they will think about a drink and sometimes go right to the bar. In my 30 years working with people with alcohol and drug addictions, the record for most DUIs was held by a guy who had 11 over a 23-year period. Based upon reason and logic, you would think this person would have learned after one or two arrests. But the nature of addiction transcends the bounds of reason and logic. That is why it is so baffling for a coach to encounter an athlete who is more addicted to their drug of choice than to their sport.

What leads to this kind of addictive behavior? You may have heard about genetic predispositions, attention-deficit hyperactivity issues, chronic pain, or mood disruptions related to substance use. However, after working in the addiction field for a long time, my nitty-gritty explanation is that alcohol or drugs does for the person what they cannot do for themselves. The person who tends to abuse typically cannot relax, feels insecure, is riddled with anger, struggles with loneliness, and, regardless of the amount of success they have achieved, still feels inadequate. These are just some of the emotional states that can haunt a person. If an addict does not have the inner resources or friends to help process the emotional stuff, alcohol or drugs is the next best thing. It works, and works well to blot out from one's mind and heart some of the issues I mentioned. In Twelve-Step programs, the purpose of a Higher Power (HP) is to help the person with an addiction to be humble, humble enough to surrender to the fact they cannot manage life on their own. So they turn to a HP (and that can be something as simple as a sunset) to learn that the HP can do for them what they cannot do for themselves.

Here is a story to illustrate the controversial nature of my position on alcohol use in sports. I was consulting with an athletic department of a division I university that had teams who were quite successful on a national level. The administration was extremely supportive of coach education. This was one of the reasons I was hired—to educate the coaches about performance enhancement. One week a national expert on drinking among college students was brought in to speak. His focus and approach to college student drinking involved an approach called harm reduction. Unlike an abstinence-based model, harm reduction *attempts* to teach students how to drink responsibly and minimize the risk of a disaster happening. What he addressed and how he addressed the topic was very good, but I was squirming in my seat. I held back when he asked if there were questions. For one thing, he was talking to an audience of coaches working with athletes who were not old enough to legally drink. The other reason was I did not feel the presenter was at all tuned in to student athletes and what it takes to be a champion. Yes, he understood the non-athlete college population, but he missed the mark when it came to athletes.

Afterward, I had a brief conversation with him about the fascinating research he and his colleagues had conducted. Then I went and sat in the stands of the ice hockey rink, scribbling notes like a maniac—my reaction to the presentation. I sat on what I wrote for a while, and knew in my gut that presenting this to the coaches was not going to go over well. But I could not help myself, and asked the administration if I could share my view on alcohol use among student athletes with the coaches. Well, my gut was right. Not many welcomed my views. I was bombarded with the question, "How do we enforce no drinking?" The bottom line is you cannot. Even a parent cannot, for that matter. However, the point I was attempting to make was that a policy such as total abstinence during the season was intrinsically related to creating the kind of culture, value system, and environment needed to foster the development of gold medal minds.

Even knowing all the benefits of abstinence, the head of sports medicine told me that having such a policy could interfere with recruiting. He felt that the school would be much less attractive if athletes knew the coaches had an abstinence-based policy. Here again five-ring fever reigned supreme and trumped what was in the best interests of the athletes, not only in terms of health, but also from a performance-enhancement perspective. "But what about the all-star pros who drink and drug?" the coaches asked me. I had no good answer to that question, but I did know that developing a gold medal mind is about going against the grain and resisting what may seem to be "normal."

One factor that takes front and center in the process of building a gold medal mind is sacrifice. In making the decision to be a rock star, an athlete must forego other choices in life. For example, given his or her sleep demands, an athlete cannot stay out as late as non-athletes—one form of sacrifice. Another is that the athlete cannot afford to eat the junk a non-athlete may eat. Abstaining from alcohol is probably one of the greatest sacrifices that can be made—but it is something that is not subject to debate in my mind. And by no means is my perspective driven from a moralistic or self-righteous stance. It stems from the fact that as a result of making sacrifices and going to any length, as they say in Twelve-Step programs, a person will increase his or her psychological fitness more so than if they had indulged. Those moments of indulgence take points off the psychological scoreboard. You may or may not relate to the challenge of avoiding alcohol. I hope you do not. But my real hope is that you understand that in order to go to heaven you need to die first, something you will learn about in detail in the next chapter.

I came to my relatively radical conclusion about abstinence based upon work I have done with athletes since 1987. I can tell you that those who are the most talented do not use any kind of mood-altering substance, let alone alcohol. These are athletes committed to the development of a gold medal mind. They know that through the sacrifice of not drinking, they will become more psychologically fit than if they used alcohol. Because when an athlete makes the choice to abstain, he or she will be challenged psychologically. The person will be forced to find another way to relax or have the confidence to dance, for example—lessons he or she would have missed by using alcohol.

The pre-game confidence of an athlete who makes sacrifices will soar as a result of knowing he or she did everything imaginable to be as prepared as possible. If you too have gone to any length and refused to cut corners, you know what I mean. Sacrifice leads to mental strength, which is fundamental to being a psychologically skilled athlete. If you are an athlete who drinks and performs at the national level, great. But I encourage you to experiment and challenge yourself for a year. Do not drink for a year. See what it does not only for your physical fitness, but more important, for your psychological fitness. And know that if taking a year off from using alcohol seems like too great a challenge, it might be a sign of larger things, such as a dependency issue. It may not be full-blown addiction, but not being able to take an extended vacation from alcohol may suggest that alcohol does for you what you cannot do for yourself.

If you are an athlete, I urge you to at least think about this issue. If you are a coach, do not get caught up in being the police. Instead, get obsessed with the type of "parent" you want to be, and what kind of culture you want for your "family." Teach your athletes what the gold medal mind is all about. Your athletes may drink, but you should establish a policy and learning environment that helps them learn the life skill of knowing that choices lead to consequences. And again, making choices that involve sacrifice is at the heart of a gold medal mind. I encourage you to take the challenge.

Don't Write a Check Your Body Can't Cash

As any mom would tell you, an important part of healthy living is financial stability. Think of taking care of your body as making deposits in a kind of athletic checking account. You cannot write a check if you don't have the money, right? You have to put money in the account before you can draw on it. Protein consumption, water intake, active and passive rest (as described in chapter 5), and good nutrition are all essential parts of maintaining a high athletic "credit score" throughout the season.

I have to add that it may be beneficial every now and then to eat that glazed donut, stay up till 4:00 a.m., or catch a buzz. I use a glazed donut for an example because the last time my 78-year-old mother was visiting me, she confessed she had a donut. She said, "I haven't had one in months and thought I deserved it. But now I feel guilty." Yes, at 78 years old! But, just to scratch the surface of her activity level, she plays competitive tennis year round and golfs 18 holes about four days a week in the summer. She lifts weights three days a week, swims twice a week, and is an avid walker even in the harsh winters of Niagara Falls. During my visits, she has initiated going for walks with me when the absolute temperature was -14°F. On her 80th birthday she swam 82 lengths in a 23-meter pool to celebrate. Again, this is just the tip of the iceberg when it comes to her activity level. You would guess she is 60 years old. When I am back in Niagara Falls we go to the gym together every day, and she relishes my helping her improve her weight-lifting technique and learn how to meditate while doing cardio. On top of all of this, she still wants to read every sport psychology book out there to stay mentally fit. She is my inspiration!

Go ahead, write checks, use your debit card, and take out cash advances with the best of them, but do not forget to fund the account according to the needs of your body. You have to be even more serious about rest, for example, if you participate in endurance sports. After you run 100 miles, your account needs big deposits. But no matter what your sport, if you have a gold medal mind, you should strive to maintain a credit score of at least 750 or more, depending on the needs and demands of your body.

Your bank account is made up of both physical and psychological resources. It is up to you to decide how you want to handle that account and what type of credit score you will have. Operating consistently with a gold medal mind is about making large deposits on a regular basis, knowing that being a star requires making huge physical and psychological withdrawals. The starting point is attending to "what your mother would say" when it comes to dietary habits, water intake, sleep, and alcohol and drug use. Living wisely will not only make your body stronger, it is also the foundation for having the equivalent of eight percent body fat in terms of psychological fitness.

CHAPTER 14

Dying and Going to Heaven

I was sitting across from the new head coach of a division I men's soccer team about midway through the season at Virginia Commonwealth University. This coach had quite a challenge ahead of him, because the former head coach had no control over the team. Players were getting in trouble with the law off campus due to drug and alcohol use, and many were on academic probation. Their performance on the field reflected their lack of discipline, commitment, and determination. Basically, they were getting their butts handed to them, game after game. There were a few superstars who seemed to forget there is no "I" in "we"—or, put another way, no "me" in "we." You get the picture.

The new coach had been the goalkeeper for the Trinidad national team and served in the army after that. My first impression was that he had a huge heart, but was tough as nails. For example, he wanted his players to have their shoes tied at all times, pants up around their waists, and hats off when in his office. They were to address him with "yes, sir" and "no, sir." That might not seem like much, but I can tell you that these expectations were 180 degrees different from those of their last coach, who used to drink with the players.

After welcoming the coach to the university I asked, "How can I help?" Without hesitation, he replied, "Doc, the problem is my boys.

They all want to go to heaven, but they don't want to die first." I loved the way he put that. Here it is, a little more than 25 years later, and I remember that moment as if it were yesterday. And I knew exactly what he meant. "Coach, this makes perfect sense," I said. "You and I both know the history of the team, and the disasters both on and off the field." Although I am a person who likes to explore prior to diving in, we did not have time to waste. We got right down to business, and I was thrilled to do so.

I can honestly say my teammates and I trained harder in high school than this division I team had been training. I recall biting my lip while watching them in the weight room. It was not my place to throw in my two cents about physical conditioning; I was there to help them use the time in the weight room to train their minds. But I was working with a group that did not even want to be in the weight room. In my opinion, this was a symptom of a larger issue. Therefore, when it came time for our first meeting, I made the weight room the focus. I exclaimed, "Men, the weight room is where it all starts. This is the place championships are won!" These words were not received with open arms, but they did not fall on deaf ears. Slowly, by starting to train with reckless abandon in the weight room, the team began to appreciate that in order to get playing time ("heaven") they would need to "die" first. Focusing on the weight-room work ethic was one of several steps the coach, the two captains, and I used to teach this team the concept of dying and going to heaven.

Crystal Clear

One of the most profound examples of an athlete who embraced the fact that he had to "die first" before achieving victory is provided by the skater Apolo Ohno, whom I mentioned earlier. He is the poster child of the expression "going to any length." Apolo displayed exceptional qualities in many areas, but I share the following example to shed further light on the topic at hand.

Shortly after the short-track speed skating team finished an on-ice morning session, the coaches would leave. The athletes were instructed to cool down with a light jog and a series of stretches. Among other things, this cool-down served as a step in the direction of preventing injury. Apolo was the only athlete who would go for a light jog prior to stretching. The rest would sit around and stretch, but they typically did not focus on the stretches, do the repetitions, or hold the stretches for the recommended amount of time. Instead, it was a time for them to laugh, to engage in a playful manner. They were very, very funny, but not at all focused or committed to that aspect of the training program.

Apolo, on the other hand, would run for about 20 minutes, listening to music to keep the passion flowing. At times we would walk briskly together, because I could not run. Then he would go back into the rink, or, if it was warm enough, stretch outside in a textbook manner consistent with the training program. This was just the tip of the iceberg when it came to his discipline, commitment, and hunger. I can tell you it is no accident that he won eight Olympic medals. It is the result of a work ethic like nothing I had ever seen before. In short, Apolo was willing to go to any length with every aspect of his training program, including the psychological.

You must choose to live in the spirit of sacrifice and determination, because that will serve as the basis of your psychological fitness. There is no other option when pursuing a gold medal mind.

A Conversation About Dying and Heaven

The following conversation is from a session I had with an athlete who had expressed a motivation to develop a gold medal mind. He was all ready to go to heaven, but his efforts did not reflect a willingness to die first.

Dr. Jowdy: You are saying one thing and doing another. You want to get a scholarship to a division I program, but your actions are not consistent with your aspirations. So do you mind if we talk about heaven?

Athlete: What?

DJ: You know, heaven, where God, his disciples, and all the angels live? The place we go when we die?

AT: Sure, but I don't believe that.

DJ: Okay, but bear with me. This is just a metaphor we will apply to the task at hand.

AT: Okay.

DJ: Based upon what you have heard, how do we get to heaven?

AT: We gotta die first.

DJ: Right. So how might this apply to you as an athlete?

AT: It doesn't.

DJ: (Long silence.)

AT: I don't know what heaven has to do with this. I don't believe in it.

DJ: But what would heaven be when it comes to sport?

AT: I guess getting a full ride.

DJ: I know that's what you want. And based on what your coaches say, you have the physical horsepower to do it.

AT: That is what they say.

DJ: So a full ride would be heaven to you?

AT: Right, yes.

DJ: Okay, now how are you going to get there? In terms of this sport, what would "dying" be for you?

AT: You know, what we talked about, eating right, sleeping well, and doing the mental stuff.

DJ: So when it comes to the mental training, do you think you are dying?

AT: I guess not. Not really.

DJ: What makes you say that?

AT: I am not keeping track of my goals all of the time, and I don't practice that concentration training much.

DJ: Anything else?

AT: I only do visualization training about twice a week before going to bed. I have only read part of *The Way of the Peaceful Warrior* and haven't watched *Seven Days in Utopia* like you told me to.

DJ: Anything else?

AT: No, I don't think so.

DJ: What about focusing in a determined way in the weight room?

AT: Not really.

DJ: So the mental training certainly is not a priority for you?

AT: Well, it's just that everything has come so easily for me. I have dominated for years, and things are going great, so I don't see how that would really make the difference.

DJ: I can see that, but your coaches believe that more mental horsepower will be needed to get you to the next level. You know, to get to heaven, as we have been discussing.

AT: Yeah, I know, but it doesn't seem like it.

DJ: How about I give you an example of an athlete who was willing to die in every way possible in order to get to heaven?

AT: All right, who?

DJ: I can tell you this because he wrote about it in his autobiography. His name is Apolo Ohno.

AT: Oh yeah, the speed skater.

DJ: Yep. At the end of the first season I gave all the skaters an 18-page questionnaire to fill out, and one of the questions at the end was, "What can you do to improve your psychological skills?" I'm going to read just part of his answer:

> For me personally, I need to be much more consistent when doing my meditation, really work on how I meditate, feel my chi more focused but relaxed at the same time. I really want to start learning chi gong and [begin] using it every day to improve my imagery, healing, circulatory skills. I want to be at a competition, and when I am not jogging, I need to be meditating. I believe that when I prepare mentally for a workout beforehand, I am much more efficient during the workout and I feel much more confident. On a visual basis, I am pretty good with self-talk. I think that I need to mentally start using the meditation skills for recovery. I have to learn how to push myself but at the same time be very smart about my recovery. This all leads to the Olympics. For me to become an Olympic champion I need to be doing mental work all day every day. While eating...while working or [doing] schoolwork I really need to be focusing on the moment. Most important—consistency.

DJ: See what I mean? He had already won medals at world championships, and these were some of his goals for the off-season.

AT: Pretty intense.

DJ: Yep, it was intense, but he knew what it would take to reach heaven. And in his mind, heaven was medals at the Olympics. He knew he needed to die first.

AT: I can see that. He was hungry.

DJ: Now I don't want to push you at all. My job is not to be another coach. I just want us to be sure you are on a path that is going to increase the likelihood you will achieve what you are striving for. And as you told me, there is room for improvement. I want you to think this over during the next week, and we will start next time with you telling me what you decided to do.

AT: Okay. I'll do it.

Remember, absorption is a cardinal feature of the gold medal mind. The gold medal mind is about being in the moment, present, absorbed and in a zone-like state. One breath at a time...breathing in, breathing out...over and over, again and again. If you are eating, focus on eating. No television, no computer, no texting. Just you and the food. One bite at a time. Chew the food well, enjoy the flavor, and move slowly on to the next bite. And again, an even a more radical perspective: for two hours at some point during the day, do not check or use your cell phone. It is probably above your pay grade to be so available anyway. Use the precious time you save to become more aware of what you tend to think and not think about and the feelings you experience. Become aware of how difficult it is to resist the impulse to look at your phone. Use that impulse as a cue to shift to your breath and yield freely to the present moment.

How to Die, Regardless of Your Heaven

1. Use strength training and conditioning as an opportunity to strengthen your mind (see chapter 12 for details). Lift with intention to improve your ability to focus and refocus

by allowing yourself to be absorbed in the moment, one repetition at a time.

2. *Get mentally prepared for practice on a daily basis.* This can be accomplished in a variety of ways. For example, after breakfast, take 15 minutes to practice the concentration exercise (see chapter 8), take time to review your goals for the day, and visualize yourself achieving your goals. Listen to music if that helps you get your head in the right space. Review your goals once again prior to practice, and think about inspiring others. (Yes, you need to look beyond yourself here. Remember, there is no "I" in "we.")

3. Know what you want and need and ask for it. Ask your coach, ask your teammates, ask the trainer, ask your partner or parents, and ask your sport psychologist. I am reminded of an 11-year-old basketball player I had been working with. The third time I saw him, he sat down and said, "Today I want to learn how to keep my composure, because after I miss a shot I lock up and get angry." Blew me away! Rarely have I heard an athlete ask for what he or she wanted in such a proactive manner, so early in the process of working together. Identifying what you need or want and asking for it is a life skill.

4. Set goals like never before and stick with them. Read chapter 7 again and put the suggestions about goal setting into practice. (To further help with this process, consider using both the goal-setting form and the practice and competition reflection form I've provided in appendixes 3 and 4, respectively.) Setting goals in the way I described is one of the clearest ways to "die." There is no substitute. Doing so will lead you to the heaven you are looking for. But it takes effort and commitment—both life skills.

5. Attend to the basics. Approach your dietary habits and sleep as if you were a body builder. They own the market when it comes to these behaviors. I may be exaggerating a

bit with this, but at least make the effort to eat clean and sleep like a baby, as described in chapter 13.

6. Identify the degree to which you have a gold medal mind and list the steps you need to take to make that way of thinking, feeling, and behaving second nature to you. Chapters 1 and 2 should help with this process.
7. Keep a daily journal identifying your progress, or lack thereof. Allow your warrior journal to become your "bible" (see appendix 5 for instructions on creating and using a warrior journal). At night, visualize yourself performing as if you had a gold medal mind—see it, feel it, and trust it, over and over again.
8. Practice concentration training on a daily basis. Get up in the morning and take your seat. Go to bed earlier so you can get up earlier to make it happen. Follow the guidelines in chapter 8. Get the audio version I offer if that will help with commitment. There is absolutely no substitute for sitting still every day, practicing the concentration training exercise, to learn how to control your thoughts, especially the highly critical ones that you allow to occupy oceanfront property in your mind. Taking time to sit still everyday is a powerful way to "die." Among other things, you will learn to befriend Self 1, and this will result in your getting to heaven more quickly and having more fun doing so.
9. Consider completing the companion workbook to *The Gold Medal Mind* with a "team," as I describe in the workbook. (See appendix 2 for more information on *The Gold Medal Mind Workbook*.)

Don't Decelerate Until it is Time

I am giving this "way to die" special emphasis, because there is no better way to describe dying in sport.

What do I mean? Think of running sprints or doing intervals in practice. As an assistant coach of Penn State's men's ice hockey team, I would typically see the majority of the players begin to decelerate prior to reaching the finish line. For example, in hockey, when skating "suicides," the players would start to decelerate shortly after crossing the blue line and way before reaching the goal line. Not okay! Dying is about running, skating, skiing as hard as possible toward and *past* the finish line. This does not necessarily mean you should accelerate before reaching the end. That may be unrealistic when lactate is squirting out of your ears. But not slowing down prior to crossing the finish line is realistic, and a psychological victory. "Dying" in this way nurtures the inherent determination, commitment, persistence, and fire that live deep down inside all of us. It is a way of going to any length that will yield dividends and allow you to perform beyond your expectations. I have seen it time and time again.

Note that pushing yourself to not decelerate will require you to take recovery time afterward, because the overload will be intense. Chapter 10 describes how to transcend pain and fatigue, and chapter 5 speaks to the importance of rest and recovery. Embrace this non-deceleration stuff, because you will see the benefits not only in your sport but also in life.

My intention here is not to imply you are not training hard enough. I am not suggesting you are lazy, unmotivated, or uncommitted. My point is that achieving your goals, the heaven you dream of, will require investing effort consistent with the demands of your North Star. The process requires you to be rigorously honest with yourself. The more honest you are, the more will be revealed. On one hand, a harsh reality may emerge. You might discover you are not willing to make the sacrifices needed to reach your heaven. This might lead you to adjust your outcome goals or perhaps pursue other options. But on the other hand, you may find your level of passion to perform beyond your expectations is off the charts.

One realization is not better than the other. What is important is that you are rigorously honest not only with others, but with yourself first. Honesty with oneself is yet another essential characteristic of a gold medal mind. Getting rigorously honest with yourself and taking a daily inventory of every aspect of your training program will shed light not only on where you can improve, but also on your strengths.

In Shakespeare's *Hamlet,* Polonius advises his son Laertes on the value of being honest with himself as he leaves home for the first time:

> Neither a borrower nor a lender be;
>
> For loan oft loses both itself and friend,
>
> And borrowing dulls the edge of husbandry.
>
> This above all: to thine own self be true,
>
> And it must follow, as the night the day,
>
> Thou canst not then be false to any man.
>
> — Shakespeare, *Hamlet,* Act 1, Scene 3

So powerful! The words "to thine own self be true" appear on the back of the chips given in A.A. to mark specific lengths of sobriety. Behaving in a way that transcends addiction starts with breaking through denial by being rigorously honest with oneself. Too often I have seen both athletes and non-athletes betray themselves by doing what they think they *should* do versus what they want to do. Wanting comes from a place of personal truth. A gold medal mind requires living from a place of "want" instead of "should."

Believe me, as you embrace and become strict with this stuff, you will grow in ways that you might never have imagined. Again, this goes back to the truth that you can learn more about yourself through sport than in any other arena in life. The court, course, or field is your classroom. And when you seize this dying and heaven concept, the lessons to be learned will reach well beyond sport. So get ready to start dying, and prepare to love it!

CHAPTER 15

The Only Performance-Enhancing Drug

I wonder what you are thinking right now. "Here comes a lecture on the dangers of steroids, andro, HGH, EPO, diuretics, creatine, and stimulants." "The mental stuff can only go so far. He is finally going to tell us the truth." "Maybe he will tell us how to beat the drug tests." Or, "Maybe I will just skip this chapter." Well, I can tell you with certainty the truth is "none of the above."

Taking conventional performance-enhancing drugs is a walk on the wild side for an athlete. In most cases, using PEDs is illegal and maybe considered immoral, along with having serious adverse physical and psychological consequences. Then why do athletes take this walk? That's easy: it is about winning at all costs—five-ring fever. After all, if the solution is just an injection away, why not take that step to get the edge? There are more choices today than ever: anabolic steroids, stimulants, human growth hormone (HGH), androstenedione (andro), creatine, diuretics, erythropoietin (EPO). Doesn't it make sense to simply take chemicals that will allow you to train harder and recover from workouts more quickly? The list of pros is wide and deep. But so are the possible cons of using illicit drugs. The chase for winning is no different from the chase for a cocaine high. Both involve the pursuit of a feeling, a high, and a rush in spite of potential negative consequences. Plain and simple, it is all about five-ring fever, the scoreboard, and fueling the desires of the ego no matter what the price. This is addiction, in every sense of the word.

If I were to do a full-blown scientific study to get the facts, one hypothesis I would test is that obsession with winning is a drug. The obsessive and desperate pursuit of winning shares many features with drug addiction—and cardinal features of drug addiction are the development of tolerance and loss of control. Tolerance means that over time, a person will need more and more of the drug to get high. And loss of control means that in spite of negative consequences and even the desire to stop, the person will continue to use the substance. Take a certain famous athlete, for example. He got high on winning and needed more and more of it to get high (i.e., he developed a tolerance). This resulted in him taking more and more PEDs, indicating a loss of control in spite of negative consequences such as health risks, betrayal of fans as well as those closest to him, and getting stripped of all awards. The way this plays out with most athletes is that in spite of an injury, the athlete will denounce doctors' orders and risk reinjury. I see this all the time in the Boulder/Denver area, even with recreational runners.

Winning can be a drug, because by its very nature it is intoxicating. I can recall in detail winning a championship over 40 years ago, when I was 13 years old. The feeling was outrageous. Before going out to play Lindsay Photo (the opposing team) for the championship, our captain began blasting the Queen songs "We Will Rock You/We Are the Champions." At the end of the first song, "We Will Rock You," he stopped the tape. The second part was "We Are the Champions," and we were not the champions yet. But after we won, 3-1, and came back to the locker room, the captain pressed play, and "We Are the Champions" blasted through the room. We went nuts, absolutely nuts. Right up to this day, when that song comes on the radio, I get chills. When I am really into it, I get tears in my eyes as I recall the buzzer going off and us piling on top of each other near center ice. It is powerful stuff, sport and winning.

But a person willing to cheat by using PEDs is an addict driven by the fear of failure. When an athlete will go to any length for the high that winning brings, it is clear sport and winning have become an addiction. A person like this typically lives life as if on a treadmill, moving without going anywhere, never satisfied. Being an athlete and having to win becomes something like needing oxygen, the very thing that keeps us alive. Such a person will not let anything or anybody get in the way. And his or her conscious choice to use PEDs is met with no hesitation, doubt, or uncertainty—because some athletes get to a point at which losing feels like death.

We have all heard of the person who has a cigarette four days post-quadruple-bypass surgery. This is what being hooked is all about. Five-ring fever has its hooks in the athlete who uses PEDs. Again, the addiction comes out of a fearful heart. And being driven by fear is the exact opposite of having a gold medal mind. The gold medal mind is about having a courageous heart, a heart filled with passion—which I believe is the most powerful PED out there.

Heart: The Drug Like No Other

The scene: Cisco and I were in the locker room after our respective workouts. Cisco was a professional triathlete, and I was still trying to be an athlete despite all my injuries and my body saying, "No!" While packing our bags and getting ready to leave the locker room, he turned to me. "Can you get me some EPO?" he asked. "What do you need that for?" I wondered. He said, "I have some big races this season and I want to move to the next level." Maybe that makes sense, I thought to myself. After all, everyone else is doing it. He went on, "I think they should just legalize it all and let athletes do whatever they want. They are going to use it anyway. Why not level the playing field." Perhaps I would be thinking the same way if I were in his shoes, I mused. But actually, I had a whole different opinion. I said, "You already have the most powerful drug out there. You have had it for a long time." He gave me a strange look and said, "What are you talking about?" With my right fist, I pounded lightly over my heart. "This is the most powerful," I said. "Once your heart is fully engaged, anything is possible!"

Cisco smiled. He said, "Yeah man, a couple months ago I was at a race. This woman I had just started to date was with me. I was so happy and relaxed. The race was important, but I was so happy to be with her. My training had been going well. My confidence was high and I could feel my passion coming back. My heart was in it more than ever. And what do you know, I set personal records that day in the bike and swim." I nodded my head in agreement and said, "Yep, there is nothing like it. No greater feeling. When your heart is engaged, you easily get into the zone with no worries, fears, doubts, or concerns. When you're absorbed in the moment, there's nothing else like it!" I lightly pounded my chest over my heart again and said, "You've got it, every day, every moment."

A silence fell. I picked up my bag and started to walk out of the locker room. He called after me, "Don't tell anyone!" I stopped, looked at him, and replied, "I won't, unless anyone else asks me for some EPO."

The Grinch in Dr. Seuss's *How the Grinch Stole Christmas* provides a powerful illustration of this principle in action. On Christmas morning, the Grinch was puzzled to see all the Whos in Whoville full of cheer and singing, even without all the glitter and gifts the Grinch had stolen to ruin their day. Suddenly he realized there might be more to Christmas than he had thought.

And what happened then? Well in Whoville they say
that the Grinch's small heart grew three sizes that day.
And then the true meaning of Christmas came through,
and the Grinch found the strength of ten Grinches,
plus two!

The moral of the story is so strongly related to having a gold medal mind and performing beyond your wildest dreams, I encourage you to watch it once or twice and then reflect in your warrior journal on how the story of the Grinch finding "the strength of ten Grinches, plus two!" applies to you as an athlete. In your writing, consider tying in how this story is directly related to how I believe your heart is the strongest performance-enhancing drug.

The Heart Versus PEDs

The heart is the hardest working muscle in the body. It pumps out two ounces (71 grams) of blood with every heartbeat. That adds up to at least 2,500 gallons (9,450 liters) of blood daily. The heart has the ability to beat over three billion times in a person's life. Can PEDs do that? Wouldn't you rather have cardiac muscle on your side? Well, you have it, every day and every millisecond of the day. It is just a matter of using it—engaging it.

Up to this point, I have not even addressed the emotional strength of the heart. I will not go into detail, but we can boil it down to the power of one simple emotion: love, the feeling of love. I know some experts out there believe love is a verb, and it can be. But for now, I am using it as a noun. Just think of how immensely powerful this emotion is. For a great example, see the movie *March of the Penguins.* You will be amazed at what parent penguins do out of love for their chicks. (This movie exemplifies the gold medal mind, among other things. Please give yourself the gift of watching it with some of your teammates.)

Think about the feeling of love: the love of a pet, a friend, a sunset, or painting with watercolors. Whatever it is, once you are motivated by love, the possibilities are limitless. And when you play for the love of the game, your psychological immune system is amazingly strong. You will be immune to the viruses and bacteria that attack secondary to five-ring fever and the opinions of sports writers. An energy will flow from within, leading you straight to a zone-like state and in turn to performing beyond your expectations with every move.

While at practice once with a gymnastics team preparing for regionals, the coach sent an athlete over to talk with me. Shortly into our chat, she said, "I have this feeling I will be awesome this weekend. It is this tingling feeling. I feel strong. My mind is clear and I'm just excited. The last two days...I can't explain it. I know I will be competing at nationals." After listening to her, I had nothing to say but, "Well, let's talk about that paper you are writing about identity development of the female athlete. That seems most important right now." Intuitively, I knew there was no need to talk any further about her heartfelt sense she was ready for nationals. So I took the time to talk about her life, the student part of the student-athlete. I think we both knew that was the most constructive way to use our time. And she was right—she went on to compete at nationals.

As a coach, you will simply know when an athlete's heart is fully engaged. It is something you will sense. It is your job to learn how to help athletes find this most profound and enjoyable state. But first, you need to learn how to do it yourself. I imagine a big reason you coach is because you want to inspire your athletes to become better people. If that is truly the case, it is essential to coach with your heart fully engaged. I believe that to teach it, you need to master it. Thus, before you try to teach your athletes how to engage their hearts, I highly recommend you learn to engage your heart when coaching. Striving to have a gold medal mind yourself is what will make the difference in your ability to help your athletes become psychologically skilled.

Engaging Cardiac Muscle— The Physical and Emotional Heart

Here is some of the advice I offer athletes to help them learn to engage the hardest working muscle in the body.

1. First, keep your motivation for playing the game in the forefront of your mind. My hope is that your primary motivation is to learn about developing a gold medal mind. Yes, the scoreboard is important, but your reason for playing is to develop a mindset that is strongly linked with victory. To take this a step further, the reason you play is to learn about yourself, inspire others, and create fantastic, positive memories. That is why you play. Your motivation is also about the scoreboard, but not to the degree that you catch five-ring fever.

2. Maintain your love of the game, the deep, intrinsic feeling that you simply love the fight, challenges, intensity, and enjoyment of learning to move your body through space and time in more and more amazing ways. Love all the ways you are getting faster, stronger, more accurate, and more precise in your movements. You are playing for the inherent excitement that is deep down inside of this thing called sport. For an athlete, nothing else comes close to awakening that joy.

3. Focus on getting satisfaction and fulfillment from inspiring others. Understand that your presence—just your presence, aside from your physical talent—inspires others to become more skilled. What you do and say touches others so that they will want to keep coming back and working to become more skilled. You help others appreciate their

gifts, regardless of whether they are gold, silver, or bronze medal material. You encourage others to join you on the journey to develop a gold medal mind. Start hugging your teammates more often. And yes, I am talking to the males out there. Just having that contact with another will make your heart sing.

4. Practice concentration training (explained in chapter 8) on a regular basis to get deeply in touch with the essence of the real challenge. Sport requires the ability to be absorbed in the moment to achieve a zone-like state. Most of the time, if not all of it, athletes want to be in the zone automatically, without working for it. The reality is that you are in the zone at some times, and not at others. When you are absorbed in the moment, your heart is engaged. And when your heart is engaged you will be in the present moment. It goes both ways. Concentration training teaches you how to be in the moment one breath at a time, one second at a time, one point at a time.

5. Remain excited for the journey to improve your ability to get into a zone-like state, regardless of the points you are scoring or games you are losing. Idealistic? Maybe, but try it before concluding anything. Contempt prior to investigation will rip you off every time. Allow yourself to become intrigued by the way letting go and non-striving work to get you into a zone-like state. Consider that developing this ability will be the most challenging aspect of being an athlete. And remember that embracing this facet of your psychological development can be really fun, because it will require you to engage your heart, not just your mind. Your passion (or aliveness) lives in your heart, and tapping into it will trigger the fire that burns deep inside. When you lose touch with the fire, your psychological strength can suffer. The fire is just like the sun. On a cloudy day, you might conclude the sun does not exist. But no, it is just behind the clouds. It is always there, like the fire inside

you. This fire too can get lost behind the clouds if you do not attend to stoking it.

6. Volunteer in some capacity, at least four hours per month. Sport can become a selfish and self-centered pursuit, to the point you can forget about the desperate needs of others in the world. The opportunities for volunteering are endless, and the right fit for you will jump out at you once you open your heart to donating your time with no expectation of getting anything in return. It is hard to put into words how much this one step will keep your heart fully engaged. But believe me, it will. It is helpful to recognize that so many things more important than sport are going on in the world. Once you plug into this reality, Self 1 will shut its mouth, and you will need less and less effort to get into a zone-like state. By putting things in perspective, volunteering will bring you back to the essence of your sport. And that essence is about playing the game. By its very nature, play is fun. Out of fun comes being in the zone and winning on the scoreboard. Who would have thought that walking dogs at the shelter for an hour a week could be such a powerful part of your training program? If you start going on the same day at the same time, you will find the dog sitting there waiting for your smile. When you see the wild excitement of that wagging tail, the last game you lost will quickly become a distant memory.

High on Heart Rate

When one is on the path to developing a gold medal mind, the heart is full of excitement, intensity, and passion, because the focus is on psychological victories. And psychological victories are the measure of success. Five-ring fever is not part of the landscape. Of course, you cannot help but aim for the podium and having that medal placed around your neck. But the majority of your brain cells are obsessed with the process, engaging Self 1 and Self 2 in a playful manner.

Success is a matter of achieving and maintaining a state of mind. Can this pursuit become an addiction? Well, I guess so, but taking this path is not about fear, intimidation, insecurity, and inadequacy—the real hallmarks of addiction. Instead, it is about personal development on all levels. Who does not have room for improvement? And who can say they are done growing? We all have what some call our "growing edges." For example, for people who have experienced vicious injustices early in life, learning to forgive others can be an important growing edge.

Let's face it, mainlining chemicals that will enhance performance might be easier than practicing the techniques I describe in this book. But as a result of battling, struggling, fighting, and coming back for more goal setting, visualization, and concentration training, you will know the power of a natural high. You will come to accept on a deeper level the knowledge that you are your toughest opponent. It is you against you. And learning to win the inner game has more far-reaching, positive consequences than I can even begin to describe.

For now, please just embrace this information on faith. Have confidence that you will find more meaning and satisfaction in sitting for hours on end practicing concentration training than you would with any chemical. It all boils down to heart. You will learn to engage your cardiac muscle in ways you would have never dreamed if you had not pursued a gold medal mind. But for now, simply realize there are more ways to measure the power of your heart than with a heart rate monitor.

CHAPTER 16

Coaches: The Leaders of the Pack

The story I am about to tell sheds light on how a disjointed Olympic speed skating team that chose to work together became a relatively healthy family. Because of one particular athlete, one of the coaches of this team did not believe working in unity would be possible. The coach thought the athlete was a moron and was threatening the team's integrity and potential. But as you will see, in the end this coach's limiting belief about the athlete finished second, because the process of team bonding won the race.

Coaches can fall into a destructive trap of labeling athletes—deciding an athlete is mentally weak or plays poor defense, for example. And a coach's limiting belief can and will undermine an athlete's potential. In the worst-case scenario, it can lead an athlete to quit. When athletes end up in my office, I find their self-limiting beliefs are largely a function of what coaches have and have not told them over the years. Coaches hold an enormous amount of power, and sometimes, just "the look" can make an athlete's confidence go south. In the situation I am describing here, the coach went beyond the look. He verbalized, without reservation, exactly how he felt about the athlete.

Here's the story. I had just started working with the US speed skating team, and during the first week, I received a call from one of the coaches.

> Coach (in a heavy European accent): Welcome to our organization.
>
> Me: Thank you, it is an honor to join the teams.
>
> C: I want to tell you a bit about one of the teams and a particular athlete.
>
> Me: Sure, go ahead.
>
> C: The athlete's name is Kyle [not his real name]. He is a moron.
>
> Me: Oh. What do you mean?
>
> C: He is stupid and causes trouble. The other skaters do not like him.
>
> Me: Hmm, sounds like something I will look into.
>
> C: I am not sure if it would be worth your time. He is an idiot and I think I will fire him from the team.
>
> Me: Sounds like it might be a quick decision.
>
> C: Yes, but the best. It is his first year and I don't want him to interfere with the others training hard to win medals.
>
> Me: That makes sense, but can you give me some time to check things out?
>
> C: Again, I don't want to waste your time, but go ahead. Good luck.
>
> Me: Thanks. I'll keep in touch.

I got off the phone and thought, oh boy, this is not good. If this is the coach's assessment, this athlete does not have much of a chance to chase his dreams. But there is more to the story.

When I showed up to the first training camp in Milwaukee, it became clear very quickly which athlete the coach was referring to.

I observed practice, and afterwards talked to another coach about the athlete. Although this other coach was a bit more forgiving, he was far from optimistic that this athlete would make it more than a couple of weeks. The athlete was a black sheep, and definitely the team scapegoat. My guess is he was a black sheep in other arenas of life, too. It was sad, because he did not seem to have ill will toward anyone. And he was far from being the moron the coach thought he was—in fact, I found him to be a fun-loving and jovial soul. My first impression was that there might be more hope for this athlete than the coach thought.

The first several team meetings were focused on developing unity and a healthy team identity. Needless to say, team members raised the issue of their difficulties with the athlete in question frequently in our meetings. We decided to implement some suggestions to break through the troubles the team was having. One goal was to create an environment in which everyone was accepting of each other. This involved dealing with self-centeredness, and how we all, at times, expect others to conform to our standards. These suggestions were all placed in the context that everyone was chasing his or her dream, and they could achieve more together than on their own. You know the saying, there is no "I" in "we." But think about it. These athletes were training together, but at a certain point would be competing against each other in the Olympic trials. The probability that each would be lining up against a friend for a spot on the Olympic team was high. It was a very challenging situation.

With some ground rules in place and regular meetings to celebrate progress, we set new team goals and dealt with the obstacles, and ultimately, the culture improved. The team developed an identity based on selflessness and what I will call love, even though that word is not used much in the world of sport. I emphasized that they were a family, and that a cardinal feature of healthy families is love. Some of the men resisted the word love and preferred unity. No problem—whatever worked was fine with me.

The team embraced the athlete once called a moron. He had some skills the others did not have, so he could contribute to others' skill development. And in turn, some of the more talented athletes took time to teach him skills in areas in which he needed to improve. In the end, he made the Olympic team and played a crucial role when it came to maintaining unity, support, and love among the team members. This was one of the more beautiful events I have witnessed in working with a team. To see the athletes hugging each other, though it did not happen often, was touching. To see Kyle laugh and feel a part of the family was moving.

By this point, I wondered what the coach thought. I never asked, and he never said anything about the change for the better. But I was tempted to say, "You failed this athlete miserably. Think about it. And let's talk sometime if you want to know how much more to it there is than meets the eye when evaluating human beings." I did not, because I knew I would be doing it more for my own satisfaction than his benefit, and that would be selfish on my part.

There is a moral to the story for coaches, and even for athletes in the throes of an experience like the one I just described. Coaches, be careful when it comes to developing impressions of your athletes. Your premature judgments—contempt prior to investigation, if you will—can crush an athlete's ability to develop a gold medal mind and perform beyond expectations. When you label a player as not being a starter, for example, you bias your own perception of the athlete. This will manifest itself in practice, both verbally and nonverbally. Athletes can be highly sensitive, especially those who believe they have been labeled less-than-average, weak, or a head case. Think about how you parent your kids and the profound impact your beliefs have on their development in all arenas. Think of your athletes as if they were your kids. And treat them no differently. I say this knowing there are indeed athletes who will put your patience to the test. Welcome these experiences as opportunities to foster psychological fitness.

Some potentially damaging ways to label athletes include (but are not limited to):

- Identifying an athlete as someone who cannot deal with pressure
- Believing an athlete will never develop a particular skill or ability
- Feeling an athlete just wants to be a pain in your butt
- Thinking an athlete does not really want it or lacks hunger (probably the most destructive label of all)

Coaches, strive to stay aware of your perceptions and attitudes about athletes with whom you have lost patience or confidence. You never know when a moron will turn into an Einstein as a result of your inspiration, love, and positive team culture. Sit with the athlete and encourage him or her to take the steps I outline here (see For Athletes below). Get your entire staff on board. Remember, even if this athlete has not scored one goal in the season, you can help him or her develop in a more important way—psychologically. Please know that psychological victories will have a more lasting impact on your athletes. Yes, scoring points and winning tournaments are important. But when you have helped an athlete develop a gold medal mind, you have given them a gift for life. One of my high school coaches blessed me with this gift. I tell Dickie Nolan whenever I can that he is one of the top three most influential people in my life. When feeling brave, I kiss him on his bald head and tell him I love him. He hates that, and I will not tell you what he says in response. But the reality is I would not have written this book had it not been for the belief Dickie had in me years ago.

There is always more to an athlete than meets the eye. Remember, deep down inside, every athlete is chasing a dream. As a coach, it is your responsibility to believe in, inspire, and nurture the person's growth and development as an athlete, and more important, as a human being. You are in a most powerful position to be an influential force, either positive or negative, in an athlete's life. Embrace it and run with it, and you will find that touching the lives of others will be more rewarding than any win on the scoreboard. That win will be forgotten shortly after the season is over. But you will always remember an athlete contacting you 20 years later to ask for guidance or just to say hello. That means more than words can say.

For Athletes

Now for you athletes who believe your coach has labeled you, or put you in a little box you cannot seem to break out of no matter how hard you work, I know how painful it is. I have seen it time and time again, and it is challenging for me to help an athlete keep his or her head up, to continue to believe they will start, for example, when they have not played at all. Confidence gets shattered, motivation suffers, and Self 1 goes on a rampage. At this point, it is normal for you to feel like a helpless prisoner of your doubts, fears, and insecurities. So what do you do?

If I were to answer this question cynically, based upon what I have seen through the years, I would say something like, "This is wrong. You should not be having this experience. But you are going to have to learn to deal with it. Short of having a stroke, your coach is never going to change." But I hate even thinking like this. What, then, is my truth? It is embracing and practicing the following suggestions, because they are the signs of a gold medal mind.

1. Be a team player, and work to inspire others. Become a force, to the degree your teammates want to improve because of who you are and the example you set.

2. Work your butt off, from the time you start to warm up until practice is over.

3. Become insanely committed to your growth both on and off the field.
4. Train psychologically to develop your mind. Your actions will speak louder than words. People with a gold medal mind radiate enthusiasm and hunger. Be the person who takes the lead in this regard. It is highly possible that you can shift from feeling like the "weakest link" to being a major force on the team.
5. Get support from those who inspire you to overpower the negativity you may be experiencing from your coach. I have found that three of the hardest words for an athlete to say are, "I need help." Well, it is time to embrace these words as a reflection of how courageous you are. Those words are a statement about how strongly you want to take action, instead of wallowing in self-pity or feeling like a victim.
6. Potentially, talk with your coach. However, think this one through with an objective party who can guide you along this path should you chose to take it. Depending on your coach's own level of emotional development, he or she may not have the patience to listen. And it can make the situation worse—sad but true. If so, it is a life lesson, because someday you may have a teacher or employer with a similar style.
7. Keep in mind that being an athlete is just one aspect of who you are. You are a person who has chosen to be an athlete. It does not define you. This will keep you off the emotional roller-coaster. I admit this is much easier said than done. My identity was wrapped up in being an athlete long after I stopped playing competitively.
8. Believe that taking these steps is a psychological victory, regardless of whether you get to start or even get playing time. It is about your character, and your character is reflected in how you face adversity. Never forget this!

9. Read this book three or four times, complete *The Gold Medal Mind Workbook*, and incorporate all of my suggestions on a consistent basis. Make developing a gold medal mind your objective. This will allow you to take some of your focus off your coach's limitations.

This last point is intimately tied in with the heart of the gold medal mind. When a coach fails to get past an initial negative impression, it can devastate an athlete's confidence and self-image. Not being recognized as a potential force on the field after working your butt off in every way possible can be painful. To some degree, it would be easier to let your motivation suffer and perhaps wallow in self-pity. But when you keep your head in the game and follow the steps I have suggested, you will earn a spot on the podium regardless of what anyone else thinks.

You may already know that you are your own toughest opponent, and a coach's negative opinion can up the ante. But the lessons you will learn by continuing to go to any length in spite of what your coach thinks will spill over into the game of life. The experience will test your character and what you are made of, and teach you how to weather the storms that are inherent in relationships with friends, family members, and partners. You will come to believe that nothing will stand in the way of you developing a gold medal mind. Remember, we are still talking about winning—winning the inner game. It all comes down to a choice: to focus in a way that allows you to transcend the challenges and win, or choose otherwise and lose the inner game. Embrace—at least for now—that winning the inner game is the real victory.

CHAPTER 17

The Parents' Job Description

One of my favorite professional activities is speaking to parents of a son or daughter who has chosen to be a competitive athlete. I am not sure parents necessarily enjoy listening to me, but I enjoy speaking to them. Still, I thought long and hard before even including this chapter. Believe me, I know a plethora of books about being a parent of an athlete already exists. The number of websites on the topic has exploded. There is so much that could be said—but at the same time, there is not much to say. It depends on how you look at it all.

In the end, because my approach to advising parents is quite simple, I decided to include the chapter. My hope for parents who read this book is that it will help them in one of two ways. They will either receive validation that they are gold medal material and on the right track with their young athletes, or they will decide to go back to the locker room and ask some important questions. For example: "How can I help with the development of my child's psychological fitness?" "What is the best way to respond when my child is absolutely dejected after a poor performance?" "What is my definition of success?" "What should I do if my partner is critical of my kid?" "Do I play the role of a coach, to even a small degree?" "Am I too wrapped up in my child being an athlete?" "Is my involvement in my kid's sport a way to avoid problematic issues in my own life?" And the list goes on.

A few years back, I gave a lecture to parents on this topic as part of a swimming camp their children were involved in. These kids were 14 years old or under and ranked in the top 25 in the state for their sport. After reviewing with the audience specific psychological principles related to performance enhancement, I invited questions. One parent asked, "How do I get my daughter to visualize? I know it works from my own experience, but she just won't do it." I could have given her a quick, scientific answer about changing behavior through positive reinforcement. A century of research in behavioral therapy shows that providing positive reinforcement (in this case, a prize or treat or sticker) on a variable interval schedule will result in the highest rates of response (in this case, more visualization training). But was this really the right answer for her question? It was not, given the fact that a kid should not be treated like a lab rat.

I did start my answer with a little chat about B.F. Skinner (the father of behaviorism) and his studies with pigeons and rats, as well as my personal experience with Kiera (the name I gave the rat I had in experimental psychology lab). She learned to press a bar 25 times to get a little drop of sugar water when a red light was on. It was insane what the animal would do for a reward. Old B.F. was onto something. In fact, his research in operant conditioning is the basis of what we call behavior modification, which has become the foundation of interventions we see used in institutions ranging from schools to prisons to hospitals.

But then I went in another direction to answer this concerned mom's question, and talked from a human resources perspective. "The best way I can answer that question is based on your job description for being a mom. Your job is to support, love, nurture, care for, teach, hug, and have tons of fun. Not necessarily in that order, but these are the basic job requirements for being a parent. And," I added, "after reading the human resources manual that describes the requirements for your position, I did not find that getting your child to visualize is part of your job description." Immediately, she asked, "So are you telling me I should not care?" I answered, "No, not at all. But care in a way that is consistent with your role. Leave visualization training up to the coach or sport psychologist. Mental training is no different from physical training. You certainly are not going to monitor the position of your child's head during the backstroke. So be careful not to get pulled into a coach's role. If anything, you might meet with the coach and your daughter to talk about the use of visualization, and then let the coach take it from there." I finished by suggesting that a major part of her job description was to take her daughter out for ice cream frequently (something I will talk more about a bit later).

I firmly believe in parents sticking with this idea of their job description. For parents who have difficulty figuring out exactly what their job description is, here is my advice: if it falls into the category of love, game on. It is simple. In families, love conquers all, just as the books and songs tell us. A parent's job is to love, love, and love, above all else. (This does not mean you should not have clear expectations and enforce consequences in every arena of your kid's life, including the dinner table!) Can a parent encourage visualization training in a loving way? It is certainly possible. But the mother in the example I just related asked the question from a heart filled with frustration and impatience. Those emotions had kicked love to the curb for her. And it is even possible that she was trying to meet her own emotional needs through her child's success. You know, the old "parents living through their kids" kind of situation. Entire books have been written on the subject. I am not going to elaborate here, but for those interested in the gold standard resource on the subject, read *The Drama of the Gifted Child* by Alice Miller for insight on how a parent might slip into exploiting a child in this way.

Kids are brilliant, and they can tell if your best intentions are coming from love or not. Let love be your guide, and you will know what to do and say. Here is an example that may shed light on what this might look like. A few years ago, a parent asked me what she should say to her child before a competition. I shared the following with her as an example of what she could say, but added, "Consider this one option among many."

Parent: Guess what?

Child: What?

Parent: We are going for ice cream if you swim fast.

Child: Sounds good.

Parent: Guess what else?

Child: What?

Parent: We are going for ice cream if you swim slowly.

Child: Oh, okay.

Parent: Know what that means?

Child: We are going for ice cream no matter how I do, right?

Parent: Nope.

Child: Well, then what?

Parent: It means that I believe you are an amazing person and I love you so much. Ice cream is a sign of my love for you. Swimming is something you do. It does not define you as a person. I know how competitive it is, but ice cream is going to be our code word to always remember that swimming is just something you do.

Child: Where did you get that, from some Buddhist book or something?

Parent: No, I had a dream last night, and that is what you told me when I said that you were going to be a state champion.

(I told you I would talk about ice cream.)

Here is a sad example of parental love gone awry. A mom and dad referred their 16-year-old daughter, who played basketball, for help with a range of issues. Her problems included frequent doubts in her ability, trouble letting go of mistakes, being incredibly hard on herself, and conflicted relationships with some teammates. I learned that Dad had coached her from age 6 until she was 13. He was a former athlete and invested in her development. She was genetically gifted, coming from a long line of athletes on both sides of the family. Her genetic gifts, in combination with her passion for the game, had resulted in a highly talented athlete. Many club coaches sought her out. However, when she came in for help, her performance was suffering. Self 1 was raging with no mercy. The struggle had been going on for at least a year, and by now she was thinking of quitting. Her dreams of playing in college were in the distant past. At this point, she simply was searching for a way to escape the torture chamber of her own mind. Sadness, bordering on serious clinical depression, was crashing on the shores of her consciousness.

Over the next year, as we worked together, she made progress. She doubted herself less and took more risks on the court. Her shooting percentage increased, and when she missed two or three shots in a row, she was able to refocus into a zone-like state more quickly than she had in the past. Relationships with teammates improved because she was less angry, irritable, and impatient. However, we ran into a roadblock of sorts. Her father continued to monitor her every move.

The young woman generally was reluctant to have her parents meet with us, but there were a few occasions on which we all met. The focus of those meetings was allowing the athlete to tell Mom and Dad how they could help her on her journey of recovering from intense emotional injury. It seemed, for the most part, that her father honored her request that he not offer feedback unless she asked. We had set some basic ground rules, such as no talking about an upcoming game, starting the night before and continuing until the day after the game. This proved to be a challenge for him, but his "free-throw shooting percentage" improved over time, at least to the degree that his daughter could continue to heal and learn to have fun again.

But midway through the season of her senior year, Dad broke all the rules. My understanding is that the athlete had an awful game filled with "stupid and uncalled-for errors," according to her father. It had been a while since we had met with her parents. Without my suggesting they join us, she said, "Dr. Jowdy, I gotta talk to my dad in here. Can we do it this week?" I said, "I will make myself as available as possible. Talk to your parents, and ask them to get in touch to set a time." Later that evening I received an e-mail from her mom, and we set a time. I viewed the fact that the young woman initiated this meeting as a huge sign of her personal development. But I was not sure what she had on her mind for the session.

There we were, the four of us. Dad was sitting on the couch at a comfortable distance from his daughter, and Mom was sitting in a chair across from the couch. The theme for the session was similar to past meetings, but this time, I did much less to facilitate the conversation. The athlete took the lead. She seemed to have a spring in her step I had not seen before. She talked about the last game and the way her father attacked her on the car ride home. As Dad attempted to justify his actions, the athlete burst into tears, shaking her head. Dad continued to talk. I put up my hand, strongly suggesting he stop; this provided the necessary space for her to express her pain. As her sobbing began to subside, I said, "It hurts." She nodded her head in agreement, wiping away tears. I said, "What do you need from your dad?" Without hesitation, slamming her fist against the arm of the couch, she looked him in the eyes, and shouted, "I don't need a coach anymore, I need a father! I need a father!"

Silence fell. What followed was shocking. She began to cry again, holding her face in her hands. And neither Mom nor Dad said or did anything. Tears began to fill my eyes as I waited for her father, sitting right next to her, to wrap his arms around her and say, "I love you so much. There is nothing more I want than for you to have fun. I messed up; I did not honor your request. I have hurt you more than I could ever have imagined, and I am so sorry. I understand why you are enraged with me. I will learn to become your father, because that is what I want to be. I just have been so excited at the progress you have made, and my competitiveness got the best of me." But neither parent said a word. Her dad did not even take her hand. Anger filled every cell in my body, but I held my tongue. Finally I said, "You can start being a father right now by giving her a hug." I still wonder if that was the most therapeutic thing to say, but I could not think of anything else at that moment. He gave her a hug. But years later, as I write this, I still get tears in my eyes over how painful this kid's experience was.

The good news is these parents did come to realize they needed to learn how to parent in a manner more consistent with their job description. They benefited from meeting more frequently with their daughter and me. Although I have been referring mostly to the athlete's father, Mom became empowered and learned to have a voice in her relationship with her husband. This was new territory for her, and yet another opportunity for Dad to grow. Focus on the athlete's sport now took place in the context of developing healthy relationships based on love. And with the emphasis taken off her performance, she continued to heal and grow, slowly developing a gold medal mind with the help of her parents. Having fun became her North Star.

One of my favorite things to do when working with a young male athlete is to ask him if he wants a hug from his mom and dad. A hug, right then and there in my office, for no reason except for love.

Oh, the guys usually do not like this idea; they shake their heads in disagreement or just say no. But I insist they give both parents a hug. They look at me as if I am nuts, but typically follow through. Then, when the athlete and I start setting goals, I introduce daily hugs with both parents as part of the training program. To date, I have not encountered displeasure with or resistance to this suggestion from either parents or kids. I think that says something about the power of hugs. If anyone outright resists, I recommend that on the first Sunday of every month the athlete make a huge breakfast for the entire family. I will let you guess how that is received!

The moral of the story? Parents need to learn to play their positions in much the same way the kids do in their sport. My hope is that kids can develop the insight and courage to know when to tell their parents they are out of position. Kids: be mindful that your parents may have good intentions but simply do not know how to follow through. Competitiveness hijacks their brains, just as it does yours. But you can help them grow and learn to become psychologically skilled parents. We want parents with gold medal minds, too. The process can be scary at times. If it is, please get support or professional help from someone who can "hug" you until you receive the hugs you should be getting from you parents.

Human Resources: From Theory to Practice

I certainly do not mean to imply that all parents of athletes are confused, lost, and unable to hug. There is a sad stereotype of parents of athletes being overbearing, overinvolved, and overidentified with their kids. The word on the street is that some parents are living vicariously through their kids' sports. Right? Think how often you hear, "That dad was a frustrated athlete who wanted to be a star. Now he is living through his son." However, I have worked with many parents who could write this chapter much better than I. Regardless of whether or not they have an athletic background, instinctively they know what to do and say.

When I start working with an athlete younger than 18, I typically meet with both the parents and athlete for the first session, and then occasionally together as I continue to work with the athlete. As often as not, I am blown away by the rock-star parenting skills I am blessed to witness. I have been tempted to ask some parents if I could interview them to find out what they did to raise such an amazing human being. There was one kid, a wrestler, who inspired me so much that I felt I should have paid him and his parents for the time we spent together. He never ceased to amaze me with his insights and willingness to go to any length to develop a gold medal mind. Without my even making the connection, he frequently saw the implications his sport had to his life. For example, the concentration exercise became as routine for him as brushing his teeth. I will never forget him saying, "Now, if I don't practice the concentration training, I feel like I missed something. I just feel better and more focused during the day when I do it. It makes me happy. It is helping me with school and friends. I feel more balanced." Textbook stuff! He had become a warrior in every sense of the word.

Watching how this young man coped with recurrent injuries that sidelined him his senior year blew me away. This was the year he was expected to go undefeated and win the state championship—something his brother had done four years earlier. He dreamed of seeing his picture hanging next to his brother's in the trophy case at school. Then he was injured again, and was unable to compete in the state championships he was expected to win. But what could have been a devastating tragedy instead inspired him to become a better person. (In contrast, it took me years to entertain the idea that my injuries were teachers in disguise.)

This athlete returned home after his first semester in college, after grayshirting for a variety of reasons, and I continued to work with him. Because of his recurrent injuries, he wanted to do some soul searching about whether or not to retire from his sport. During this time, I sometimes saw him and his father at the gym. We had amazing little chats. But once I ran into the dad by himself. He thanked me for the work I had done with his son, and told me about the changes he had noticed. I replied, "I've been thinking of telling you this for some time. It is an honor to be a part of your son's journey. He has inspired me in so many ways. What an amazing young man you have raised. I am sure you know he is crazy about you!" It was something I had wanted to say years ago, and I was glad the Universe at last provided the right moment for me to express my gratitude to this wonderful parent.

The impact of good parenting in youth sport performance (including college) is immensely powerful. The truth is parents do not get the recognition they often deserve in this area. I hope my words can help change this state of affairs. To you athletes out there, young and old, be generous with the hugs you give your parents. And to you parents of athletes, never forget your job description is not about coaching, but about love. That is the best contribution you can make to the development of a gold medal mind.

CHAPTER 18

Beyond Expectations

It was the summer before the 2002 Winter Olympics. I was with the US speed skating team at Fortress Mountain, a lodge about two hours north of Calgary, Alberta. The lodge was a huge building that looked as if it might come crashing down with a strong wind. However, its character and charm offset the fear factor. The team would spend several weeks here this summer to train, both on and off the ice. In the morning we would drive to the oval in Calgary, and later in the afternoon there was some sort of dry-land training. Some days the athletes would go for a 100-mile bike ride. And this was after a morning skate! I usually met with the coaches over some iced tea or lemonade during the athletes' afternoon workout. About twice a week, in the evening, we would meet as a group—players and coaches—to discuss issues related to the gold medal mind.

I was meeting with the sprint team one evening when one of our most powerful interactions occurred. To this day, I can remember it vividly. I can visualize who was sitting where. What went down sealed the deal for me that there is no substitute for what I call the belief factor, the *feeling* deep down inside that one has what it takes. Whereas confidence is cognitive—thinking you can do it—the belief factor is an inner knowing, a burning felt deep inside. It is what psychologist Eugene Gendlin, PhD, called a "heartfelt sense."

The belief factor is that overwhelming feeling in the body, mind, and spirit when you know, maybe the day before an event, that you will be outstanding. There is a zone-like quality to it that settles into your heart before the gun goes off.

That particular afternoon, the athletes, coaches, and I were sitting in a circle talking about the upcoming season and, ultimately, the Olympics. The conversation ranged from talking about work ethic in the weight room to the family—the family being a term we used to describe the athletes living in harmony. It was one of those times at which I had no agenda, when I simply had to trust that important issues would be raised without forcing anything. What happened next had a powerful impact because it came not from the coaches or me, but from the athletes themselves.

While talking about the Olympics and getting on the podium, one athlete blurted out with intensity, "I just realized I train as hard as anyone else in the world, so there is no reason why I can't win a medal." Dead silence followed his epiphany. I looked around the room, smiling. "So what does everyone think?" I asked. What followed was fruitful chatter about the truth in the statement. First, we focused on the fact that the athletes really did train as hard as anyone in the world. Next, they had to trust the training program. And finally, we arrived at the idea they had to believe—to believe in their *hearts* that anything would be possible with a gold medal mind. (As you may recall, I believe the heart is the most powerful performance-enhancing drug.)

This led us to talking about the power of belief and performing beyond initial expectations. I say initial expectations, because typically, initial expectations are not close to what an athlete is capable of. Initial expectations can be powerful, for sure. But in the spirit of the gold medal mind, we are talking about transcending limiting beliefs and performing beyond expectations. For example, if you are thinking about getting a lot of playing time in the next season, why not engage every cell in your body to believe you will start? You may say that starting is not want you really want. But sit back and imagine what it would be like being on the floor to start the game in a jam-packed gym on a Saturday night. The little kid inside you would be jumping for joy. Yes, I am talking inner child stuff. The truth is, we all have one. And your inner kid has probably been dreaming for ages not only of playing, but also of starting and getting a lot of playing time. Think of all the hours you spent shooting hoops pretending you were Michael Jordan, Kobe Bryant, or LeBron James. They all started. And starting is within your grasp too. You must simply make specific choices to smash your limiting beliefs and use your mind as an ally.

Self-Limiting Beliefs

What makes it so hard to perform beyond initial expectations, to think in terms of possibilities and put your mind ahead of the experience? Plain and simple, our self-limiting beliefs hold us back—mere thoughts handicap us. In the Alcoholics Anonymous "Big Book," there is a line that says, "Some of us have tried to hold on to our old ideas and the result was nil until we let go absolutely" (58). The belief in A.A. is that to achieve and maintain sobriety, the person with an addiction to alcohol must reject old ideas—for example, that they will not be able to cope without the "fire water," as we used to call it. For athletes, a common example of an old idea might be something like, "I am only as good as my accomplishments." With this belief, a major competition could pose a real threat to your self-worth. It will certainly not be the exciting challenge it is meant to be. For many athletes, such a belief is largely unconscious. Part of my work with athletes is to help them do the work of bringing these unconscious beliefs into consciousness and smashing them.

Another prime example of an old idea is this: "If you work hard and live right, good things will happen." Do you believe that? I hate to say it, but that belief is fiction. Look around you. Think of friends you know who have lived well, trained like crazy, and, within a couple weeks of the season's start, suffered an injury that put them out for the year or ended their career. It is not fair, and totally inconsistent with the fiction that some call the "life of blessings." This term, coined by the writer Larry Crab, PhD, refers to a belief that if one lives in a right and good way, life will always bring good things. We all were led to believe this in one way or another as children. But it is an old idea that needs to be smashed, because holding on to it will lead to perpetual disappointment, frustration, and anger. These are feelings that are not pleasant for anybody. But in the case of a person who is used to drinking to blot out feelings, it is unhealthy to think in ways that only promote heartache. Holding onto self-limiting beliefs will interfere with achieving long-term sobriety (another way of performing beyond expectations).

Life is hard enough without manufacturing our own misery, as they say in Twelve-Step programs. So getting rid of old ideas and beliefs will lead to a less painful and lower-stress existence. This process is also at the heart of both the physical and psychological breakthroughs that will allow you to perform beyond your expectations time and time again.

Self-limiting beliefs in sport can be extremely damaging. One clear example is when an athlete believes he or she can make the Olympic team, but will not be able to win a medal. Or the athlete believes it is possible to win a medal, but not a gold. If we take it a bit further, the athlete may believe he or she can win one gold, but not two gold medals. I have seen it and worked with athletes who held such limiting beliefs. And these are just individual examples. We all have limiting beliefs in all areas of our lives. I was certain I could not succeed when it came to calculus—no way, no how. I am not sure where I got this belief, because I had done well in math up until that time. But my belief resulted in a C- in pre-calculus and a D+

in calculus, and my professor would assure you this was not due to lack of effort. You may have a limiting belief that you will never get along with a specific person in your life. Well, that belief will simply put a wall around your heart, making it impossible to get close to that person, maybe even preventing you from forgiving him or her.

During the group discussion with the sprint team, we decided to use the expression "smash" in reference to the limiting beliefs. The beliefs needed to be smashed. The coach liked the word and used it often after that point. Using the word in practice when an athlete was discouraged and believed he would never get it right made a huge impact. It is so easy for us to get impatient with ourselves. As a result, we can jump to the conclusion that we will never be able to "come out of the turn with power," to use speed-skating terminology.

Patience is crucial to the process of smashing self-limiting beliefs. Old beliefs die hard. Changing your "mental swing" can be much more difficult than changing your physical swing. Be prepared to get frustrated when your old thinking patterns resist new ways of thinking. When working with a competitive person, I often talk about the "p" word and point out when his or her "patience muscle" is underdeveloped and needs to spend more time in the gym. Self-limiting beliefs are defiant and stubborn, for good reason. In many ways, they have worked quite well in allowing you to accomplish great things. Expect the dogs of rebellion to come out barking, as they say in Twelve-Step programs, during the process of smashing your self-limiting beliefs.

We can adopt a self-limiting belief quite easily, especially if we have been struggling with something for a few days with a Herculean effort. The danger is if we let it grow long enough, it will become a weed with roots that travel wide and deep. Then it will be much more difficult to smash that belief.

Uprooting Self-Limiting Beliefs

During college, my brother Vin and I had a business called D&V Services (for Doug and Vin). Our specialties were landscaping and house painting. However, we also sealed driveways, detailed cars, washed windows, repaired roofs, dabbled in light electrical work, and at times watched our customers' kids while they ran errands. We did quite well, so well that I proposed to my parents that I not continue with my formal education and instead make D&V Services my life's work.

I was not a fan of school, and after earning a 2.1 grade point average my freshman year, I thought the decision to cut me loose would be a no-brainer. But it wasn't. To my surprise, they insisted I earn a bachelor's degree. Although I was not happy at the time, I became forever grateful. My parents' insistence that I continue with school forced me to come face-to-face with my self-limiting beliefs. They were weeds with roots that ran wide and deep. I used to think some of the roots traveled as far as China. Isn't that what we did as kids digging in the dirt—tried to get to China? It seemed the roots of my self-limiting beliefs almost touched China.

They ran especially deep, I believe, because at a relatively early age I had a "coach" of sorts who smashed my confidence as a student. Father John Lindsay, an oblate of St. Francis de Sales, was my English teacher. He told me that based upon my PSAT and ACT scores, I would struggle to get an undergraduate degree and never succeed in graduate school. Can you imagine, a young student hearing that from a messenger of God? What happened to mercy and grace?

Needlessly to say, the grass in my psychic yard was soon overrun with weeds. Even as co-owner of D&V Services, I had no clue where to start uprooting them. I had been a connoisseur of sport psychology for a couple of years by then, but nowhere had I read about self-limiting beliefs. Even today, much of what you will read in this area advocates using positive self-talk. You know: "I think I can. I think I can. I think I can." I call this the lawn mower approach: just run over the weeds, and poof, they are gone—or so it seems, until you are in a pressure situation and the weeds sprout up all over again.

Little has been written about pulling mental weeds out by the roots. Based on my personal and professional experience (and Father John Lindsay was not the only coach who rained on my parade), I approach this subject with passion. I know from experience that these weeds can interfere with the development of a gold medal mind. But in reality, the self-limiting beliefs I am calling weeds are just opportunities to practice the skills required to get closer to a gold medal mind.

When I let go of how he hurt me at the time, Father John Lindsay's words led to a fierce determination to blast through any obstacle, mental or otherwise, that stood in the way of achieving my goals. I can tell you getting into and doing postdoctoral training at Stanford University School of Medicine was not a conscious goal of mine at the time. If you had told me after my first year of college (during which I earned a 2.1 GPA) that I would go to Stanford, I would have thought you were psychotic. But after pulling weed after weed, this became a reality. Had Lindsay not wreaked havoc in my psyche, I might not have developed the persistence to overcome the many different forms of adversity I encountered along the way.

The time to start pulling weeds is when doubts, fears, and worries first get a foothold. As I mentioned, there is a lot more to overcoming self-limiting beliefs than positive self-talk, which I liken to quickly running over the weeds with a lawn mower only to have them grow back. I am also not suggesting pouring kerosene on them, but rather using a kind of heavy-duty grade of Scotts Turf Builder. Here are the steps I suggest you take to help get rid of your mental weeds for good.

1. Make friends with your self-limiting beliefs. I could say they are there for a reason, but this would lead me on a philosophical and theoretical tirade you probably would rather not hear. For the sake of this explanation, just accept that limiting beliefs can help you grow in ways that would not otherwise be possible. Embrace that your limiting beliefs will be your teachers. They are the kind of teachers that can be harsh, critical, and demanding. But they will serve as a catalyst that allows you to perform beyond your expectations. When you hear them entering your house uninvited, just say, "Oh, glad to see you, come in. I know all you want is for me to win, and win more. But I also know you are coming from a place of fear—fear that I will fail. Let's talk about that. What would you like to drink?"

2. Adopt an attitude that your participation in sport is all about learning. If you win you learn, if you lose you learn, if you tie you learn. Having such an attitude is one good way to stay off the emotional roller-coaster. To use the lawn analogy again: we treat our lawns in the spring so there will be no weeds in the summer. Same with cultivating your attitude. View every day as an opportunity to learn and be grateful for what you learn, regardless of the results. And remember to look for progress, not perfection, because some days this learning idea will seem like happy horse crap.

3. See the work that it takes to pull weeds out by the roots as a journey—a lifelong journey. Because after removing one weed, you will find another. A pitcher may not have confidence in his curve ball against a left-handed batter when the count is 3-0. Both the pitcher and the catcher know the curve ball is the pitch of choice in that situation, but the pitcher has a deep-seated doubt and so compensates by throwing a different pitch. With work, the pitcher can learn to believe in and rely on the curve ball regardless of the situation. However, next the pitcher will run

into another self-limiting belief—that he cannot throw an off-speed pitch when the pressure is on. And the process will continue, with more and more weeds to pull. This is the beauty of the journey. As you can probably guess, this philosophy also applies to the game of life.

4. Sit with your coach or sport psychologist and make a list of your self-limiting beliefs, no matter how embarrassing they may seem. Put them under the microscope. It works the same way as shining light on gremlins and dousing them with water—it kills them. (See the movie *Gremlins* if you do not remember.) Bringing your limiting beliefs into the light will immensely help you understand the process. Only when you put them front and center will you and others appreciate their strength. And doing so will free you from their toxic effects.

5. Start to set daily goals to develop confidence that you have the skill set you need to perform beyond your expectations. Yes, set specific daily goals to improve every aspect of your game, leaving no stone unturned. As you move the sticks, so to speak, your limiting beliefs will begin to dissolve. The weeds will start to dry up as they would if they had not been fed or watered for months. Not quickly, because they are much more tenacious than Kentucky bluegrass. But they will start to die. For details on setting and pursuing goals, reread chapter 7 and check out the goal-setting form included in appendix 3.

6. Visualize yourself achieving your daily goals. As your confidence improves, start visualizing exactly where you are smashing your limiting beliefs. Over and over again, day after day, visualize in such a way that you see, feel, and trust yourself performing beyond your expectations. And as you do so, believe in what you are experiencing. To take it a step further, at the end of your visualization session, take a few minutes to silently remind yourself what you know is true about your skills, gifts, abilities, and talents.

Let the words soak in deeply. While you are in a state of relaxed concentration, your words will serve as a better weed-killer than positive self-talk strategies. Self-talk will typically bounce off the trampoline of your mind while protecting the limiting beliefs, whereas this deep visualization process will help you root them out where they live. (See chapter 9 for details on visualization training.)

7. Allow yourself to ask for help and to receive regular hugs. By this I mean develop a team—a band of brothers and sisters—that understands your journey and believes in you. They might believe in you more than you do yourself. In my experience, being stubborn and driven by a competitive, self-willed style kept me from asking for help. I did not assemble the kind of team I needed on my own, but somehow these teammates emerged in my life at interesting times and stood by my side as I attempted to pull weeds. Just when I would say, "The beliefs are too deep. They are in my blood, in my bone marrow. This is the way it is," these teammates, Dennis and George in particular, would smile, shake their heads in disagreement, and give me a hug. It was enough to inspire me and give me hope. On my own, I could have never done it. And you cannot and do not have to do it alone either. So take off your armor, put your sword in the ground, and surrender to win. Accept that the act of enlisting support is an act of courage.

8. Take time to rest, because the process of change can be exhausting work. Pace yourself, get a massage, listen to nurturing music, have regular acupuncture treatments, go for long walks, indulge in the progressive muscle relaxation exercise. (An audio recording of this exercise is available for purchase on my website, www.goldmedalmind.com.) Get after it, crush it—but also rest, being mindful this is a lifelong process.

The Truth About Self-Limiting Beliefs

Smashing self-limiting beliefs and performing beyond your expectations are what I think sport, and life, are all about. Sport, with the emphasis on the scoreboard, provides an ideal place for self-limiting beliefs to surface. Because there are objective measures by which to evaluate yourself, the pressure can be immense. This state of affairs leads to Self 1 running wild, challenging you to the core. Faced with a situation in which you must achieve a certain score in gymnastics (or figure skating or diving) will put you to the test. If you have to execute a skill you are not entirely confident about, doubts and worries can arise, and if they are strong enough, they will take you out of your zone-like state in a matter of seconds.

The truth about self-limiting beliefs is they can be stubborn. They can bring us to our knees and bring tears to our eyes. In the presence of recurrent injuries, for example, limiting beliefs can be strengthened because you are vulnerable. Confidence is compromised when one is injured. At such a time, the idea of smashing limiting beliefs can be ridiculous to consider. And that is when it gets tragic, because when you start to believe you will not make the Olympic team, it is likely you will not. The tragedy occurs when we want to give up. In the men's locker room of my high school there was a sign on the wall that read, "The ugliest four letter word is quit." Those words are tattooed on my brain.

Let us call this state of identifying with and believing in the words that limit us a crisis. It is a crisis because confusion, frustration, and impatience can fertilize and help limiting beliefs take root. But as we learn from Eastern philosophies, crisis also leads to opportunity. When you adopt a belief in opportunity, you will become a warrior. Now you can put on armor, take up the sword, and go to war with a heart that is fully engaged. Recklessness will fuel your attack on your limiting beliefs. Surrender or defeat will not occupy a single brain cell. With people around you who also believe, there will be no stopping you. That is the real thrill of victory we used to hear about in the introduction to the classic show *Wide World of Sports.* Remember the thrill of victory and the agony of defeat? With the words "agony of defeat" came the scene of the great skier Vinko Bogataj crashing spectacularly as he came off the high jump in the 1970 Winter Olympics. (You can check it out on YouTube.) For any athlete who blows it, this kind of crisis is the time to dig down deep and come out fighting. It is an opportunity to soar with the eagles, because next time around, it will be a glorious fight to perform beyond expectations.

The mythological Greek figure Icarus was told not to fly too close to the sun because his wings would fall off and he would crash to his death. In my opinion, that is just conventional wisdom. To smash self-limiting beliefs, we must transcend what seems logical. If you fly close to the sun, flap your wings so rapidly there is no chance you will fall. Strive to fly right past the sun as she looks on in bewilderment, wondering if you have lost your mind. And that is exactly what it takes. You have to lose your mind to gain a new one, as Joseph Dispenza writes so eloquently in his book *Evolve Your Brain: The Science of Changing Your Mind.* Lose the mind filled with limiting beliefs, and gain a new one by thinking in ways that make your brain cells fire in a different direction, where you start to consistently think in terms of possibilities.

But once you smash one set of self-limiting beliefs, the beauty is you will come face-to-face with a new set. When you at last believe you can win not just one but two gold medals, you may run into a new weed that says you cannot set a world record. That is awesome! Because it is exactly where you want to be. That is the gift of sport in action. Smashing self-limiting beliefs, only to run into more. By performing with a fully engaged heart and being reckless in your approach, you will experience the blessings sport has to offer—growing and growing some more, moving through the barriers in your mind, time and time again. Is this not what life is all about?

This ongoing practice leads to the development of an athletic and personal identity based on courage. Operating with this philosophy will lead to the psychological victories I have referred to throughout this book. Regardless of whether you make the Olympic team, win a medal, or set a world record, you will know you left it all on the court. This is what being an athlete is all about. This is the epitome of a gold medal mind, striving and fighting to perform in a way in which you know, no matter what the score, that you used your mind as an ally, and resisted the temptation to give toxic thoughts oceanfront property in your mind. You won against your toughest opponent—yourself.

It is my hope you will come to realize that smashing self-limiting beliefs to perform beyond your expectations makes being an athlete really, really fun. Believing that approaching your sport with a wild heart will lead to the most fun you have ever experienced. You will create pure enjoyment and joy, something we rarely experience in life, on a daily basis. Take my word for it; this is when you will truly have a blast. So when one day you are preparing for a training run and the weather is brutal, windy as heck, and raining like crazy, you will not have a single thought of dread about the run. You will look out the window, smile, and embrace the challenge as an opportunity to surprise yourself by having one of your best training runs under the circumstances. Again, the mere fact that you opted for this perspective will be a psychological victory in every sense of the word!

This may seem like crazy thinking to some, but it is the essence of sport and the true nature of competition. Your real sport is developing a gold medal mind and becoming a psychologically skilled athlete. This is your real journey as an athlete. Play with this idea. I mean have fun with the struggles of adopting a new philosophy about what sport and being an athlete is all about. Try it, and you will surprise yourself. You will experience a shift in how you see yourself, the world, and other people. And, as a result, you truly will win more on the scoreboard as the transformation begins to happen. Remember the paradox I have talked about throughout this book: letting go of the outcome and focusing on the process is the real answer to winning on the scoreboard.

As I have said time and time again, learning the way of the gold medal mind will serve you well in all arenas. Long after your competitive career is over, the world will continue to provide you with opportunities to use your gold medal mind to navigate the rapids of life. Life will become your sport, with crisis to your left, right, and straight ahead. There will be battles to fight. But instead of getting stressed out, losing sleep, turning to alcohol, getting angry, and developing hypertension, you will smile and engage your heart, mind, and soul, using all the tools you picked up in the process of developing your gold medal mind.

A popular saying in Twelve-Step circles is, "Don't quit before the miracle happens." I believe you have what it takes to bring your "patience muscle" to the weight room every other day for the rest of your life. You now realize this muscle is what will allow you to perform beyond your expectations in all aspects of life. I take great pleasure in knowing you will experience the gift of a gold medal mind as a result of engaging your courageous heart on a daily basis. Don't try too hard. Play with the ideas and the skills in this book, get out of your own way, let go, and allow the changes to occur. Be amazed, surprised, and thrilled that you are not only becoming the athlete you wanted to be, but also the person you always imagined you could be. Trust that you have what it takes, regardless of the challenge, because there is no winning or losing, just learning, learning, and more learning. Enjoy the way of the gold medal mind, and you will have more fun than ever before, on and off the field.

APPENDIX 1

Recommended Reading

Bach, Richard. 1970. *Jonathan Livingston Seagull.* New York: Scribner.

Bell, Keith F. 1983. *Championship Thinking: The Athlete's Guide to Winning Performance in All Sports.* Englewood Cliffs, NY: Prentice Hall.

Bell, Keith F. 1982. *Winning Isn't Normal.* Austin, TX: Keel Publications.

Bode, Richard. 1993. *First You Have to Row a Little Boat.* New York: Warner Books, Inc.

Carson, Richard D. 2008. *A Master Class in Gremlin Taming.* New York: HarperCollins.

Coffey, Wayne R. 2005. *The Boys of Winter: The Untold Story of a Coach, a Dream, and the 1980 U.S. Olympic Hockey Team.* New York: Three Rivers Press.

> For the short cut, you can watch the movie *Miracle.* But I suggest reading the book first and watching some of the many YouTube videos. To learn more about the coach, Herb Brooks, read *Herb Brooks: The Inside Story of a Hockey Mastermind* by John Gilbert.

Johnson, Crockett. 2015. *Harold and the Purple Crayon.* New York: HarperCollins.

Originally published in 1955, this remains a classic for people of all ages. The moral of the story: you always have a "purple crayon" to help you create the life you want to live.

Dispenza, Joe. 2014. *You Are the Placebo: Making Your Mind Matter.* New York: Hay House.

Frankl, Viktor E. 2006. *Man's Search for Meaning.* Boston: Beacon Press.

Originally published in 1959, this book was listed in 1991 as one of the top 10 most influential books in the United States by The Library of Congress. It offers profound insights for athletes and non-athletes alike. Note some parts may be disturbing due to the amount of torture the prisoners experienced.

Gallwey, W. Timothy. 2008. *The Inner Game of Tennis.* London: Pan Books.

Originally published in 1974. This was the book that turned me onto the mind-body connection at the age of 13.

Gendlin, Eugene. 1981. *Focusing.* New York: Bantam Dell.

Gibran, Kahlil. 1923. *The Prophet.* New York: A.A. Knopf.

Hesse, Hermann. 1972. *Siddhartha.* London: Lotus Group.

This is another book with something to offer everyone, but especially the athlete 16 or older and those retiring from sport.

Hemingway, Ernest. 1952. *The Old Man and the Sea.* New York: Scribner.

Herrigel, Eugen, and Daisetz T. Suzuki. 1971. *Zen in the Art of Archery.* New York: Vintage Books.

Hoff, Benjamin. 1983. *The Tao of Pooh.* New York: Penguin Books.

In a symbolic way, this book addresses the way we typically operate—on or off the field—using more RPMs than we need.

Jackson, Phil, and Hugh Delehanty. 2006. *Sacred Hoops: Spiritual Lessons of a Hardwood Warrior.* New York: Hachette Books.

Jackson, Phil, and Hugh Delehanty. 2013. *Eleven Rings: The Soul of Success.* New York: The Penguin Press.

Support for the use of meditation by the athlete. Among other topics, Jackson explains his use of meditation with the Bulls and the Lakers. Kobe Bryant has talked on NPR about his continued use of meditation.

Kabat-Zinn, Jon. 1994. *Wherever You Go There You Are: Mindfulness Meditation in Everyday Life.* New York: Hyperion.

A user manual for the student of mindfulness meditation.

Kauss, David R. 2000. *Mastering Your Inner Game.* Champaign, IL: Human Kinetics.

Millman, Dan. 2006. *The Journeys of Socrates: An Adventure.* New York: HarperCollins.

Millman, Dan. 2000. *The Way of the Peaceful Warrior.* Novato, CA: HJ Kramer. Originally published in 1980.

Millman, Dan. 2007. *Wisdom of the Peaceful Warrior: A Companion to the Book That Changes Lives.* Novato, CA: HJ Kramer.

This book will help you learn to be your own Socrates.

Mumford, George. 2015. *The Mindful Athlete.* Berkeley, CA: Parallax Press.

The author of this book is Phil Jackson's right hand man. Jackson's wife met George Mumford at the Omega Institute in New York state (a place to consider doing retreats and/or taking classes).

Ohno, Apolo. 2010. *Zero Regrets: Be Greater Than Yesterday.* New York: Atria.

Apolo Ohno has written an inspiring story about his journey, a brilliant example of what it means to "go to any lengths" and be willing to "die before going to heaven."

Raisman, Aly. 2018. *Fierce: How Competing For Myself Changed Everything.* New York: Little Brown and Company.

The title of this book speaks for itself. It may take time for you to truly feel and embrace what a profound experience it is to compete for yourself.

Reynolds, Peter H. *Ish (Creatrilogy).* 2004. Somerset, MA: Candlewick Press.

Here's a fun example of why perfectionism is not always necessary.

Silverstein, Shel. *The Giving Tree.* 2004. New York: HarperCollins.

This book offers a clear illustration of how important it is to support and inspire your teammates and even your coaches.

Vienne, Veronique. 1998. *The Art of Doing Nothing.* New York: Random House.

At least consider these three chapters: "The Art of Breathing," "The Art of Napping," and "The Art of Listening."

Williams, Margery. 2013. *The Velveteen Rabbit.* Kennebunkport, ME: Applesauce Press.

This is a good reminder that you can be your own Nursery Magic Fairy and be open to the Nursery Magic Fairies around you. Originally published in 1922.

Wood, Douglas. 2003. *Old Turtle and the Broken Truth.* New York: Scholastic Press.

A clear explanation of the power of wisdom.

Worthington, Everett L., Jr. 2003. *Forgiving and Reconciling: Bridges to Wholeness and Hope.* Downer's Grove, IL: InterVarsity Press.

Worthington, Everett L., Jr. 2013. *Moving Forward: Six Steps to Forgiving Yourself and Breaking Free from the Past.* Colorado Springs, CO: WaterBrook Press.

Song

Kenny Rogers, vocalist, "The Greatest," by Don Schlitz, released April 17, 1999, on *She Rides Wild Horses,* Dreamcatcher Records.

Poem

Kipling, Rudyard. "If." *Rewards and Fairies.* NY: Doubleday, 1910.

APPENDIX 2

Resources

The Gold Medal Mind Workbook: Training as Hard Psychologically As You Do Physically

by Douglas Jowdy, PhD

After reading *The Gold Medal Mind*, you will have learned a great deal—enough to put into practice immediately, perhaps. However, becoming truly psychologically skilled requires rehearsal of the information contained in the book. I created *The Gold Medal Mind Workbook* to help you develop "psychological muscle memory." Think of a gold medal mind as the equivalent of a physical body that performs like a finely tuned machine. The development of your physical muscle memory took thousands of hours of rehearsal, and developing psychological muscle memory is no different. For example, achieving and maintaining a zone-like state when the pressure is on is a skill that takes practice in order for you to internalize it. "Practicing" with *The Gold Medal Mind Workbook* not just once, but a few times, will ensure this happens, and you will find yourself enjoying your sport more than you even imagined you could. *The Gold Medal Mind Workbook* is available for purchase through Amazon.

The Gold Medal Mind website

On *The Gold Medal Mind* website (www.goldmedalmind.com), I have made available a number of audio recordings to help you with your mental training. These are designed to guide you easily through progressive muscle relaxation, concentration training, and visualization exercises. I have also made available a recording of a guided relaxation exercise designed to help you get a good night's sleep.

On my professional website (www.drdougjowdy.com), you will find short articles about dealing with injury, confidence, and visualization training.

The Horse and the Man: A Short Story by Douglas Jowdy, PhD

I encourage you to read this short story I wrote to reinforce some of the principles I talk about in *The Gold Medal Mind.* The story captures the essence of the gold medal mind, illustrated by the example of the horse. The man in the story has a mind consistent with the hard-driving nature of most athletes. Questions for reflection appear at the end of the story. *The Horse and the Man: A Short Story* is available for purchase through Amazon or as an audio recording on my website (www.goldmedalmind.com).

HeartMath Institute

HeartMath Institute is a nonprofit organization that researches and develops scientifically based tools to bridge the connection between heart and mind. They offer a number of simple mental and emotional self-regulation tools that can help you on your journey to a gold medal mind. Their Inner Balance Bluetooth device, for example, uses your heart rhythm to give you real-time feedback on the degree to which you have reached a state of relaxed concentration.

After you have practiced concentration training for a while, consider using a HeartMath or Muse device (described below) to hone your abilities. The real-time feedback can make the process of learning to focus really fun.

Visit www.heartmath.com to learn more about their products, and www.heartmath.org for literature describing their theories and research.

Muse

Muse (www.choosemuse.com) provides more options for improving your ability to remain calm and focused. Muse describes their devices as "brain fitness tools" that measure brain activity and translate it into real-time feedback that guides you to a state of calm focus. See www.choosemuse.com for more information on the products and how they can help you.

Everett Worthington

Ev Worthington, a former professor of mine at Virginia Commonwealth University, has become an international expert on the "sport" of forgiveness, including self-forgiveness. I can't find words to describe the magnitude of his competence, integrity, and love. Should you need assistance with the sport of forgiveness, I encourage you to visit Ev's website (www.evworthington-forgiveness.com).

APPENDIX 3

Goal-Setting Form (a.k.a. North Star Form)

The goal-setting forms on the following pages are intended to give you a concrete method for pinpointing goals and identifying obstacles to achieving them. The forms are meant to serve as a template, and you may find it helpful to tweak them in some ways.

How to Use the Forms

The important thing to understand right now is that you will be practicing a kind of "reverse engineering" in your goal-setting process. After identifying your North Star, your level of belief that you can achieve it, and potential obstacles to getting there, you will then work backward to set yearly, monthly, and weekly goals until you arrive at today.

I cannot emphasize enough that all of your goals, both outcome- and process-oriented, should come from your heart, the most powerful performance-enhancing drug. They must be based upon the fire inside—what you *want* to do versus what you feel you should or have to do. (More on want versus should soon.) Review chapter 7, "Making Your North Star a Reality," for specific suggestions on setting daily psychological and physical goals.

Below are step-by-step guidelines on making the form work for you. There are two basic ways to use it. You can make copies of each page of the form and write on them directly, making more copies for your daily, weekly, and monthly goals as you progress. Alternately, type them up on your computer as simple templates to use again and again. Remember you can tweak the form to fit your needs. For example, if you would like to list more than my suggested number of targets and obstacles for a particular time period, feel free to do so.

Day after day, in your warrior journal, keep track of your progress. It is most crucial to keep track of your daily and weekly goals here. You can then refer back to the monthly goals and track the next week and days in the journal. Every month, identify three more goals for that month, taking it one month at a time based upon how things are going with your daily and weekly goals. And depending on your daily progress, you may find yourself changing your monthly and yearly goals to meet higher standards than the ones you had when you started your journey.

Your North Star

Identify your North Star goals—your ultimate wishes, dreams, or desires. These are outcome- or scoreboard-oriented goals. For example:

"Play professional soccer."

"Win a gold medal."

"Win the state championship."

Then identify your belief level, the degree to which you believe you can achieve your North Star goals. Rate your belief on a 1 to 10 scale, in which 1 indicates total doubt and 10 represents no doubt. Next, identify potential obstacles to achieving your North Star (e.g., getting injured, losing confidence, being too self-critical, overtraining and under-recovery, having an overtly abusive coach or poor work ethic—you get the picture). These obstacles will help inform your monthly, weekly, and daily goals. Just identify them for now.

When you start this process, it is normal to find your belief level is not on the higher end of the scale. As you work through the form and get to the point at which you are breaking down targets, identifying daily goals, and using the practice and competition reflection form, you will have more insight on how strongly you believe you can achieve your North Star and other outcome-oriented goals.

I've included space for three North Star goals on the form, but feel free to list fewer (or more). The point is to make this work for you.

Targets for a Year From Now

These four targets are outcome-oriented goals you wish to achieve by the end of next year. For example:

"Score X number of points."

"Batting percentage of XXX."

"Finish first in the league."

"Win the MVP award."

At this time, the obstacles you identify will provide you with information that may guide your monthly and weekly targets and daily goals. For example, in bowling, if you always start doubting yourself in the ninth frame, you can set a monthly goal to put that tendency to rest, and weekly and daily goals to help you achieve it.

I've included space for four targets for the year on the form, but again, you can list more or fewer as desired.

Targets for the Next Month

These five targets can have a combination of process- and outcome-oriented elements. For example:

"Meet with my batting coach twice a week."

"Run X number of miles."

"Play eight practice matches."

"Read three sport psychology books."

"Complete the first three chapters in *The Gold Medal Mind Workbook.*"

Note that these goals are outcome-oriented in that there are objective measures that will determine if you followed through or not. They also provide direction for the specific steps (process) you will take to achieve the monthly targets, which in turn will help you identify weekly goals and the steps to take on a daily basis to work toward those outcomes. For example, if you tend to neglect aspects of your program that will prevent overtraining and injury, they can become part of your daily goals. You may have the tendency to overtrain as a result of guilt you experience when you take time to rest. But you know your risk of injury will be higher if you do not rest. Your tendency to overtrain is an obstacle that will serve to inform your daily goals directly. You might set a daily goal to take your resting heart rate in the morning (or whatever your coach uses as a barometer for overtraining), and if it is too high, modify your workout. Or your daily goal may be to be mindful to have a thorough warm up and cool-down to help prevent injury, or to use heat and ice to help with your recovery. Or you may set a psychological goal to manage the feelings of guilt that cause you to overtrain in the first place.

The monthly targets are meant to inspire you to take steps on a daily basis based upon the fact that you believe, without much doubt, that they will be realized. Believing strongly that you can achieve your monthly targets frees your mind up to focus on your daily goals. At this stage of the game, if your belief level is not at least an 8, you may want to consider revising the target. It is important that you strongly believe you can achieve your monthly targets before you move forward.

Say you have a monthly goal of improving your ability to get into and maintain a zone-like state during competition (note here that you are trying to improve your *ability*—remember, progress, not perfection). Your weekly goals may include some of the following:

- Practice concentration training once a day for 15 minutes, twice if I have time.
- Use informal ways of practicing concentration training on a daily basis. For example, upon waking up, take 10 deep complete breaths before getting out of bed. (See chapter 8 for more suggestions for informal concentration training.)
- During warm ups, when stretching, use the time as a form of concentration training. (See appendix 6 for instructions on how to do this.)
- Take 10 minutes after a workout to visualize getting back into a zone-like state during the times I lost focus during the workout.

Be sure to identify the specific weekly goals that will result in you achieving your monthly target. As you keep track of your experience on a daily basis, you can then set new goals for the following week. After two or three weeks, you will have the information you need to set targets for the next month.

Daily Goals

Now the real fun starts. Daily goals are all process oriented and can address both physical/biomechanical areas and psychological targets. I encourage you to look back at the North Star chapter and review my suggestions for daily goals to see how specific they are. For example, for a gymnast on a beam, a daily physical goal might be to repeat to yourself, "rib cage up." A daily psychological goal can be "every 15 minutes, use my breath, a word, soft gaze, or an image to keep my zone level high." I used the zone example here because achieving your monthly, yearly, and North Star goals depends largely on your ability to achieve and maintain a zone-like state, and daily practice is required. Developing your zone muscle requires you to rack up psychological victories every day. Ideally, learning to achieve and maintain a zone-like state should be a daily goal for all of us!

At the end of the day, come back to the daily goal form and answer the question at the bottom: "What did I learn today?" Below are some examples of answers from fellow pilgrims with whom I have walked side by side:

> "I am very impatient when practicing concentration training. But boy, I am learning more than I thought about myself by attempting to sit still every day."

> "This is getting too intense; I need a break for a few days. Maybe even some sofa training."

> "Setting daily goals, visualizing them happening in the morning, reviewing them at night, and setting goals for the next day keeps me focused and allows me to have more fun."

> "A big obstacle is procrastination...I am not getting my homework done early enough so I am not getting enough sleep and I'm tired all day. I need to manage time better so I can get the sleep I need."

> "This idea of really feeling, in my heart, that I will achieve my monthly targets is hard. What can I do differently, so I can bring my belief from my head to my heart?"

Reflections on the Process

The purpose of pinpointing your North Star, goals for the year and month, respective obstacles, and your belief level is to help you identify highly specific, positive, realistic, believable, weekly and daily goals. As you review your progress at the end of the week (every Sunday night, for example), you will gain more information as to how to realize your monthly goals, yearly goals, and subsequently, your North Star.

This is a simple process, but there is more to it than meets the eye. Throughout my more than 30 years of professional experience, I have found that instructions on goal setting consistently fail to address the nitty-gritty: what outcomes inspire you, how much you believe in your ability to achieve them, what obstacles will inform what you do today, and how and when you will do it. The gold-medal-mind approach requires being specific, comprehensive, and methodical. Getting absorbed in your daily goals, one day at a time, is the way to amass the psychological victories that ultimately will result in achieving—if not surpassing—your outcome targets. And consistently practicing concentration training will develop your ability to focus on today, without worrying about your monthly target(s). Concentration training is intimately related to the goal-setting process, and again, I strongly encourage you to make it an essential part of your psychological training.

The North Star approach will provide the opportunity for you to be "rigorously honest" with yourself on a regular basis. If you feel you would benefit from further exploration of any part of this process, I would be happy to schedule a time for us to meet in person or via technology.

NORTH STAR GOAL

Your North Star:

1. ______________________________

2. ______________________________

3. ______________________________

Belief Level:

(Total doubt) 1 2 3 4 5 6 7 8 9 10 *(Total belief)*

Potential Obstacle(s):

____

____

____

____

____

____

____

TARGETS FOR THE YEAR

Target 1:

____

Belief Level:

(Total doubt) 1 2 3 4 5 6 7 8 9 10 *(Total belief)*

Potential Obstacle(s):

____

____

____

____

____

____

____

____

____

____

Yearly Target 2:

____

Belief Level:

(Total doubt) 1 2 3 4 5 6 7 8 9 10 *(Total belief)*

Potential Obstacle(s):

____

____

____

____

____

____

____

____

Yearly Target 3:

____

Belief Level:

(Total doubt) 1 2 3 4 5 6 7 8 9 10 *(Total belief)*

Potential Obstacle(s):

____

____

____

____

____

____

____

____

Yearly Target 4:

____

Belief Level:

(Total doubt) 1 2 3 4 5 6 7 8 9 10 *(Total belief)*

Potential Obstacle(s):

____

____

____

____

____

____

____

____

TARGETS FOR THE NEXT MONTH

Target 1:

____

Belief Level:

(Total doubt) 1 2 3 4 5 6 7 8 9 10 *(Total belief)*

Potential Obstacle(s):

____

____

____

____

____

____

____

____

____

____

Monthy Target 2:

___

Belief Level:

(Total doubt) 1 2 3 4 5 6 7 8 9 10 *(Total belief)*

Potential Obstacle(s):

___

___

___

___

___

___

___

___

Monthly Target 3:

____

Belief Level:

(Total doubt) 1 2 3 4 5 6 7 8 9 10 *(Total belief)*

Potential Obstacle(s):

____

____

____

____

____

____

____

____

DAILY TARGETS FOR THE NEXT WEEK

Target 1:

____

Belief Level:

(Total doubt) 1 2 3 4 5 6 7 8 9 10 *(Total belief)*

Potential Obstacle(s):

____

____

____

____

____

____

____

____

____

____

Daily Target 2:

____

Belief Level:

(Total doubt) 1 2 3 4 5 6 7 8 9 10 *(Total belief)*

Potential Obstacle(s):

____

____

____

____

____

____

____

____

Daily Target 3:

___

Belief Level:

(Total doubt) 1 2 3 4 5 6 7 8 9 10 *(Total belief)*

Potential Obstacle(s):

___

___

___

___

___

___

___

___

Daily Target 4:

____

Belief Level:

(Total doubt) 1 2 3 4 5 6 7 8 9 10 *(Total belief)*

Potential Obstacle(s):

____

____

____

____

____

____

____

____

GOALS FOR TODAY

Target 1:

____

Belief Level:

(Total doubt) 1 2 3 4 5 6 7 8 9 10 *(Total belief)*

Potential Obstacle(s):

____

____

____

____

____

____

____

____

____

____

Today's Target 2:

Belief Level:

(Total doubt) 1 2 3 4 5 6 7 8 9 10 *(Total belief)*

Potential Obstacle(s):

Reflection: what did I learn today?

APPENDIX 4

Practice (and Competition) Reflection Form

PSYCHOLOGICAL FOCAL POINT RATING SCALE

	(low)						*(high)*
Intensity	1	2	3	4	5	6	7
Perseverance	1	2	3	4	5	6	7
Refocusing	1	2	3	4	5	6	7
Attitude	1	2	3	4	5	6	7
Confidence	1	2	3	4	5	6	7
Composure	1	2	3	4	5	6	7
Zone	1	2	3	4	5	6	7
Enjoyment	1	2	3	4	5	6	7

Your Physical/Technical Focal Points

1. ____

2. ____

3. ____

Questions for Reflection

What did you do well? ____________________________

____

____

What would you like to improve? ______________________

____

____

What did you learn about yourself?_____________________

____

____

About the Practice (and Competition) Reflection Form

The purpose of using a practice monitoring form is to help you improve your performance through a process of increasing your awareness of and focus on key focal points, both physical and psychological. In the book, I make reference to using such a form in a number of ways. When you are setting goals, you can use the form as a way to track your daily progress. You can use the same form to reflect on your performance in practice and in competitions. How you use it will depend on your own goals and needs (both physical and psychological) in various situations. The form provided here is merely a template; you can focus on completely different areas from the ones listed here.

There is science to support the use of a tool like this for modifying behavior. The book *Self-Directed Behavior: Self-Modification for Personal Adjustment* by Watson and Tharp (2013) describes in depth how self-monitoring can lead to change. Long story short, the mechanism at work is called reactivity. Here are some examples of the principle of reactivity in action. If you are trying to drink more water, your chances will be much better if you increase awareness of your water intake by writing down the amount you drink every day. People experiencing a depression will become more aware of negative, helpless, and hopeless thought patterns by writing down exactly what they are telling themselves when the thoughts strike. Simply writing them down decreases the frequency, intensity, and duration of negative thinking. To help people stop procrastinating, I have them write down what they are thinking and feeling at the exact moment they believe their procrastination starts. This alone decreases procrastination.

Why does it work, and how will it help improve your performance? When you know you will be rating various target areas after performing, you will bring a higher level of awareness into practice or competition. Yes, it is that simple, and that powerful.

The Psychological Focal Point Rating Scale

The purpose of the rating scale is to increase your level of awareness of what I call focal points. These are factors that you identify as key to helping you improve in your psychological target areas. A heightened awareness of important psychological factors that are relevant to you will significantly increase the likelihood of you performing beyond your expectations.

I have chosen to call these psychological factors focal points for a specific reason. If you think back to my instructions on concentration and visualization training, you may recall I ask you to start your practice by looking at a focal point with a soft gaze. I suggest you be aware of this focal point, but not overthink it. I want you to apply the same approach to the psychological focal points you have identified here. Think about them with a "soft gaze," remaining aware of them but not overthinking. This will lead you to the same state of absorption I described in the text. As you know, absorption is at the heart of the zone-like state you want to achieve. Be patient, as this may take time and practice.

On the sample form I have provided here, I have listed the psychological focal points that were most helpful for a particular athlete with whom I worked. You may find them useful too, but it is up to you to identify the specific areas that you want to develop. After reading the book (and especially if you complete the accompanying workbook), you should be highly in touch with what your psychological targets are. If you still are uncertain, ask a teammate or coach what he or she thinks you would benefit from improving. I can say with certainty that "zone" is a target that applies to everyone, because this is always a work in progress and can be extremely difficult for many people. I suggest you strongly consider making "enjoyment" part of your lineup too, simply because the zone comes naturally when you are having fun and in a good mood.

Using the 7-point rating scale to look closely at the psychological attributes consistent with ideal performance will help you "lock in" to factors you have identified as critical to your performance. What shows that you are locked in? Ratings of 6 or higher on the scale might indicate you are aware of your daily targets and are executing in a manner consistent with composure, for example. You can think of a 1 as absolutely forgetting about your target areas, while a 7 would mean you are remaining conscious and mindful throughout practice or competition when using a strategy to refocus, for example.

For those of you who will benefit from operationalizing the 7-point scale, you can think of the numbers in the following way.

1–2: You are not thinking much about your focal points.

3–4: You are aware of the areas during practice or competition, but not locking in consistently (maybe only 50 percent of the time).

5–6: You are really keeping your focal points in the oceanfront property of your mind, and doing your best to meet your standards.

7: Your focus is great, not perfect, but great. If you allow yourself to "color outside the lines," an 8 or higher would be closer to what you believe is perfection.

Note that your rating can be higher than 7. Don't hold back. I know many of you will have a hard time giving yourself a 7, regardless of how well you do (this includes me, too). Kick that tendency to the curb. Rating yourself a 7 (or 8, or even 9) is not about perfection, but rather about celebrating the effort you made to focus your attention on intensity, for example, as consistently as possible during a given practice or competition. Giving yourself credit where credit is due is at the heart of developing a gold medal mind. But I have worked with many athletes over the years who would not, under any circumstances, give themselves a 7 on certain focal points (confidence being a big one). Remember, one way your inner critic will manifest is by not allowing you to circle the 7 (or 8 or 9). This is something to reflect on. If you find you are having a hard time giving yourself high scores, ask yourself the question: "What is the invisible force that kicks my pen off the 7 when I know I deserve it?"

If you find that your ratings are consistently on the low side, and that you are at a loss for what to do, several options are available. Reread the section of the book or workbook that relates to your focal point. Listen to the recordings available on the Gold Medal Mind website to improve your focusing skills. Think of your ability to concentrate as if it were a muscle. The more you train that muscle, the more likely you will have ratings of 5 to as high as 8. Reviewing the goal-setting form may help you modify some of your focal points. Another idea is to speak with a fellow athlete who is also on the path of the gold medal mind and using this form. That person may offer suggestions that will be helpful. Consulting with your coaches also can potentially assist you in increasing your ratings. And finally, strongly consider consulting with a sport psychologist.

Your Physical/Technical Focal Points

These focal points will be specific to biomechanical factors you want to improve on. A gymnast on beam may identify "chest up" or "rib cage up" as physical focal areas. A runner could focus on "drive with my back leg" when going up hills. And a tennis player may target "rotation" during a serve. These are the very specific and sometimes subtle mechanical factors your coach harps on constantly. When you bring greater awareness to these ways of moving your body, your skill level will increase. With an increase in skill level, consistency will follow, triggering a boost in your confidence and belief factor.

For several weeks, you may focus on a particular physical focal point until you internalize it and it becomes automatic. Then you can change your focus to something else you are not doing on a consistent basis.

Questions for Reflection

Your answers to these questions can apply to both physical and psychological targets.

What did you do well? Just as circling a 7 or higher on the rating scale may be difficult for competitive folks, identifying and writing down what you did well can be challenging. This is an opportunity to not take for granted what you are doing well. For example, even if your performance was not perfect, you might note that you made friends with Leroy and maintained ideal mechanics when you would have rather gotten sloppy because the pain was too much to handle.

What would you like to improve? Here you should identify areas for improvement from a perspective of patience and ease for yourself. This is not the time to take yourself to the whipping post. I have seen some athletes write things like, "I will never get my shot right." "When am I going to learn to keep my head down?" Or "I sucked today!" I understand these statements, but whipping yourself into right action typically does not work. Statements such as the following are most consistent with what I am suggesting as areas for improvement:

"Use visualization more consistently after coach gives me feedback."

"Trust myself more and taking those 3-point shots when I am hesitating."

"Use deep complete breaths prior to every jump."

"Use my calming cues words to avoid retaliating after a cheap shot."

"Leave my phone in the kitchen at night to help improve my sleep."

"Keep my hands up on defense."

"Focus on myself more during warm ups."

The idea is to be specific and honest about what you can improve on. Identifying areas for improvement can help with daily goal setting. It can set the stage for visualization training after practice, so you will be better able to see, feel, and trust yourself making the adjustments. If you see that the same behaviors keep creeping in, maybe it is time for private lessons, watching more video, staying longer after practice, talking with your coach or a sport psychologist, or some other strategy for improvement.

What did I learn about myself? This one may be challenging at first, but as your awareness increases, with time it will become second nature. When you entertain this question during practice or competition, you will start to notice you are becoming more open minded and teachable. Your thirst for learning about yourself as an athlete and a person will soar. Some examples:

"I am much more talented than I give myself credit for."

"I tend to be at my best when I just observe Self 1, and not try to fight with it."

"When I am more conscious during strength and conditioning, I really enjoy it."

"When I bring a smoothie to practice and drink a quarter-cup every hour, my energy is much better."

"I truly am a leader."

"There is no question I have what it takes to make this team."

"Using the soft gaze during warm-ups helps get me into a zone-like state."

If you find yourself uncomfortable stating something like, "I am a leader," but in fact truly believe you are a leader, write it down. Then reflect in your warrior journal about what you think leads to your discomfort in identifying your strengths. The athletic culture is one that emphasizes what you did not do and what you are not, and does little to encourage celebrating your psychological victories and strengths. This is up to you.

How to Use the Form

Make copies of the form and put them in different places (for example, in your athletic bag, locker, or warrior journal) or type it into your phone or computer. Remember that the form included here is merely a template; it is meant to be flexible, so you can alter the focus to explore whatever targets you are working on currently. What will remain the same are the questions posed at the bottom of the form: What did you do well? What would you like to improve? What did you learn about yourself?

Deciding when and exactly how to use the form will be up to you. You can use it when goal setting as a way to track your daily progress, or after competitions to review how consistently you focused on your psychological targets. The basic idea is to use it whenever you want to become more aware of improving in specific target areas—either physical or psychological. But how you use it will vary according to your situation. This is a bit challenging to address because of what we call "individual differences" in psychology. What works for one person might not work for another. When I am guiding someone on the journey of developing a gold medal mind, I have the opportunity to consistently monitor how the athlete is using the form and how it is going. Obviously, I cannot do that here. But having said that, here are my suggestions for making the form work for you.

1. Start out by using the form every day after practice for three weeks, and then evaluate your progress.

2. If it seems helpful, stay the course, modifying or changing your focal points as you internalize them, and continue to use the form after every practice. You can delete focal points you feel you are consistently doing well with over the course of several weeks.

3. As long as the form continues to be helpful, use it every day after practice in the spirit of knowing there is always room for more improvement—consistently staying in the zone, for example.

4. After you believe you have mastered a certain focal point—maintaining a high level of confidence during practice, for example—and have taken that focal point off the list, several weeks later you may find you are slipping back into negative thought patterns. If this happens, put confidence back on the list. Remember this is a work in progress with no finish line.

5. After about a month of consistently using the form after practice and experiencing results, start using the form after competitions.

6. After three or four competitions, evaluate and make any modifications or changes you feel will be beneficial. Asking for feedback from teammates and/or coaches may help you make the modifications you need to escalate your growth and development.

You may wish to consider consulting with a sport psychologist to facilitate your progress with the form. Remember, the form is not meant to be a test, but rather a mirror that reflects the degree to which you are internalizing your focal points. This process will be as enjoyable as staying the course with the goal-setting form that is also included here. Using the two forms in unison can increase your mastery of psychological and physical skills far beyond your expectations. Consider your use of this form as part of a work in progress.

My hope is you will use a modified version of the form well after "the dance is over," allowing your process of growth and development to continue over the course of your life. Enjoy!

APPENDIX 5

How to Create and Use a Warrior Journal

Throughout this book, I make reference to your warrior journal and suggest various writing assignments for it. Below are the instructions for creating this masterpiece, which you will probably have for quite some time, perhaps longer than any textbooks you might read over the years. Feel free to improvise in any way you think will most profoundly serve your growth and development.

1. Buy a hardcover, 8.5 x 11 inch journal with blank pages. You can find blank journals online, at art supply stores, or at Barnes & Noble and other bookstores.
2. On the inside of the cover, paste a picture of a person (e.g., a former teacher or coach), a place (e.g., a forest in the fall), or a thing (e.g., the Olympic rings) that provides you with inspiration or triggers good feelings—happiness, excitement, bliss, passion, joy, calm, peace, enthusiasm, courage, or any other positive mental or emotional state. You can always change or add to the image later.
3. Leave pages 1 and 2 blank for now. The purpose of these pages is to write down, every now and then, aspects of your life that you are grateful for. When you run out of space on these two pages, you can start from the last blank page in the journal and work forward. When your gratitude list

collides with your journal entries, you can start a journal dedicated to gratitude and appreciation. (Down the road I plan to write a book about these immensely powerful emotions and how they can change your life.)

4. On pages 3 through 5, write down some of your favorite quotations—lines that remind you what you believe, value, cherish, embrace, feel. You might want to include a few lines from a book you recently read, a poem, a Bible passage, song lyrics, lines from a movie—you get the idea.
5. On pages 6 through 8, add something *you* have written, something original. For inspiration, think of a word or two describing a concept that is important to you—for example, discipline, commitment, focus, the zone, challenge, letting go, mental toughness, love, belief, North Star, focus, composure. Write a few lines that bring your chosen concept to life so that you can actually *feel* (not just think about) the good sensations you associate with it. What you wish to write about may change as you learn and grow. In other words, what you write does not have to be perfect, and you can change or add to it later. Sit back, breathe easily, listen to music or watch a video that inspires you, and write what comes from your heart and mind. It may be helpful to chat with a teammate to explore the wide range of possible sources of inspiration that exist.

Here are some of my own favorite quotations:

> Just because a man lacks the use of his eyes doesn't mean he lacks vision.
>
> — Stevie Wonder

> The Lord that I serve says the impossible is unacceptable.
>
> — Stevie Wonder

(As a reminder, Stevie Wonder has recorded more than 30 US top-10 hits and received 25 GRAMMY Awards—the most ever awarded to a male solo artist. Stevie Wonder is blind and an outrageously accomplished keyboard player. Watch some YouTube clips of him in concert to really appreciate his talent.)

> Every good rowing coach, in his own way, imparts to his men the kind of self-discipline required to achieve the ultimate from mind, heart, and body. Which is why most ex-oarsmen will tell you they learned more fundamentally important lessons in the racing shell than in the classroom.
>
> — George Yeoman Pocock

> Our deepest fear is not that we are inadequate. Our deepest fear is that we are powerful beyond measure. It is our light, not our darkness that most frightens us. We ask ourselves, who am I to be brilliant, gorgeous, talented, fabulous? Actually, who are you not to be? You are a child of God. Your playing small doesn't serve the world. There's nothing enlightened about shrinking so that other people won't feel insecure around you. We are all meant to shine, as children do. We were born to make manifest the glory of God that is within us. It's not just in some of us; it's in everyone. And as we let our own light shine, we unconsciously give other people permission to do the same. As we are liberated from our own fear, our presence automatically liberates others.
>
> — Marianne Williamson

> Some of us have tried to hold on to our old ideas and the result was nil until we let go absolutely.
>
> — *The Big Book*, Alcoholics Anonymous

> If you can't fly then run, if you can't run then walk, if you can't walk then crawl, but whatever you do you have to keep moving forward.
>
> — Martin Luther King, Jr.

> Engrave this upon your heart: there isn't anyone you couldn't love once you heard their story.
>
> — Mary Lou Kownacki

The last one is my all-time favorite. Really understanding and embracing Kownacki's words will help you access the zone-like state on a consistent basis. Get down and really grapple with her words to gain insight into how intimately they relate to your own struggle to perform beyond your expectations. We can explore this in detail should you decide to meet with me in person or via FaceTime or Skype. In the meantime, just allow curiosity, wonder, and even amusement to guide your reflections on how her words might apply to sport.

6. Starting on page 10 of your warrior journal, identify the following:

    - Your end-of-season goals and the degree to which you believe you can achieve each of them (use a 1 to 10 scale in which 1 represents total doubt and 10 total belief)
    - What you see as the major obstacles to realizing your goals
    - Specific goals toward overcoming these potential obstacles
    - Your goals for the next week, both physical and psychological
    - Obstacles you may encounter in pursuing your goals for next week, and how you will overcome them

- Your goals for the next month, both physical and psychological
- Obstacles you may encounter in pursuing your goals for next month, and how you will overcome them

Reread chapter 7, "Making Your North Star a Reality," if you need extra help with the goal-setting process. I strongly suggest you use the goal-setting form I provide at the end of the book as a guide, as it will be a tremendous help with this aspect of your warrior journal.

7. On the inside of the back cover of the notebook (the hard cardboard page) write the lyrics of a song, paste in a photo, or add anything else that represents what you believe will occur as you take the path of the gold medal mind. You can add to this as you continue on your journey. My hope is that in some way, shape, or form, whatever you choose to paste in that spot will reflect the feelings of thrill, bliss, euphoria, satisfaction, meaning, and conquest you will experience as a result of becoming psychologically skilled.
8. On a daily basis, at the very least, write down the most beautiful thing you experienced that day and explain the impact it had on you.
9. Use the remaining pages, in no particular order, to work on exercises from the book. For example, when you feel it would be helpful, you may choose to answer some of the following questions:

- How is my concentration training going? What has been the impact on my performance both on and off the field?
- Have I been using my heart as a performance-enhancing drug? How is that going?
- What am I learning from this injury? What is helping me strengthen my patience muscle?

- How am I feeling about being more conscious of inspiring others?
- What have I been learning from my experience volunteering?
- How am I thinking about my North Star now?
- Are there ways I can have more fun?

Enjoy the journey!

APPENDIX 6

Additional Methods for Mental Conditioning

Formal concentration practice is about sitting still and sitting some more, as I described in chapter 8, "Thinking Less: A Psychological Lobotomy." But there are many ways to engage in what might be called informal practice. In chapter 8, I listed some simple suggestions for incorporating informal practice into daily life—for example, stopping to take a few deep breaths at various times during the day. Here are some other methods you can practice in order to develop your ability to focus and refocus in ways you never imagined possible. These informal methods will complement your formal practice and give you the additional advantage of being able to practice in a variety of places, including the gym.

Stretching

When you are stretching, allow your focus to settle entirely on the muscle group and connective tissue you are stretching. I encourage people to close their eyes while stretching a particular muscle group, for example, the hamstring. Breathe into the muscle and feel the fibers and tissue lengthening. Keep your attention on that area, and when your mind wanders, bring it back to total absorption in that muscle group. Breathe in and out of the muscle and hold the stretch for the recommended length of time (typically 20 to 30 seconds). Using a 1 to 10 scale, with 10 being painful, stretch until you experience a 6 or 7; there is no need for stretching to be painful. After holding the stretch, release and feel the muscle relax. The muscle fibers and connective tissue will release and potentially feel warm as blood flows into the area. Then focus again on holding the next stretch. Doing this at home before bed after a hot bath or shower can be a great way to settle your mind into a state conducive to deep, restorative sleep.

Weights and Resistance Training

See chapter 12, "Moving Steel," for detailed guidelines on incorporating concentration training in the gym when lifting weights, using bands, or practicing other forms of strength training.

Cardio

While working out on exercise equipment, such as the treadmill, you ordinarily may listen to music, watch videos, or chat with someone else to pass the time. You may do something similar when you are running or biking outside. To make concentration practice part of the workout, start by leaving your phone in the locker room. As you exercise, focus in on your body at least every few minutes. Notice the movement of your legs—the relaxation and contraction of your quads and hamstrings, for example. Enjoy being absorbed in how these muscles work in sync with one another. Feel the movement of your arms, your feet in contact with the ground or pedals, the sweat dripping down your back. Focus on your breath and body, and when (not if) your mind wanders, bring your attention back to your body and breath, just as you would in your formal practice. Do this for a minute or two.

The idea is to practice shifting your attention back and forth to strengthen your ability to focus and refocus. Staying aware while you are moving can be much easier than when you are sitting still at home, so if you have trouble with formal practice, this may be the best place for you to start. Use the time as another opportunity to tell your mind, "Okay, right now I will focus on my body and breath." This will also help you push through pain and fatigue during workouts when you are engaged in overloading your cardiovascular system—both the aerobic and anaerobic systems. See chapter 10, "Learning to Love Leroy," for more details on making friends with pain and fatigue.

Core Strengthening

Core work is one of the best places to experience the power of your mind. I will use planks as an example, but what I share here can be applied to any core exercise. During planks, you have probably noticed that toward the end of a set your legs, core, and arms start to shake to some degree. You may push your butt in the air or let your midsection sag due to the pain and fatigue. The pain can be intense, and it is meant to be—you just hold for dear life until the set is over.

Actually, core work should not be as painful as you might think. That extra burn is not necessary to develop a strong core and can do more harm than good. But the majority of athletes seem to buy into the idea it is hard, boring, and something to push through just to get it over with. This is groupthink, the gravitational pull toward what the majority of people are thinking in any given situation. But sport psychology is about questioning conventional wisdom.

In my opinion, your bellyaching over core training is fantastic, because it affords you another opportunity to learn to use your mind as an ally. Again, taking planks as an example, try the following. Before getting in plank position, take two deep belly breaths, allowing your attention to move from your mind down into your body. When you get on your elbows and toes, visualize and feel a steel bar going from the top of your head down through your spine and legs—a steel bar that will not bend. You could also visualize a beam of light, a laser than is unbendable. During the set, do your best to breathe easily, focusing on your body and the steel bar. No bending, no moving—just breathing in and out, slowly. When you feel the pain, resist the temptation to bring your shoulders up toward your ears. Keep your shoulder blades back and down, attached to the steel bar. Breathing in and out, relax your neck and shoulders as much as you can. This will work for you biomechanically, too; you will build greater strength if you do not hunch and contract your neck and shoulders.

It will take discipline to lock in this way. You will not be focused on how much time is left. Instead, you will be allowing yourself to be absorbed in feeling the steel bar and your strong and unbendable body. Your neck and shoulders will be relaxed as you breathe in and out slowly. As you become better at this, you may find that when the set is over you feel as if you could have held the plank 20 or 30 seconds more.

Have fun with this and experiment! Here are a couple of other visualizations you can use during planks:

- Imagine the floor is supporting your body, as if you are actually lying on the floor and it is holding you up.
- Picture ropes attached to your back and legs holding you up. Lock into that sensation as your mind registers the fatigue and pain.

Remember, records are made to be broken! Through core work you are strengthening your mind as well as your body. Your limiting belief in this case might be that you hate and dread certain core exercises.

But if you are stubborn and focus your attention in the way I describe, you may be surprised to find you are you are enjoying them—all because you have experienced the power of your mind.

REFERENCES

Alcoholics Anonymous, ed. 2001. *Alcoholics Anonymous, 4th Edition.* New York: A.A. World Services.

Chartrand, Judy M., Douglas P. Jowdy, and Steven J. Danish. 1992. "The Psychological Skills Inventory for Sports: Psychometric Characteristics and Applied Implications." *Journal of Sport and Exercise Psychology* 14, 405–13.

Dispenza, Joseph. 2008. *Evolve Your Brain: The Science of Changing Your Mind.* Deerfield Beach, FL: Health Communications.

Flavell, John H. 1979. "Metacognition and Cognitive Monitoring: A New Area of Cognitive-Developmental Inquiry." *American Psychologist* 34, 906-11.

Gallwey, W. Timothy. 2015. *The Inner Game of Tennis.* London: Pan Books.

Gendlin, Eugene. 1981. *Focusing.* New York: Bantam Dell.

Gladwell, Malcolm. 2007. *Blink: The Power of Thinking Without Thinking.* Newport Beach, CA: Back Bay Books.

Loehr, James E. 1982. *Mental Toughness Training for Sports: Achieving Athletic Excellence.* Lexington, MA: The Stephen Greene Press.

Maguire, Daniel C. 1979. *The Moral Choice.* New York: HarperCollins.

Mahoney, Michael J. 1991. *Human Change Processes: The Scientific Foundations of Psychotherapy.* New York: Basic Books.

McCann, Sean, Douglas Jowdy, and Judy Van Raalte. 2002. "Assessment in Sport and Exercise Psychology." In *Exploring*

Sport and Exercise Psychology, edited by Judy Van Raalte and Britton W. Brewer, 291-305. Washington, DC: APA Books.

Miller, Alice. 1996. *The Drama of the Gifted Child: The Search for the True Self.* New York: Basic Books.

Morris, Tony, Michael Spittle, and Anthony Watt. 2005. "Psychophysiological Research on Imagery." In *Imagery in Sport,* 153-74. Champaign, IL: Human Kinetics.

Murphy, Shane M., and Douglas P. Jowdy. 1992. "Imagery and Mental Rehearsal." In *Advances in Sport Psychology*, edited by Thelma S. Horn, 221-50. Champaign, IL: Human Kinetics.

Ohno, Apolo. 2010. *Zero Regrets: Be Greater Than Yesterday.* New York: Atria.

Orlick, Terry. 1982. *In Pursuit of Excellence.* Champaign, IL: Human Kinetics.

Peale, Norman Vincent. 1952. *The Power of Positive Thinking.* Upper Saddle River, NJ: Prentice Hall.

Peck, M. Scott. 1978. *The Road Less Traveled.* New York: Simon & Schuster.

Peck, M. Scott. 1998. *Further Along the Road Less Traveled.* East Roseville, NSW: Simon and Schuster Australia.

Tutko, Thomas, and Umberto Tosi. 1980. *Sports Psyching: Playing Your Best Game All of the Time.* Los Angeles: Penguin Putman.

Vienne, Veronique. 1998. *The Art of Doing Nothing.* New York: Random House.

Winter, Bud. 1981. *Relax and Win: Championship Performance in Whatever You Do.* Corcoran, CA: Oak Tree Press.

ABOUT THE AUTHOR

Douglas Jowdy, PhD, is a licensed psychologist with offices in Boulder and Denver, Colorado, where he sees both athletes and non-athletes. He works via TeleHealth as well as in person. Dr. Jowdy is currently on faculty at the University of Colorado Hospital in the department of orthopedics. He has coached athletes at the collegiate level and worked for the US Olympic Committee, serving as the team psychologist for the US speed skating team. Dr. Jowdy's passion for the mind-body connection began at age 13, when he read his first sport psychology book. *The Gold Medal Mind* is based upon academic research, professional experience dating back to 1986, and personal involvement coaching and as a competitive athlete. For more information about his background visit his website, www.goldmedalmind.com.

Made in the USA
Middletown, DE
15 December 2021

56037607R00179